THE MARCONI
SCANDAL

BLOOMSBURY READER

Discover books by Frances Donaldson published by
Bloomsbury Reader at
www.bloomsbury.com/FrancesDonaldson

A Twentieth-Century Life
Child of the Twenties
Evelyn Waugh
Freddy Lonsdale
The Marconi Scandal
The Royal Opera House in the Twentieth Century

THE MARCONI SCANDAL

FRANCES DONALDSON

BLOOMSBURY READER

LONDON · NEW DELHI · NEW YORK · SYDNEY

This edition published in 2013 by Bloomsbury Reader

Bloomsbury Reader is a division of Bloomsbury Publishing Plc,

50 Bedford Square, London WC1B 3DP

First published in Great Britain 1962 by Rupert Hart-Davis

ISBN: 978 1 4482 0585 1
eISBN: 978 1 4482 0554 7

Visit www.bloomsburyreader.com to find out more about our authors and their books
You will find extracts, author interviews, author events and you can sign up for
newsletters to be the first to hear about our latest releases and special offers

Printed and bound by CPI Group (UK) Ltd, Croydon, CR0 4YY

Contents

Introduction vii

  I   The Contract with the Marconi Company 1

  II   Opposition to the Contract 8

  III   The Debate of October 11 21

  Behind the Scenes

  IV   1. The Isaacs Family and the Marconi Shares 38

  V   2. The Eye-Witness 54

  The Select Committee

  VI   1. The Contract 67

  VII   2. The Journalists 75

  VIII   Le Matin 87

  The Select Committee

  IX   3. Sir Rufus Isaacs 99

  X   4. Mr Lloyd George and Mr Herbert Samuel 124

  XI   5. Godfrey and Harry Isaacs 137

  XII   6. Four Important Witnesses 157

  XIII   Ghastly Record: Isaacs v. Chesterton 172

The Select Committee

XVI   7. An Absconding Stockbroker 193

XV   The Reports 201
XVI   The Final Debate..208
XVII   Aftermath 238
    Author's Reflections..259

Appendices

A   An Open Letter to Lord Reading 267
B   Report of the Select Committee of Inquiry................................271
C   Lord Robert Cecil's Report 279

List of Works Quoted and Referred To 307
A Note on the Author 309

Introduction

I confess to being unable to abstain from an attempt to narrate the Great
Marconi Mystery, though it would tax the pen of a Conan Doyle,
assisted by the brain of a Sherlock Holmes, to do anything approaching
justice to it.   L. J. MAXSE

There is no great mystery about the Marconi case. It is not like the
Tichborne or the Dilke cases, where any solution that explains one set of
facts is unthinkable in relation to another, and where the fascination is in
the secretive past which may never now disclose itself. On the contrary, it
is fairly easy to discover how one event led to another and even to determine the motives behind them. Yet, if there is no mystery, nor is there any
agreement. The Marconi scandal was so deeply felt by those it concerned
that it crops up again and again in biographies of the period, always
without conclusion.

In 1936, twenty-three years after the close of the case,
G. K. Chesterton wrote:

> It is the fashion to divide recent history into Pre-War and Post-War
> conditions. I believe it is almost as essential to divide them into the
> Pre-Marconi and Post-Marconi days. It was during the agitations upon
> that affair that the ordinary English citizen lost his invincible ignorance;
> or, in ordinary language, his innocence . . . I think it probable that
> centuries will pass before it is seen clearly and in its right perspective;

and that then it will be seen as one of the turning-points in the whole history of England and the world.[1]

Six years later the second Lord Reading wrote in his biography of his father, Rufus Isaacs:

> Nobody reading the story . . . today can believe that there was ever the most shadowy foundation for the allegations . . . which were so glibly made . . . So great a mountain of controversy was erected during these few months that it is difficult now to see the original molehill which was the basis of it all.[2]

The Marconi case is not likely ever to be seen as a turning-point in history, but it was not founded on a molehill. It has escaped the attention of serious historians because it had no consequence; yet it repays a careful curiosity. The past may be illumined in various ways, and, if the story of this old scandal adds no line to the form of history, it contributes unexpectedly to the colour and texture.

For eighteen months, in the years 1912 and 1913, the Marconi case excited the public violently, while it ravaged the spirits and endangered the careers of men without whom the world might indeed have been different. Nevertheless, because of the title which has always stuck to it, I cannot say too soon that the one person whose reputation was never assailed or lowered was Signor Marconi himself. Nor must anything in this story of fifty years ago be taken as reflecting on the reputation of the great company that bears his honourable name today.

It is difficult to present the facts with clarity and justice because of the mass of material among which one is forced to discriminate. My task has not been further complicated, however, by any personal bias, because my affections have not become engaged on either side. The case was prosecuted viciously and without humility or charity, while the niggardly defence was unredeemed

---

[1] *Autobiography*, 202.
[2] *Rufus Isaacs*, 1, 273.

by any act above self-interest. As I followed this strange story through news-paper files and Parliamentary and Law Reports, my interest continually increased. I could never quite relinquish the thing because it grew upon me that there was, after all, a small mystery—the mystery of human behaviour.

F. D.

(1)

The Contract with the
Marconi Company

1

In 1912 the word "Marconi" meant what it means today. A reasonably informed child of twelve asked to explain the word "wireless" or alternatively the word "Marconi" would inevitably have used the other in his reply.

Guglielmo Marconi was born in Bologna in 1874. His father was an Italian businessman and his mother an Irishwoman. From the earliest age he showed the vision and application of genius, and Professor Righi of the University of Bologna initiated him into all the earlier discoveries in his field and allowed him the use of experimental apparatus. It is a simplification to say that he invented wireless telegraphy because sixty years of research work contributed to his discovery. But he saw, as no one else had seen, the end to which the scattered finds of other men were pointing.

His earliest experiments were conducted with the aid of his brother and the local peasants in the house and garden of his home, and later across the surrounding countryside. At the age of twenty-two he had achieved a crude form of wireless communication and he offered his invention to the Italian Government. This was refused and, as a result, he crossed to England. Here

Sir William Preece, Chief Engineer to the Post Office, and Sir Oliver Lodge were close to the secrets of the new science, and they welcomed the young man, Preece allowing him the use of instruments as Righi had done.

By 1897 Marconi, who had applied for and received his first patent, formed a company to exploit his inventions and this was capitalised in the City of London. From the beginning he surrounded himself with the ablest men and employed first-class engineers. In the same way he bought all patents of value which he could acquire, among others Edison's. He progressed steadily and never promised anything he did not perform, or made public new inventions until they had been thoroughly tested. In 1900 he took out the patent No. 7777 which protected the vital invention that made possible tuning, or multiplex telegraphy on a single aerial. Then in December 1901 he made wireless history by signalling across the Atlantic. Nevertheless, he was working on a new science and one which required a great deal of money for its research. He had a long way to go before it became financially profitable, and for years his backers had little or no return.

In 1908 the Marconi Company had been twelve years in existence and was in very low water. £500,000 had been sunk in experimental work, no dividend had been paid on the ordinary or preference shares and none was in sight. During 1908 the price of the ordinary shares had dropped to *6s. 3d.* and holders who had paid £3 or £4 were not in a mood to make further advances. At the same time Marconi, tiring of the financial side of the business, which kept him from his real work of research and development, looked about him for someone who could be taken into the company as managing director.

Now Godfrey Isaacs appeared on the scene. Just turned forty, he was one of the younger sons of the large family of Joseph Isaacs, a fruit-broker and general merchant with a big and profitable business. Godfrey had no obvious qualifications for the post Marconi desired to fill, since at this time he had no knowledge of wireless telegraphy. But his father's business, which he had entered as a young man, maintained contacts with exporters on the continent, and Godfrey, who had been educated at Hanover and Brussels University, spoke several languages and had extensive acquaintance with European finance houses. He had tremendous energy and enterprise, and Marconi, to whom he was introduced by the inventor's brother-in-law, seems

to have taken an immediate liking to him. He was offered the post of managing director and, after working six months with Marconi to learn the business,
he assumed full control of the management of the company.

> Godfrey Isaacs, managing director of the English Marconi Company,
> was the king-pin of the organisation [said one of the early members of
> the company]. As an extravagant promoter he had an insatiable love
> for power; he was the salesman of wireless with the business strategy
> and enthusiasm necessary to promote such a radically new communica-
> tion system.[1]

Wireless telegraphy had by now begun to be proved by practical demonstration. In January 1909 the S.S. *Republic,* bound from New York to the
Mediterranean, was rammed by the S.S. *Florida,* and for the first time in
history ships were turned in their course to rescue the crews. The possibilities
of the Marconi apparatus, which was already fitted to ships of the Royal Navy
and to shore stations, began to be understood.

Godfrey Isaacs applied himself energetically to the problem of capitalising
the expansion of wireless telegraphy and started litigation all over the world
to prevent infringement of patents. By 1912 Marconi had companies in
Russia, Spain, the Argentine, Canada and America, all using the same patents
and all associated with the British Company, which usually held the majority
of the shares and placed directors on the board.

2

In March 1910 the managing director of the Marconi Company submitted
to the Colonial Office an imaginative plan to link the British Empire by a
network of wireless stations, by means of which different portions of the
Empire would all be put into communication with one another at greatly
reduced rates. He proposed to begin with a series of eighteen stations,
taking in Egypt, India, Malaya, China, Australia and Africa. At this time

---

[1]   Dunlap, *Marconi,* 204.

3

he was asking for licences for the stations and for the support of the Government in obtaining licences from self-governing Colonies. The company, he said, was prepared to erect, maintain and operate stations entirely at its own expense.

This plan was considered by a Standing Committee called the Cables (Landing Rights) Committee, which in March 1911 reported against the suggestion that the Marconi Company should own and operate the stations, but recommended that a state-owned system connecting the Empire was desirable and that the Marconi Company should be approached to erect it. In June the Imperial Conference endorsed this suggestion and a committee was formed, with the Postmaster-General in the chair, to negotiate with the Company on behalf of the Post Office. Negotiations began in the autumn of 1911, and on 7 March 1912 a tender was signed between the Post Office and the Marconi Company which provided for the erection of the first six stations.

3

The Government concerned was the second Asquith Government of 1910. The Liberals had come to power in 1905 and this had been confirmed in the landslide election of 1906. They had, both by their victory and by the measures they introduced, inspired political anger not exceeded in this century. Theirs was the first of the modern Governments of the Left and it laid the basis for the Welfare State. The leaders were drawn far more than was usual from the middle classes and the intelligentsia, less from the aristocratic ruling class, and they were determined to improve the conditions of the poorer people.

From the first the Tories made it plain they would not easily consent to the Liberals using the power they had won constitutionally. In an election speech A. J. Balfour, Leader of the Party and recently Prime Minister, had said that it was the duty of everyone to see that the "great Unionist Party should still control, whether in power or whether in opposition, the destinies of this great Empire."[2] This was understood to mean, and did mean, that the

---

[2] Nottingham, 15 January 1912.

House of Lords would be used to block unwelcome measures passed by the Liberal majority through the House of Commons. For nearly four years every measure of importance was rejected by the Lords, and when in 1909, against all precedent, they rejected the Finance Bill, it might have been described as a counter-revolution except that there had been no revolution.

Then there began the long struggle to curtail the power of the Lords which involved two general elections, an undertaking by the King if necessary to create peers on a vast scale, and the exhaustion of the Liberal Party, culminating in the Parliament Act of 1911.

In 1911 there was also introduced the National Insurance Bill, the foundation of subsequent social achievement, which, while not severely opposed in the House of Commons, enraged many sections of the community.

During all this time the Irish question, which for nearly thirty years dominated Parliament and aroused more passion than any other issue, remained in abeyance. In 1910, when their majority was much reduced, the Liberals governed only with the aid of the Irish Members, who gave their support because they recognised that the Parliament Act was a necessary preliminary to a resumption of their own struggle.

It was a time of political emotions with no comparison in modern history. The ill-temper of the Opposition who believed in their inherent right to rule was equalled only by the invective used and the storms that regularly took place in the House of Commons. To this day when politicians wish to find a parallel for bitter, passionate or reckless controversy they go back to the Parliament of 1910.

The most hated politician was David Lloyd George. He first incurred much anger by his opposition to the Boer War. Then he was responsible as Chancellor of the Exchequer for the People's Budget (the Finance Act of 1909) and for the controversial Insurance Act. Lloyd George was sincere in his desire to improve the conditions of the people of England, but he had the provocative temperament of the born fighter. He went out of his way to create the conditions of warfare, and he rejoiced in the attack on institutions held sacred.

In the spring and summer of 1912, when the contract with the Marconi Company aroused so much controversy, the Parliament Act and the Insurance Act were only one year old, while the Third Home Rule Bill, which roused opposition that threatened civil war, was before the House. All these events took place in the atmosphere of uneasiness created by the menace of Germany's growing strength.

4

Among the members of the Liberal Government who were to figure in the Marconi controversy, Asquith had succeeded Sir Henry Campbell-Bannerman as Prime Minister in 1908, and at the same time Lloyd George followed Asquith at the Exchequer; Mr Herbert Samuel was Postmaster-General and Sir Rufus Isaacs, brother of the managing director of the Marconi Company, was Attorney-General.

In an age of great advocates Sir Rufus had risen to the top of his profession with unusual speed. When, in 1898 and at the age of thirty-seven, he took silk after only ten years at the Bar, he was, in terms of length of call, the youngest Q.C. so far created. Seven years later he entered the House of Commons as Member for Reading.

As a backbencher he did not shine. He had no great power of language and he relied as an advocate on his unusual intelligence[3] and on a self-control which constantly gave him command in a court of law. He had, however, a beautiful speaking voice, and it seems likely that his public utterances, which read badly, gained immensely from his impressive character and personal charm.

In March 1910 he became Solicitor-General, an appointment welcomed by his colleagues at the Bar, among whom he was much admired and respected.

In the autumn of the same year Sir William Robson, the Attorney-General, resigned his office, and, after only seven months as Solicitor-General, Sir Rufus succeeded him as senior Law Officer and official leader of the Bar.

Then in June 1912 Lord Loreburn resigned the office of Lord Chancellor

---

[3] When the late Lord Birkenhead, as F. E. Smith, introduced Rufus Isaacs to his wife, it was with the muttered aside: "I may say that I consider this man quite as able as I am myself." (Birkenhead, *F. E.*, 77.)

and Lord Haldane succeeded him. This was a break with tradition, since the office normally reverted to the Attorney-General, and Sir Rufus "indignant, not only for personal reasons but on account of the break in the traditional rights of his own office,"[4] expressed his resentment to the Prime Minister. Asquith replied that when Lord Haldane had accepted the War Office it was on the understanding that he should succeed to the Woolsack whenever a vacancy occurred. In order to show that the appointment was not due to any disrespect for Sir Rufus, Asquith announced the inclusion of the Attorney-General in the Cabinet. The date of his entry into the Cabinet, later to become a matter of importance to Sir Rufus, was precisely three months after the signing of the tender with the Marconi Company.

---

[4]   Reading, *Rufus Isaacs*, 1, 224.

(2)

Opposition to the Contract

1

In the autumn of 1911, when, eighteen months after they first submitted to the Government a plan for an Imperial Chain of wireless stations, the Marconi Company began seriously to negotiate with the Post Office, they gave as much publicity as they could to these negotiations. In March 1912, when the tender was signed, they sent a circular to their shareholders setting out the terms that had in principle been agreed, and this again was published in the newspapers. During all this time the Post Office issued no statement.

The tender, which was often referred to as the contract, was a formal statement of the clauses later to be embodied in a legal contract. Because it related to mails and telegraphic communication it came under a Standing Order that required it to be ratified by the House of Commons. This was sufficiently unusual for the Attorney-General later to say: "I think I did know it required to be ratified, not because I had in mind that there was a Standing Order, but I think I read it at some period when the contract and the acceptance of the tender was announced." On March 7 most people believed that the contract had been signed and the matter concluded.

During the spring and summer, questions were asked of the Postmaster-General in the House of Commons, indicating that opposition to the contract was growing, although some of them expressed merely the irritation felt by Members of Parliament because the terms had been made public by the Marconi Company, while the Post Office continued to leave the House without official information. Members pressed Mr Samuel to say when the agreement would reach the House and when there would be an opportunity to debate it. To these and other questions Mr Samuel replied that the contract would be tabled in the House of Commons as soon as it was ready.

The Government regarded the erection of the stations as a matter of some urgency, and it was assumed that formal ratification would be given in the summer session. By the time that, on July 19, the contract was at last tabled in the House it was apparent that the opposition had become so strong it would be necessary to give more time for debate than could be crowded in at the end of the session. Motions had already been put down for a Select Committee to consider the whole matter.

The Marconi Company and wireless telegraphy generally had now become a matter of lively interest to the public. In April, soon after the signing of the tender, the great liner *Titanic* had been sunk on its maiden voyage, and in the shock of the tragedy one hopeful thing emerged: those passengers who had been saved owed their lives to the wireless apparatus on board ship. The opposition was not to the establishment of an Imperial Chain of stations, but to the contract with the Marconi Company.

When Mr Samuel asked the Government Chief Whip the reason for the unexpected strength of the opposition, he was told that it was probably due not so much to the contract as to the rumours surrounding it.

If this was the first time the Postmaster-General had heard of the existence of the rumours, he lived in a state of ignorance of public concern and opinion which is unusual even in a Minister hard pressed by affairs of State.

The rumours had begun in the same month that the tender was signed, and were caused partly by a great gamble that took place in the shares of the Marconi Company. In August of the preceding year these shares had stood at £2. 8s. 9d. and by December they were £3. 6s. 3d. In March 1912 they shot up to £6. 15s. 0d. and by April to £9. After this they fell rapidly and never again reached such heights. In April an issue of new shares in the Marconi Company of America was also introduced on to the market and these again enjoyed a short but startling boom followed by a fall.

Gossip started in the City and in the House of Commons. From both places it sped to the drawing-rooms of fashionable London. It was detailed, sensational and widespread. Quite quickly two distinct charges emerged—both against Ministers of the Crown.

In the House of Commons it was said that, from the details publicised by the Marconi Company, the contract was inexplicably generous to the Company and injurious to the interests of the nation. The delay in reaching agreement on a matter of public urgency had seemed endless and had culminated in an unbusinesslike and unworkable contract. In addition, while the Company had published the terms of the contract, the Postmaster-General continually thwarted discussion in the House. A charge was made—although it had not at first very wide circulation and one wonders how it achieved such as it had—of grave and improbable corruption based on the following facts: the managing director of the Marconi Company was Mr. Godfrey Isaacs, while the Attorney-General in the Liberal Government was his brother, Sir Rufus Isaacs. The Postmaster-General was Mr Herbert Samuel and (an extraordinary weight was put on this) all three were Jews.

The gossip from the City was different and it was angry. Some people had lost money in the fall that followed the boom in Marconi shares; many more had failed to get in on the rise. All over the City it was said that the market had been "rigged." It was widely suggested, and by many people believed, that Ministers of the Crown had used their privileged knowledge of the negotiations for the contract to speculate in Marconi shares.

So matters stood when, on July 19, the contract was tabled in the House of Commons. On the following day these rumours, which for months had been enlarged and enriched by word of mouth, for the first time reached print.

2

A journalist named Wilfred Ramage Lawson was the first person openly to refer to the rumours surrounding the Marconi contract. On July 20, the day after it was tabled in the House of Commons, he published an article in a weekly journal named the *Outlook* in which there occurred the following sentences.

> The Marconi Company has from its birth been a child of darkness. Its finance has been of a most chequered and erratic sort. Its relations with certain Ministers have not always been purely official or political.

After referring to Godfrey Isaacs, the managing director of the Company, Lawson continued:

> All the world knows that a similar surname exists among the members of the Asquith Cabinet, and the House of Commons may naturally wish to learn if there is any relationship between the two. It is also a matter of common knowledge that the Postmaster-General for the time being bears the honoured name of Samuel. Here we have two financiers of the same nationality pitted against each other, with a third in the background acting perhaps as mutual friend. If expedition and equity could be looked for anywhere, it was surely in such a combination of business and political talent. . . .
>
> The Marconi Company have published their version of the contract more than once, and on the strength of it their shares went up from the 6/3d of 1908 to about £9, yet the Postmaster-General is still busy dotting its i's and crossing its t's.
>
> The House of Commons of course saw through the comedy which the Government were playing so very clumsily. At all costs the contract was to be kept back until the last day or two before the summer recess, in the hope that it would be forgotten before the House met again in the autumn. Thanks, however, to the persistence of Sir Henry Norman, that game is going to be defeated.

Then, after saying that the Government could not decline to explain the peculiar conditions under which the contract was negotiated, Lawson concluded:

> The personal relations which undoubtedly existed between a Cabinet

11

Minister and the board of the Marconi Company may or may not have been in the public interest. If they were, there should have been no reason for shrinking from publicity and legitimate criticism. The problem of wireless telegraphy is quite complex and difficult enough in itself without being mixed up with family party negotiations.

Four weeks later Lawson began a series of weekly articles on the Marconi affair in the *Outlook,* and in these he set out all the technical objections to the contract. For the sake of clarity the contract will be dealt with separately, and, for the moment abandoning chronology, the following sentences are quoted from Lawson writing in the following October, this time in the *National Review.* (This article was important for two reasons—because it was an extension as well as a resumé of the insinuations made by Lawson in the *Outlook,* and because it ensured that L. J. Maxse, editor and proprietor of the *National Review,* was engaged in the Marconi case.)

Referring to Dr Muirhead, one of the two holders of the Lodge–Muirhead patent in wireless telegraphy, Lawson said:

> He never suspected that members of the Government which had bluffed him for four years and tried to steal his invention were all the time in league with the Marconi clique—his bitter and relentless competitors. He knew, however, that when the Attorney-General gave notice of objections to the extension of the Lodge–Muirhead patent he was really acting in the Marconi interest. . . .
>
> Any Parliamentary Committee that wishes to get to the bottom of it will have to investigate the mysterious relations which have obtained between certain members of the Government and the Marconi Company ever since Mr Godfrey Isaacs took to wireless telegraphic finance. . . .
>
> The Postmaster-General must have known when he was negotiating [the contract] that he was aiding and abetting the creation of a monopoly certain to prove prejudicial to the public interest, the commercial public in particular . . . He has served the Marconi interest so effectively that the Government now find themselves in an awkward and puzzling dilemma. . . .

Such is the sordid story of the Marconi scandal of 1912. In a small way it has been a repetition of the South Sea Bubble. Ministers implicated in the South Sea Bubble were impeached and severely punished. What is to happen to Ministers who directly or indirectly may have been responsible for the Marconi Scandal?

And lastly:

For this sardonic Treasury Minute the Chancellor of the Exchequer is, of course, officially responsible. It will therefore be necessary for the proposed Committee of Inquiry to have him before it. He will naturally be anxious to tell it all he knows about the wireless mystery. Altogether three members of the Government have figured more or less in this suspicious episode—the Chancellor of the Exchequer, the Attorney-General and the Postmaster-General. What have they to say to the unflattering comments that are being made on their conduct as public trustees?

In the middle of that summer, and before all but the first of Lawson's articles had appeared, a series of articles was also published in the *Eye–Witness*, a weekly journal founded and for some time edited by Hilaire Belloc, who had recently resigned the editorship to Cecil Chesterton, a brother of G. K. Chesterton. The first of these, which appeared on August 8 was entitled "The Marconi Scandal" (a title that was to stick) and in it occurred the following paragraphs:

What progress is the Marconi Scandal making? We ask the question merely from curiosity and under no illusion as to the inevitable end of the affair. Everybody knows the record of Isaacs and his father, and his uncle, and in general of the whole family. Isaacs' brother is Chairman of the Marconi Company, it has therefore been secretly arranged between Isaacs and Samuel that the British people shall give the Marconi Company a very large sum of money through the agency of the said Samuel, and for the benefit of the said Isaacs. Incidentally the monopoly that is to be granted to Isaacs No. 2, through the ardent charity of Isaacs

13

No. 1 and his colleague the Postmaster-General, is a monopoly involving antiquated methods, the refusal of competing tenders far cheaper and far more efficient, and the saddling of the country with corruptly purchased goods. . . .

Another reason why the swindle, or rather theft, impudent and barefaced as it is, will go through is that we have in this country no method of punishing men who are guilty of this kind of thing. . . .

Meanwhile we would ask our readers to note the following facts. At the beginning of 1911 the shares of the Company stood at 14s. By the end of that year, doubtless after an intimation had been conveyed from Herbert Samuel, Cabinet Minister, through his colleague Isaacs to Isaacs' brother, of the intention of the Government, their value multiplied by nearly *five,* standing at close on 70s. Between January and March 1912, they rose to just under 100s, which would be about their natural price, supposing the abominable scandal of the contract to be allowed to stand. After this price had been reached the news was deliberately allowed to leak out and the stock was thus forced up to a fictitious value. At the end of April they stood at £9. Then, of course, they sagged just as was intended.

In the two succeeding weeks further articles appeared in the *Eye–Witness,* neither less specific in matter nor more controlled in language, but, since an article appearing later quotes the more relevant passages from each, it is convenient to ignore the first two and to quote from the third at considerable length.

Last week a reader of the *Eye–Witness* sent the subjoined letter to a number of London journals, including the principal organs of Harmsworth, Pearson, Cadbury, Levi, Mond and other bosses of the great capitalist Trusts that control our Press.

"Copy of my original letter to the Daily Mail.

"Sir,

"Possibly many of your readers who, like myself, have been disgusted, if not surprised, at the silence with which the British Press has treated the recent

Telephone and Marconi scandals, may be interested to read in the *Eye–Witness* of August 22nd the striking article headed 'The Marconi Scandal Again.' In this article, which should be read by all who view with apprehension the increasing jobbery and corruption in the public life of England, the following passage occurs:

" 'Two men, co-opted into the administration, one called Samuel, the other called Isaacs, have acted in the following fashion: Samuel, having it in his power to determine what the English people shall pay for services in connection with their postal arrangements, has arranged that a concern run by the brother of Isaacs shall have a privilege and a monopoly. Isaacs, whose brother is thus favoured at our expense, is the man who has at his discretion the prosecution of his fellow citizens—and virtually their punishment—especially in political cases. He has, further, the exceedingly valuable arbitrary power of *preventing* such prosecution and punishment. The gift which Samuel is making to Isaacs' brother is not a small or debatable one. His mere proposal to help Isaacs' brother out of the public pocket has already multiplied the property of that brother, in the concern with which he is connected, by anything between *five* and *eight* times. Finally, Samuel arranged that this deal, which he privately carried through behind our backs, should be formally passed through the House of Commons under conditions when there could not be any effective debate. This last enormity was only prevented by the suspicion and jealousy of other men of his own kidney, envious of such facile successes.

" 'All this stands. Samuel is still left drawing his great salary and in absolute power over a great public department. Isaacs is still in exercise of arbitrary power over the most dreaded department of "justice." What is more, the other Isaacs and the commercial concern it is proposed to benefit are so confident that there is no power in modern England capable of punishing these abuses that their shares still fetch *more than seven times what they fetched in the open market before the intrigue was begun.*

" 'There is no palliating such things. There is no excusing them. There is no explaining them. They constitute a perfectly clear case of—well, we won't say what—committed at the expense of the public by the guardians of the public interest.

" 'As there are no two ways of looking at dangerous nastiness of this kind, so there is no doubt as to the issues involved . . . Either Isaacs and Samuel will be allowed to put the thing through, in which case we shall have passed a certain boundary which nations when they pass it are not allowed to recross, and we shall have sunk to a certain level from which the public life of a people does not recover; either that—or the authors of the proposed raid upon our pockets will be checked before the profits are scooped in, which is as much as to say that they will have lost the position and the rights they have exercised so dishonourably and obtained by no consent direct or indirect of the English people.'

"In the next number of the *Eye–Witness*, August 29, in an article headed 'A Pause for Thought,' the following passage is particularly worthy of the attention of all thoughtful readers . . . 'If Samuel and Isaacs force their deal through (as is exceedingly likely), it will be in the teeth of a public opinion that regards them simply as criminals.'

"As an outsider, possessing no first-hand knowledge of the jobbery which seems to have become a commonplace of English political life, I submit that it is impossible for men filling public positions to ignore the accusations contained in these articles. Either they are true or they are false. If false, they cannot be ignored in silence by the men against whom they are directed. If true, it is inconceivable that two Hebrews unable to refute such accusations should continue to occupy positions hitherto supposed to be filled by honourable English gentlemen.

"Trusting you may see your way to give publicity to my letter.

"I am, Sir, faithfully yours, Christopher Sandeman.
"Beaufort Gardens London S.W. Sept. 4., 1912."

No paper inserted this letter. By the kindness of Mr Sandeman we have had access to the replies which he has received. Most of them attribute the suppression of his letter to 'lack of space.' That is Levi's answer, and also that of Lloyds, who control the *Daily Chronicle*. The most amusing communication is from the gentleman who transacts such business for Sir Alfred Mond. From this we learn that 'he regrets he is already *so well supplied with MSS of this nature* that he is unable to accept *more* at the present time!' From which we gather that the daring and incisive exposures of political and financial corruption which we read every evening in the *Westminster Gazette* are a mere sample of those which Sir Alfred has safely locked up in his desk and which he is prepared to produce when the public interest requires it.[1] That at least is good hearing. The one answer which goes anywhere near meeting Mr Sandeman's challenge is that of the Harmsworth organ. The Editor of the *Daily Mail* replies asking him (1) what definite allegations he is prepared to make and (2) what means he is prepared to adopt to substantiate his charges. To this Mr Sandeman has replied by pointing out, very properly, that it was we and not he that had brought the accusations, and adding the very pertinent remark: 'If false, I do not see how they can and why they should be ignored in silence by the persons against whom they are directed!' He then refers Harmsworth to us.

Well, what we have written we have written. We have nothing to withdraw: we have a good deal to add. From time to time we shall let our readers hear more and more about the Marconi scandal until we have made it impossible for the Isaacs family to put the deal through. Meanwhile what we have written remains; and our readers may be assured that it was not written without a full sense of responsibility or without an intimate acquaintance with facts which are not only notorious in political circles, but which we happen to be in a position to substantiate. And where we have stepped in we do not think that Lord Northcliffe with his great wealth and influence need fear to tread.

It is curious that, although most people would agree with Mr Sandeman that it would be utterly impossible for men holding ministerial appointments to overlook the accusations contained in these articles, the Ministers did in fact ignore them.

Two other points provoke thought. First, one would like to know more about Mr Sandeman. When considering his letter and the discussion given it in the *Eye–Witness*, one cannot escape the faint suggestion of collusion between himself and those responsible for the paper. Secondly, it seems strange that none of the editors to whom his letter was sent gave the obvious and truthful answer: that, had they published it, they would have become liable to a charge

---

[1] The *Westminster Gazette* was one of the chief Liberal papers. The Editor, J. A. Spender, was probably the journalist closest to the leading Liberal politicians.

of libel. By not making this reply, to which there seems no objection, they gave the editor of the *Eye–Witness* the chance to suggest that, with the exception of his own paper, the whole of the press of England was in league to conceal corruption, or, at least too craven to expose it; and, at the same time, the pleasure of rolling the names of newspaper-proprietors round his pen with the insolence that was, in its political pages, the keynote of this journal.

In spite of the virulent and explicit terms of the articles, it is doubtful whether many people believed these particular charges. It is impossible to overstress, however, the extent of the rumours or the credence given them on the other matter; and for an explanation of this, here is a further quotation from Lawson.

A very considerable number of the shares [of the Marconi Company] are in pawn to all sorts of banks—London, provincial, Irish and foreign. The real owners of such shares could not be traced unless a Committee of Inquiry were armed with legal powers to cross-examine the bankers and compel discovery.

Neither would it be easy to find out the principal holders of the 100,000 bearer shares. The riggers, whoever they may have been, were no doubt acting under expert guidance. Whether or not they had confederates in high quarters, they seem to have always made a good guess as to what was going on behind the scenes. From whichever side they obtained their special information, there can be no doubt that it was both early and valuable. Among other things they also seem to have known the right moment to get out. . . . Transfers for blocks of 22,000 shares went through on March 18th, and a block of 52,000 followed a little later. In March, April and May a great stream of transfers was going through the office. The official records of the Company suggest a serious question as to whether its shareholders are the right sort of people to be entrusted with an all-British scheme of wireless telegraphy. One half of them hail from the Nationalist section of Ireland with a very small sprinkling of Ulstermen. Another fourth of them are foreigners, and perhaps not always friendly foreigners. Of the remaining fourth comparatively few are Gentiles. Altogether they are a decidedly polyglot multitude to have financial control of the wireless telegraphy by which the operations of the British Army and Navy may have to be directed, with the fate of the Empire at stake on them.[2]

It would have been better perhaps both for Mr Marconi and the British public if he had been paid a handsome sum right away for the exclusive use of his invention in the United Kingdom rather than let it be a stalking-horse of a huge gamble in which hundreds of thousands have been lost and won. By that simple means monopoly and scandal would have been equally avoided.[3]

Apart from Lawson only the *Eye–Witness* adopted this tone of virtuous relish, but in graver terms other journals were giving publicity to the same suggestions. On September 14 the *Spectator*, the most respected of the weeklies, concluded an article on the Marconi affair with these words:

In conclusion, we ought not to omit to say that some critics of the Government have suggested that, owing to private opportunities, the Marconi Company have been able to bring about a 'boom' in their shares, which but for these opportunities would not have been possible. It is pointed out, in evidence or illustration, that the Joint Managing Director of the company is Mr Godfrey Isaacs, brother of the Attorney-General.

We may say at once we do not believe for a moment that either Sir Rufus or Mr Samuel has lent himself consciously to any sort of secret financial manoeuvre for the enrichment of friends. That they should both have been outwitted by shrewd business men is, of course, always possible in such a case. . . .

Probably the presence of Mr Isaacs on the Board of the Company made no difference one way or the other. As, however, stories about the Marconi gamble have a wide circulation in the City and elsewhere, the Liberal Party, if they consent to the appointment of a Select Committee, will no doubt see the desirability of referring to it also some questions

[2] *Outlook*, 31 August 1912.
[3] *Ibid.*, 7 September 1912.

under this head. The Ministers themselves would, of course, be glad of the opportunity to kill all unfair personal charges.

So matters stood on October 11 when the House of Commons met to debate a motion to appoint a Select Committee of Inquiry into the Marconi contract. Those newspapers which commented on the suspicious aspects of the boom in Marconi shares were neither contributing anything new to scandal, nor attempting to guide public opinion. They were merely reflecting a body of rumour that had been growing throughout the spring and summer, that was spoken of incessantly in the City, the House of Commons, in the west-end of London, even in the law courts. A witness at the Inquiry was later to say that he had heard it said over luncheon in the Inner Temple that Rufus Isaacs had made £160,000, and Mr Samuel was told by one of his own relations that he was commonly believed to have made a quarter of a million.

(3)

The Debate of October 11

1

All that summer the terms of the agreement with the Marconi Company were furiously discussed, and, while the rumours of corruption and gambling kept alive the public interest, serious criticism of the contract itself inflamed opposition to the Government. Major Archer-Shee[1] began the press campaign with a letter to *The Times*. Later he wrote an article for the *National Review*. Lawson, who came to be regarded as an expert on wireless telegraphy, contributed a series of weekly articles to the *Outlook* in which every detail of the contract was scrutinised, and later, at the request of the editor, he summed up the arguments against it in the *National Review*. Papers with a larger circulation gave it less space but also adopted a critical tone.

On August 7, before the recess, Mr Samuel did explain the Government's case in the House of Commons and answered many of the points. Comparison

---

[1] Martin Archer-Shee, a half-brother of the Osborne cadet who was the original of *The Winslow Boy*, had appeared as a witness in the famous case in 1910 and was cross-examined by Sir Rufus Isaacs, prosecuting for the Grown.

of his first speech with that of October 11 shows that, although the latter was fuller and angrier, they were otherwise virtually the same. But M.P.'s had been much provoked because they believed he had deliberately left discussion of the subject to the last minute before the adjournment, thus muzzling criticism in the House. They were not in a mood to listen to his arguments or understand the interpretation he put on facts. The atmosphere was such that he was forced to offer an adjournment, so that the debate could be resumed when Parliament met again in the autumn, and the Prime Minister announced that a Select Committee would be appointed if the House of Commons desired it. All through the recess M.P.'s and others continued their criticism in the press, and the strength of the opposition grew.

While Godfrey Isaacs had been in negotiation with the Post Office, he had also had negotiations with the Lodge-Muirhead Syndicate, the only other English wireless company, and, before the tender was signed, he had bought their patents. This left only two other serious competitors in the field, the Poulsen Syndicate, associates of a Danish company, and Telefunken, which was German. So synonymous in 1912 were the words "Marconi" and "wireless telegraphy" that it was originally news to the ordinary public that there were other companies, but by the time of the October debate Poulsen and Telefunken were household words. When the M.P.'s who opposed the contract reached the House of Commons on October 11, they were so well-informed on matters relating to wireless telegraphy that it was clear they had been well briefed. This, however, is in the ordinary course of events and it is proper that, in a case where one company has signed a contract with the Government, members of the Opposition should be approached by their rivals and should seek to present their case.

According to the contract tabled on July 19 the Marconi Company were to build six stations within the Empire—in England, Egypt, the East African Protectorate, South Africa, India and Singapore—at a cost of £60,000 for each station. It was further agreed that they should receive a royalty of ten per cent of the gross takings of each station for a period of twenty-eight years, although there were several clauses in the contract relating to conditions which must, in that case, be fulfilled. The main criticisms of the contract were as follows:

(1) That by contracting with the Marconi Company to build these

stations the Government were not fulfilling the recommendations of the Cables (Landing Rights) Committee that wireless stations should be State-owned. The Admiralty itself was already possessed of certain patents, might have acquired the rest, and might have undertaken the work.

(2) That the contract had not been put out to tender and the claims of other inventors had been ignored.

(3) That the Marconi Company had been given an undisputed monopoly for five years and for the first six stations: and a virtual monopoly for twenty-eight years. (A clause in the contract allowed that, at the end of the five years or at the completion of the six stations, further stations could be built with other inventions, but, in that event, the Marconi Company were given the right of inspection to ensure that their own patents were not infringed. Critics maintained that in the first instance other companies could sell their inventions only by coming "cap in hand" to the Marconi Company, but that, if later stations were built by a different company, its secret processes were laid open to the Marconi right of inspection.)

(4) That the price of £60,000 was much too high and allowed the Marconi Company a middleman's profit. A wireless station was to consist of site and equipment, the latter to include masts, buildings, engines, boilers and dynamos to be supplied and erected by sub-contractors, while only the wireless apparatus itself would be supplied by Marconi.

(5) That the royalty of ten per cent was much too high and the duration of twenty-eight years much too long. A great point was made of the fact that the Marconi Master Patent No. 7777 was due to expire in less than three years, when it would be necessary for the Company to apply to the Courts for a renewal. "If the disputed contract should then be in operation the Postmaster-General will also have a divided duty to perform. He will be a working partner of the Marconi Company, and at the same time it will be his official duty to oppose renewal of the patent which is the corner-stone of the Company's system."[2]

(6) That a stage of evolution had been reached, and that it was

[2] Lawson, *Outlook,*, 24 August 1912.

monumentally stupid to choose this moment to tie the country to any one system. Far better to have a short delay than to be permanently saddled with inferior equipment. "Any day a new discovery may be announced which will knock out the Marconi system."[3]

2

On October 11 the debate on the motion to appoint a Select Committee was primarily an opportunity to discuss the criticisms of the contract, but it was expected that Ministers would speak in reply to the accusations of corruption and gambling. Direct charges had been made against Sir Rufus Isaacs and Mr Samuel, and in the gossip of the City a third Minister had been almost equally implicated. It may be remembered that Lawson in one of his articles referred to a Treasury Minute, and then, after naming the Chancellor of the Exchequer as its official author, remarked that it would therefore be necessary for the proposed Committee of Inquiry to call him along with the other Ministers. This was a device. Lawson did not connect Lloyd George's name with those of the other two Ministers because of the Treasury Minute. On the contrary, he introduced the Treasury Minute because, in the gossip of the City, Lloyd George's name had already been connected with theirs. It was expected therefore that the Chancellor would reply to the charge of gambling in Marconi shares.

Three of the chief spokesmen against the Government were Liberals—Sir Henry Norman, Sir George Croydon Marks and Mr Godfrey Collins. The speakers for the Conservative Party included Major Archer-Shee, Lord Robert Cecil and Sir Frederick Banbury. In a crowded and excited House they made in great detail and with much repetition all the points against the contract which six months' preparation had provided.

Sir Henry Norman, who opened the debate, began his speech with some remarks which were to be repeated in one form or another by all the Opposition speakers. He said that the contract had been criticised on two grounds—first that it was a bad bargain and second that it was a bargain tainted by corruption.

---

[3] Ditto, 28 September 1912.

I have mentioned the second of these grounds, and with great reluctance, only for the reason that if I omitted all allusion to it it might afford an opportunity for some evil-disposed persons to suggest that I had a lurking sympathy with such charges. I mention it only to say that I dissociate myself in the strongest possible manner from any criticism of the kind. I believe that it is not only without a shadow of foundation, but that it is preposterous. I regard it as a lamentable falling off from the high standard of public controversy in this country, and I hope that the Select Committee which will doubtless be appointed . . . will take an early opportunity of exercising its powers of summoning before it persons who have published and written charges of this kind, and affording to them on oath the opportunity of stating publicly the grounds upon which they felt themselves to be justified in bringing these charges against honourable men.

After Major Archer-Shee had made a statement of the same kind he also rejected charges that he had been concerned in the slanders and that he had an interest in rival companies. Only Lord Robert Cecil spoke of the rumours in impersonal terms. He said:

It is as well to tell the truth plainly to this House. These stories are extraordinarily prevalent all over the place. I say this . . . as much in the interests of members of the Government as of anybody else—a mere denial by the Government before this House will not meet the case at all. There must be a full Inquiry. . . . members of the Government must take great care . . . to submit themselves to examination and cross-examination in the fullest possible way. We all have an interest in this, not only members of the Government, but the whole House of Commons, and the life of the nation is bound up with our respect for our public men and their personal integrity. That must be preserved, and, unless it is, we are done for absolutely.

In spite of the intense interest and excitement, it was not until George Lansbury was speaking that serious interruption began. He remarked that the agreement had been "riddled with somewhat deadly criticism" and then went

25

on to say that the fact that the House had had no information, while other people outside it had, did give grounds for criticism.

"I hope," he said, "there will be no kind of shrinking on the Committee with regard to this matter."

Mr Lloyd George. I hope, too, there will be no shrinking on the part of those who make the allegations.

Mr Lansbury. The irritation expressed on the Treasury Bench this afternoon when people are making speeches is, I think, not a very nice sign at all. I am entitled to say what other hon. Members have said this afternoon without interruption, that there have been very grave rumours all over the City that people have made money out of this business who ought not to have made money out of it. I am entitled to say that without interruption.

During the course of an interchange that became steadily more acrimonious, Lloyd George made the statement—afterwards to be constantly quoted—which was his only important contribution to the debate.

Mr Lloyd George. The hon. Member said something about the Government, and he has talked about rumours. I want to know what these rumours are. If the hon. gentleman has any charge to make against the Government as a whole, or against individual members of it, I think it ought to be stated openly. The reason why the Government wanted a frank discussion . . . was because we wanted to bring here these rumours, these sinister rumours, that have been passed from one foul lip to another behind the backs of the House.

Lansbury, undaunted by the ferocity of the Chancellor's words and manner, stuck to his point and continued:

If these undertakings are to be taken over, and if more and more of the Government are to spend huge sums of money in matters of this kind, I contend that some means ought to be devised to prevent gambling in the shares, and if the House of Commons does not think that a proper proposition, I at least do.

Then Sir Rufus Isaacs rose to speak. Having remarked that it would be the purest affectation for him to pretend (a phrase much beloved at this date) that he was not in some way implicated by what the hon. Member had said, he observed that he was not so much concerned with what had been said in the House but with the insinuations outside.

> I want the House to understand what the charges are . . . so far as I have been able to gather reading through the various newspapers that have been brought to my notice, and weekly journals. I make them out to be two or perhaps three.
>
> The one is that some person has used his influence to obtain a contract for the Marconi Company with the Government, or has in some way acted to the advantage of the Marconi Company in the negotiations which took place with reference to this contract. I want to say in refer- ence to myself that I have never, from beginning to end, in any shape or form, either by deed, act, or word, or anything else, taken part in the negotiations in reference to this company. . . . I never knew there was such a contract in contemplation until a few days before, when I was told at a private social function by the managing director of the company, who is my brother, that he did hope to get a contract with the Government, and was in negotiation with them for it.

Sir Rufus said that the first intimation he had that the contract had been got was an announcement in the press. Then he continued:

> Let me go to the next charge, which is, I think, a worse charge. It is that some member of the Government, not named but hinted at— some member or members of the Cabinet—knowing that these negotiations were taking place, knowing that there was a contract in contemplation, and thinking the shares would go up when the announcement of the contract came to be made . . . bought shares in this company at a low price in order to sell them at the higher price when the contract was announced.

I desire to say frankly, on behalf of myself, that that is absolutely untrue. Never from the beginning, when the shares were 14s. or £9, have I had one single transaction with the shares of that company. I am not only speaking for myself, but am also speaking on behalf, I know, of both my right hon. friends the Postmaster-General and the Chancellor of the Exchequer, who, in some way or other, in some of the articles, have been brought into this matter.

Two further rather trumpery charges had been made against the Attorney-General. The first, which could hardly have been believed even by Lawson who made it, was that, in the Lodge–Muirhead application for renewal of patents, he had intervened on behalf of the Marconi Company. The second, introduced by Major Archer-Shee, related to a telegram he had sent on the occasion of a public dinner to Marconi in New York. Asked for a message of congratulations, he had replied with these words:

> Please congratulate Marconi and my brother on the successful development of a marvellous enterprise. I wish them all success in New York, and hope that by the time they come back the coal strike will be finished.

There is no doubt that this had been a minor indiscretion, but the Attorney-General was a man of high reputation and it needed a lunatic uncharity to see it as a calculated move in a hidden game. (The oddity of the last sentence inspired the boy-scout-minded to conceive the possibility of a code.) Sir Rufus had no difficulty in disposing of Lawson's allegation, and, referring to the telegram to New York, he made the following statement.

> What happened was this. I was asked whether in conjunction with a number of other public men I would send a telegram, because there was a banquet to be given by the *New York Times* to Mr Marconi and others. . . . They had made arrangements to have a Marconi apparatus fitted up on the table . . . and as a matter of interest to guests they wanted to see how long it would take to get the messages through to the dinner table.

After explaining that he had been only one of several public men who sent messages, he referred again to the rumours that he or his colleagues had speculated in shares and ended with the sentence: "As I have said, there is not one single vestige of foundation for any one of those statements."

When Mr Samuel rose to speak he said immediately what a relief it was to be able at last to answer the insinuations and accusations of the last months.

I should like, in the first instance, to confirm in unqualified terms what has been said on his own behalf by my right hon. and learned friend the Attorney-General, and I can do it not only on my own behalf but on that of every member of the Cabinet . . . Neither I myself nor any of my colleagues have at any time held one shilling's worth of shares in this company, directly or indirectly, or have derived one penny profit from the fluctuations in their prices. It seems shameful that political feelings can carry men so far, that lying tongues can be found to speak and willing ears be found to listen to wicked and utterly base-less slanders such as these.

To refute the charge of corruption in the placing of the contract, Mr Samuel relied on a description of the number of departments and committees that had played a part in the negotiations, and without whose agreement the tender could not have been signed.

All those departments formally expressed their approval of the terms. Therefore, is it not ludicrous, as well as wicked, to suggest that I, even if I desired it—God forbid that I should—was in a position to show undue personal favour to any company in this matter.

Then Mr Samuel turned to the serious business of the debate.

3

The Postmaster-General's replies to criticism make it plain that his opponents had seriously overplayed their hand. They had blandly ignored his explanations of August 7 and built up a case so slightly underpinned it could be demolished by the first wind of truth. But the Government had left it too late. All through the recess the most arrogant and ill-informed criticism had perforce remained unanswered, and the confidence of the critics, their sincere belief that the Government, if not corrupt, was incompetent could no longer be upset by argument. It was to be many years before history, blunting emotion, persuaded the Opposition that, in the circumstances of the time, the Government had no choice.

Mr Samuel suffered a little from the weakness of all politicians that—possibly with reason—they will admit nothing. A mixture of truth and specious evasion allows the Opposition to choose what they will from the points of a speech. On this day he began rather weakly to defend himself from the charge that, while the Marconi Company had published the terms of the agreement, the House had been left without information. He said that the agreement of March 7 had been merely an exchange of letters and it had never occurred to him to lay these before the House. If any Member had asked for the Papers he would have given them.

> *Major Archer-Shee.* The right hon. gentleman has just said that nobody asked him for the Papers of the agreement of March 7. I would remind him that I asked him in March for the agreement, and he said it would be ready as soon as possible. He never offered to give the Papers.
>
> *Mr Samuel.* The hon. Member asked for the contract. The answer is that the contract was not completed until July 7.

Mr Samuel then referred to Lansbury's speech.

> The hon. Member for Bow and Bromley says today that this contract . . . has been "riddled in debate." A contract has been riddled in debate, but it is not the contract I signed. . . .
>
> Hon. Members have said here again and again that the Government have bound themselves to pay a royalty for twenty-eight years of ten per cent on the gross receipts, . . . and they have asked, "What are we to pay royalty for when the Marconi patents may expire within a year or two?"

The hon. and gallant gentleman [Major Archer-Shee] was the first to make this assertion in *The Times* of July 27. . . . On August 7 I denied this and said, if we were not using the Marconi patents—if the patents expired—from that date we ceased to pay any royalty. . . . If the patents are essential to the working of the stations, it is right that we should pay a royalty—that is, assuming a royalty is to be paid at all. If the patents are not essential to the working of the stations, we can turn them out.

Sir C. Marks. I only state that the provision for twenty-eight years is obviously beyond the life of any patent. Therefore why pay the royalty?

Mr Herbert Samuel. On any individual patent. But there are scores of patents touching wireless telegraphy, and new patents are being taken out every day. . . . Hon. Members have said what are you buying for this royalty? In the first place I have pointed out that we are buying the use of all their patents so long as they are valid, and when they are not we cease to pay the royalty. We are buying much more than that. We are buying . . . the unpatented inventions, the secret inventions, which I am told are really of considerable importance. We are buying what is more valuable still, their experience of long-range wireless telegraphy, which they alone have, for they are the only company in the world which has kept up a continuous commercial service for distances approaching those which would be necessary. Not only that, but we are buying their assistance, the technical assistance of their engineers during the whole period the royalty runs. Not only are we buying the existing patents, but all future patents and all future inventions which the company either owns or uses, and, further, when the twenty-eight years comes to an end, the royalty having then also come to an end, we are buying the right to use after that period any patents that may have been used, however new, in any of the stations without extra payment.

In the course of the debate Mr Samuel also gave figures to show that the price to be paid to Marconi was not greater, in some cases smaller, than that being paid for the same services by European Governments.

In answer to the criticism that he had given a monopoly, he said:

I come to the second provision of this contract which has been

31

riddled because it is not there. That is the provision that is supposed to give the company a monopoly for twenty-eight years. What did the company originally ask for? They asked for licences to work eighteen stations in different parts of the Empire for which the Government had not to pay them a single sixpence . . . we rejected it for the very reason that we were determined not to give that company, or any other company, a monopoly of wireless communication. . . . The hon. Member for Blackburn [Sir Henry Norman] said that these stations will not be State-owned but State and Marconi-owned, and that the Government will not have complete control over them. The hon. Member for Finsbury [Major Archer-Shee] said that the Marconi Company will be middlemen. . . . And therefore he suggests that other inventors will have to go to the Marconi Company to get their assent for the use of their appliances. That is literally the charge. . . . Clause II of the contract says: "Upon the giving of the final completion certificate in respect of the long-distance installation, . . . the company shall hand over such long-distance installation to the Postmaster-General, and the same shall become the absolute property of the Postmaster-General or the Government [of the Dominion or Colony] and he and they shall be entitled to use, work and maintain the same in any way and for any purpose at his and their absolute discretion by his and their servants. . . ." We propose to work them ourselves. There has never been any question of the Marconi Company working them.

There was a long wrangle about the Marconi Company's right of inspection of other companies' patents should they be used on other government stations, the Postmaster-General maintaining that this did not give them a means of inspecting the secret processes of their rivals, his critics maintaining it did.

With regard to the criticism that the work had not been put out to tender, he said:

That point was referred by me at the very outset to the Committee of twenty members of which I have spoken. After discussion it was decided not to call for tenders, because all the expert members of that Committee said that it was necessary to have proof that the people could do this work and the Marconi Company was the only company carrying on operations of this nature.

Discussing the suggestion that the stations might have been built by the Government, he asked:

> But what is the Government? . . . The Post Office has a number of little stations around the coasts of this country, but it has not the staff and not the experience which would enable it to undertake a task so gigantic as this. . . . It has further been suggested that the work should be done by the Admiralty. . . . Their representatives said at one of the meetings of the Committee that they would only undertake the work in the very last resort, because they did not wish to devote what staff they had—I do not think it was a very big one—to the erection of these stations, instead of devoting themselves to the proper and normal work of the Admiralty experts of this class—putting in Admiralty installations on the ships and the land stations that belong to them.

When he turned to the question of the Poulsen Syndicate, Mr Samuel said:

> The hon. Member would have been far more candid with the House if he had told us that the company made no claim to communicate by day. As soon as I knew that it had established any sort of communication of that nature, I sent an adviser of my Department to San Francisco to test it, and there is no evidence that they can maintain that long distance by day.
>
> *Sir H. Norman.* I think the right hon. gentleman will probably desire, when he reflects, to express regret to me for what he has just said, because in quoting that experiment I added, "under extremely favourable atmospheric conditions."
>
> *Mr H. Samuel.* Why did not the hon. gentleman say by night? "By night" is two short words.
>
> *Sir H. Norman.* Favourable atmospheric conditions means by night.
>
> *Mr H. Samuel.* Only recently the Inspector of Wireless Telegraphy of

the Post Office, whose advice I cannot ignore, reported to me that it is not safe to assume without proof that the Poulsen Syndicate are able to apply sufficient power to their system to work 2000 miles by day. It is not a question of being able to do it by night, but it is a question of being able to do it also by day. . . . Lastly, there was a certain amount of uncertainty as to whether the Poulsen patents were valid against the Marconi patents. The Committee came to the conclusion that it was impossible to accept the Poulsen Company's offer without a test of their capacity to perform what they claimed to perform, and we said that if that test could be carried out in a comparatively short period, say of one month, or at the most three months, we should wait to enable them to perform the test. Their representative told me that they could not possibly make any such test within that time; that they might make a test one way in six months, both ways in a year. . . . Suppose—I put this to the House, and I hope the House will consider it candidly—I had at that time in March signed an agreement with the Poulsen Syndicate, what would have happened? That syndicate of Danish gentlemen is not carrying on any commercial work here. . . . I do not say it would have been improper at all, but they would probably first have gone to the City to raise capital on the strength of the contract to carry out the work. Then the Marconi Company would have brought an action against them for the infringement of patents, as the American Company has brought an action against the company working the Poulsen system in America. . . . Hon. Members would have said to me: "Who is this syndicate of Danish gentlemen with whom you are entering into this contract, and who are now in the City raising money in order to fulfil it? Have they proved they can cover this distance at all?" I should have had to say: "Oh! no, but they assert they can and very likely they may." I should have been asked: "Have they any staff of engineers able to put these stations in hand and complete them quickly?" I should have been compelled to reply: "No, as far as I know, they have no staff approaching anything like the scale necessary. . . ." "Are you sure their patents are valid? . . ." "No, we believe them to be valid, but they have not been tested, and the Marconi Company are now disputing them in the Law Courts. . . ." "Did your permanent officials advise you to make this contract?" . . . "No, my

34

permanent officials unanimously urged me not to do so."

Mr Samuel said that he had asked the engineers of the Admiralty and the Post Office for an estimate of the cost of building each station. The figure they gave was £60,800. The first Marconi figure had been £70,000, but they had reduced it to £60,000.

> Then the Company told us they had spoken their last word, that they would not erect the stations on lower terms. Therefore, if it was not practicable for the Admiralty or the Post Office to erect them, if we could not get any other company which had proved its capacity to do the work, if, owing to the urgency of the matter from the Imperial point of view, we could not delay, and if we could not get lower terms from the Company, I ask what other course had I? Hon. Members have made many accusations and many criticisms. Is there any charge left against the Government? There is no response. Then, sir, I have done.

The contract was to be discussed for weeks and weeks at the Select Committee and was then to become the subject of a technical committee, the Parker Committee. It was to be debated again in the House of Commons, but in July 1913 the Parker Committee were to report that the Marconi Company alone could do the work. A contract was then signed which did not differ in any of its main provisions from the original contract, and the work was put in hand, to be incomplete, however, in August 1914.

Mr Samuel had made it plain that the limitations of the agreement were no greater than is common with large government transactions. It is not necessary today to vindicate his actions because that has been done by history—the history of the Marconi Company, of wireless telegraphy and of the world.

At the time the matter was recognised as one of extreme urgency, the Liberal Government had, with the Irish members, a majority. If it had not been for the scandal that from the beginning had surrounded the negotiations with the Marconi Company, they would have used it to ratify the contract.

4

So much for the debate of October 11. The Ministers had categorically denied all charges levelled against them, while the Postmaster-General had explained the terms of the agreement. But nothing was altered. The critics of the contract continued assiduously to add to a case Mr Samuel had already demolished, Lawson and Chesterton went back to their articles, and Hilaire Belloc wrote to Maurice Baring:

Of this company Mr Marconi, his father an Italian Pantheist, his mother an Irish Protestant, was director. Nor did it pay any dividends nor had it any prospect of doing so. Mr Marconi, therefore, approached Mr Godfrey de Bouillon Isaacs and begged him to become a co-director. This gentleman accepted the post and shortly afterwards emerged as sole director, with Mr Marconi occupying the honourable position of Chairman, the leisures of which he beguiled by touring upon the Continent where only the other day he had one eye poked out in a motor-car accident.

Meanwhile Mr G. de B. Isaacs discovering that the shares of the Company fetched no more than 14s. approached the Postmaster General of England and suggested that a monopoly should be given him for establishing round the world an All Red Chain of Wireless Stations. Fired as the young patriot was (I refer to Mr Herbert Samuel) by so splendid a conception, he drove the hardest possible bargain in the public interests and the shares of Mr Godfrey de Bouillon Isaacs only rose from 14s. to one hundred. An extraordinary example of the secrecy and honour with which such affairs are conducted today is the fact that Sir Rufus Isaacs, though the very born brother of de Bouillon Isaacs (the one being named after the second Norman King of England, the second after his contemporary The Great Crusader) never heard of the negotiations at all until the day before the contract was signed! To the truth of this Sir Rufus has himself testified amid the cheers of the House of Commons and what is more proclaimed it for a second time in a loud voice before two battalions of the Royal Marines drawn up in Hollow Square for the purpose of the ceremony. Unfortunately foul tongues are at it again and suggesting that Mr Lloyd George, our popular Welsh Chancellor, though sprung from the people, had fallen into the aristocratic vice of fluttering and, having inside knowledge, had made no small profit upon the difference between the 14*s*. and the 100*s*. No one, I am assured, gives credence to this vile tale with the exception of a couple of hundred gossiping bankers in the City and some eight or ten thousand in the West End. It is even asserted, I am glad to say, that the poorer and more contemptible of those who have lent themselves to this abominable slander will be sent to prison at the discretion of some judge appointed by the Chancellor himself.[4]

---

[4] Speaight, *Hilaire Belloc*, 309–10.

(4)

Behind the Scenes:
1. The Isaacs Family and
the Marconi Shares

1

Joseph Isaacs, the merchant, was partner in a family business with his brother Sir Henry Isaacs. His son Godfrey once publicly stated that this business had an annual turnover of from £500,000 to £600,000. But Joseph was a genial, optimistic creature who, according to his grandson, could make money but not keep it. The first question his children asked when they arrived home for the holidays was: "Is the carriage up or down?" If up, their holidays would be gay and carefree, if down, they would be ruled by the strictest economy.

The hazardous finances of this family seem to have been caused not by any failure in Isaacs's main business but by a propensity for gambling outside it. He seems to have had a share of the imagination and optimism that later was so marked a characteristic of his son Godfrey.

But in his own home Joseph Isaacs was ruled by his wife and this was a matriarchal society. It was one of those large, devoted families, more common in the Victorian age than today, and all the members of it were gifted, vigorous and enterprising. They lived a full life in the company of neighbours of their own social standing and secure sense of natural worth.

Rufus, the second son, was one of those singular personalities of which there are only a few in each generation, who seem to be born at double strength. He had, in addition to a brilliant brain, unusual physical strength, vast energy and such an exceptional memory that at the age of six he won, in a Belgian school for pupils of all ages, the first prize in a competition which consisted in reading over for ten minutes two pages of French prose, and then repeating as much of it as could be remembered.

As a child he was wild and uncontrollable. He was sent to school in Brussels because his mother wanted him to learn languages, and he was accompanied by his brother Harry, who was his elder by only a year, and to whom above everyone he was devoted. Before long the headmaster sent for their father and told him that he would keep in his school either Rufus or Harry, but in no circumstances both. Later, at a school in England, Rufus gave a demonstration of his incisive mind and strong character. Another brother, Albert, contracted an illness from which he was never to recover. Rufus was convinced that the illness was more serious than the doctor or the school authorities believed, and he tried repeatedly to make them send for his parents. He was unable to persuade them, so he ran away from school, and finding his way home, told his parents of the illness himself.

When Rufus was fourteen the headmaster of the University College School expressed the opinion that he ought to stay at school until he was of university age and then read for the Bar. But this idea was quite outside the vision of his tradesman father, and he was taken away from school and put to work in the family business. This was not a success, and after some time it was decided he should go to sea. When his father took him to join his ship and he discovered that to sail as an apprentice meant signing an agreement that would bind him for two years, he refused to sign it, and nothing his father or the captain could say would persuade him. He therefore sailed in the much harder conditions of ship's boy.

The life on this ship was not brutal, but, after seven weeks at sea, on reaching port at Rio de Janeiro, Rufus decided he had had enough of it, and while on shore-leave he disappeared into the open country behind the city. Here, without food or money, he was taken care of by an elderly negress, from whose amorous advances he was forced again to run away. He was caught then and returned to the ship, and on the home voyage he was much bullied by the boatswain, until one night, still only fifteen or sixteen, he fought the bully and knocked him out.

When he returned to London, after another short period in the family business, he made one more false start. He entered the office of a stockbroker, and here he remained for four years, first as a clerk, but later as a stock-jobber and full member of the Stock Exchange. Now he encountered disaster. He was young and inexperienced, his capital was small and his ambition large. Caught unprepared in a slump, he was unable to meet his liabilities, and not only was he "hammered," but left with debts of £8000.

During his time on the Stock Exchange he acquired an enthusiasm for boxing, and while this enthusiasm lasted he broke the nose of every one of his younger brothers, while his boxing-master broke his.

He was deeply disturbed by his indebtedness and determined to repay the money as soon as possible, and he showed now some of the grandiose imagination that was such a marked characteristic of his brother Godfrey. He decided to go to Panama, which was being featured as a potential Eldorado, in an effort to get rich quickly. His mind was made up, his plans completed, and he was actually sitting in the railway carriage that was to take him on the first stage of his journey when his brother Harry rushed breathlessly on to the platform and hauled him out of his seat. His mother was at that moment indulging in a sharp fit of hysterics which she intended to continue until her beloved son was returned to her.

Now at last it was agreed that some of the advice of his schoolmaster should be followed, and Rufus began to read for the Bar. Having left school at fourteen, he was, in spite of all his adventures, only at the age at which young men from the university normally begin their legal training, but he had to make up for that part of the necessary education he had never received. It was then he did something nobody else had been able to do for him: he disciplined himself.

He married very young in spite of his indebtedness and the years that lay ahead before he could hope to make an income at the Bar. The Isaacses seem always to have married women with unusual aptitudes for getting their own way. The father of Miss Alice Cohen regarded her suitor as a youth with a past that inspired no confidence in his future, and refused to consider the match. Miss Cohen immediately took to her bed where she managed symptoms so alarming that the famous physician called into consultation instructed her father: "Give her the young man and I promise you she will recover. Otherwise she will die."

Armed then with his own great ability and the faith of this determined young woman, Rufus Isaacs worked at his profession twelve or fourteen hours a day. His rise and his career were such that in 1910, at the age of fifty-two, after a short time in Parliament, and having long since paid his Stock Exchange debts, he became Attorney-General in the Liberal Government.

By now he was unrecognisable as the wild youth who had run away from school and from his ship. Very reserved and with a quiet and modest manner, he was inclined to be ascetic and had a sad taste in food. Left to himself he would have subsisted on eggs and bacon with a baked apple, or roast chicken and rice pudding with vast cups of tea. He was sociable but not very social, and his life was devoted to his career.

It can be seen that he was a brilliant man, with great energy and self-control. It must be presumed that he was a proud man, and it should never be forgotten that he was a Jew.

England has never been hysterical about her Jews in the manner of many continental countries, because they have not been sufficiently numerous or powerful. But anti-Jewish feeling of the kind that is not cruel but merely superior, which takes it for granted that to be a Jew is to be an underdog and a person of certain markedly unattractive racial characteristics, was very prevalent in the England of that time. It must have been a surprise to the reader that Lawson should use the phrase "two financiers of the same nationality" when speaking of two Englishmen of the Jewish race, nor can it have escaped his notice that in the quotations from the press which occur in Chapter Two of this book Mr Samuel and Sir Rufus Isaacs are constantly and contemptuously referred to as "Hebrews" or in some other equivalent term. It is true that the writer in the *Eye-Witness* does not comment on the race of these men except where he quotes his correspondent, but this is because it had been his custom to speak of the Jews, and in particular of Mr Samuel and Sir Rufus Isaacs, in such outrageous terms that he had lately provoked a strong rebuke in the correspondence columns of the journal: and, although in the civilised society of the time anti-Jewish feeling was quite common, as an intellectual attitude it was already disapproved. There can be no doubt, however, that anti-semitism was a strong, disagreeable and only partly subconscious social influence. The second Lord Reading in his biography of his father, constantly alludes to it, remarking that few Jews had as yet been called to the Bar, almost no Jew had ever shone as a barrister, and so on. Probably no one not born a Jew can ever completely imagine what it was for a man, conscious of his own superior qualities, always to be at this bitter disadvantage always to be within range of humiliation on account of his race.

2

The second Lord Reading begins his account of the Marconi case with the sending of the telegram, afterwards so much criticised, to the Marconi dinner in New York. This trivial and unconsidered incident seemed in retrospect to open the long and fearful scandal which, he says, brought his father and his family nearly to breaking-point. For eighteen months the word Marconi held its place in the headlines and on the newspaper placards, while it obsessed their thoughts and their dreams. Other Ministers' careers were put in jeopardy and the Government itself in danger of defeat.

Marconi and Godfrey Isaacs, both of whom were directors of the American Marconi Company, had gone to New York in March 1912, soon after the signing of the tender with the British Government, ostensibly to be present at the hearing of an action against the United Wireless Telegraph Company of America to prevent infringement of patents; but Isaacs had already been approached in London with an offer of the assets of this rival company, and when he left London he had some hope that the action might be settled out of court. He was accompanied by a Mr Heybourn, a member of the Stock Exchange firm of Heybourn & Croft, the largest jobbers in the Marconi market.

When they arrived in New York they found the United Wireless Company in liquidation and their directors in gaol on a charge of fraud.[1] Godfrey Isaacs,

---

[1] It was always assumed that this was a case of simple fraud, and there were fraudulent practices by some of the directors. But one of them, Dr Lee de Forest, was the

whose enterprise was stupendous, realised that the tangible assets of the company included practically the whole of the wireless business of America and that this was an exceptional opportunity to acquire them.

There were certain difficulties. The shares of the American Marconi Company were standing at a heavy discount and the public had invariably lost money in wireless undertakings. When therefore Isaacs called a meeting of his directors and proposed an issue to increase the capital of the Marconi Company by more than six million dollars, the Americans, whose imagination had bounds unknown to him, were understandably taken aback. They refused to consider the suggestion unless Marconi and Isaacs on behalf of the English Company would guarantee that the whole amount would be subscribed. Isaacs would have given his word, but here Marconi baulked. He would consent to the proposal only if Isaacs would undertake to be personally responsible for 500,000 of an issue of 1,400,000 shares, leaving a balance of 900,000 to be guaranteed by the English Company.

Isaacs immediately agreed to this suggestion and called in their travelling companion, Mr Heybourn. He arranged there and then to place with him 250,000 shares at a par value of five dollars American, or £1. 1s. 3d. British currency, on the condition that Heybourn should introduce them into the London and New York markets, supplying the principal dealers in London with shares fixed at a price not exceeding £1. 5s. 0d. Isaacs also placed shares

---

inventor of the three-electrode valve. The charge contended that the company's only assets were the De Forest patents, "chiefly directed by a strange device like an incandescent lamp, which he called an audion . . . and which had proved worthless."

The district attorney said that:

> De Forest has said in many newspapers that in would be possible to transmit the human voice across the Atlantic before many years. Based on these absurd and misleading statements of De Forest, the misguided public, Your Honour, has been persuaded to purchase stock in his company. . . .

De Forest was acquitted of criminal intent, although two of his associates were found guilty. In 1947 he was presented with the Edison Medal and his "worthless" invention hailed as one of the twenty greatest of all time. (Upton, *Electronics for Everyone*, 151.)

with bankers and others in the United States, leaving 100,000 for his own disposal when he got back to England. In view of the situation in America, it is impossible to believe he could easily have placed so many shares but for the great prestige the English Company had recently acquired through the agreement with the British Government.

Before leaving America Isaacs had one further brilliant success. He negotiated an agreement with the Western Union Telegraph and Cable Company for the reception and distribution of wireless messages in America, thus removing the necessity of setting up a competitive system.

Then, elated as he might well have been, he returned to England, and on the day after his arrival, April 9, he invited his brothers, Sir Rufus and Harry Isaacs, to lunch with him at the Savoy. For an account of what took place at the luncheon-party we have the word of the three brothers.

Godfrey began by describing in detail the events of his American visit. He had already been concerned with various other schemes and businesses, none of which, as his nephew dutifully puts it, had been an unalloyed success, and this cannot have been the first meeting between these brothers to discuss some new project of Godfrey's. They were a close and affectionate family and there must have been some element of hope and concern in the attitude of Rufus and Harry, although this was never afterwards stressed. Godfrey proceeded to offer them some part of his shares in the American Company at £1. 1s.3d., the price he had paid himself.

Lord Reading says that Sir Rufus had, up to this moment, been ignorant of the affairs or even the existence of the American Company, and that his first reply to Godfrey's offer was to question him about the relation between the American and English Marconi Companies. He wished to assure himself that the American Company received no advantage, direct or indirect, from the contract with the British Government, since this would affect his position as a Minister of the Crown.

His brother reassured him. He said that, whereas the English Company was a large shareholder in the American Company, the American Company held no shares in the English and was in no way concerned with its profits or undertakings. It made no difference to the financial position of the American Company, whose operations were confined to the United States, whether the acceptance of the tender ever matured into a formal contract, or whether the

Imperial wireless chain was ever established.

Nevertheless, Sir Rufus refused to buy any of his brother's shares at this meeting, on the grounds, according to his later explanation, that he thought the proposed issue of capital very high, and that, although he saw no objection to his buying the shares, he thought it better he should have no dealings with his brother Godfrey. He then left the luncheon table, but the other two sat on for some time. During their conversation Harry agreed to take 50,000 shares at £1. 1s. 0d. and no one considering the size of this undertaking can fail to be impressed by the aplomb these brothers showed.

When Harry got home that night his wife asked him whether he could get some shares for members of her family. He telephoned to Godfrey and secured for them a further 6000. For this reason his holding is sometimes treated as 50,000, sometimes as 56,000. It will here be treated as 56,000, because, where the total number of shares placed by Godfrey is being discussed, it is essential that it should be.

Godfrey had no difficulty in placing the whole of the remaining 44,000 shares, with the exception of 2500, which he kept for himself.

During the week following the luncheon-party at the Savoy there was an unofficial boom in American Marconi shares, although they could not yet be bought on the Stock Exchange. What happened was that the applications for shares were known to be so great that there was a quick appreciation in value. When, shortly afterwards, Harry paid a call on his brother Rufus his shares were already worth £2 each.

It was apparent that the Marconi issue was going to be very successful. The shares, having risen so much before opening day, were almost certain to rise again. Harry wanted his brother to share in his luck. During the course of the interview he persuaded Sir Rufus to take 10,000 of the shares he had bought from Godfrey. The Attorney-General insisted on paying the appreciated price of £2 and conceived, so he said, that there was a very real difference in buying from this brother rather than the other.

He was a close friend of the Chancellor of the Exchequer and of the Master of Elibank, Government Chief Whip, who at this time was staying at 11 Downing Street. That night he visited the two men and told them of his transaction. He offered each of them one thousand shares at the price he had paid, remarking that they need not bother to pay him at the moment, as the shares were not yet in existence and he would give them plenty of notice when he required the money. Both men accepted his offer.

There is a benighted innocence in all this. None of these men ever attempted to conceal his name in later dealings through stockbrokers and none of them ever showed a great propensity for gambling. They seem to have given the matter little or no thought. With Lloyd George and the Master of Elibank one can understand how this might happen. They were offered a share in a good thing by a man whom they trusted, who was Attorney-General of England, had knowledge of the Stock Exchange and was brother to the managing director of the Marconi Company. They were overwhelmingly busy men and they took the whole thing on trust.

On April 18 a meeting of the shareholders in America authorised the proposed increase in capital, and the Marconi Company issued a circular in London setting out the arrangements Godfrey Isaacs had made. On the 18th there were dealings among members of the Stock Exchange which raised the price to £3, and on the 19th, when the shares were made available to the public, they opened at £3. 5s. 0d. and closed in the evening at £4.

On that day Sir Rufus telephoned to his brokers, Messrs Bourke, Schiff and Co., who advised him to sell, on the grounds that the shares were far too high. He telephoned this advice to Harry, who agreed to sell some of his shares, and Sir Rufus sold for the two of them 7000 at an average of £3. 10s. 0d. On May 5 he sold a further 1000 at £2. 13s. 9d. At the same time Lloyd George and the Master of Elibank sold half their holdings. Later, however, they invested again, buying together a further 3000 shares.

They then apparently gave the matter no thought until in June they heard, as did everyone else, the rumours that were causing so much excitement in the City. Sir Rufus then went to Mr Samuel and told him of these transactions.

3

Mr Samuel had by now plenty of troubles of his own. He was not, it is fair to say, in the least perturbed about the contract he had made, only about the extent and form of the criticisms of it. This contract must be seen against the background of the German naval rearmament which had begun in

1910. Mr Samuel was aware that there was only one company who might have rivalled the Marconi, and that was not the Poulsen on whose behalf so many Members took up arms, but the Telefunken, the a German company. He had consulted his Cabinet colleagues when the Marconi Company had refused to reduce their terms, and here is a reply from the Home Secretary, Mr Winston Churchill.

I think it is very undesirable to give Government patronage to foreigners. The circumstances may arise which render it necessary, but each case must be judged on its own merits. Very strong and special reasons would be required to convince me of the propriety of giving an order to a foreign firm. Of course when the question arises quite nakedly whether you should pay more to a British firm than you would have to pay to a foreign firm for exactly the same quality goods, a very awkward dilemma is created. The good administration of a Department by the political Chief ought in nearly every case to prevent such an unfortunate conjuncture being created. These little stupid attempts to save twopence tend to bring the whole structure of the Free Trade argument into discredit with the working-class electorate.

At any rate, no Department for which I am responsible shall, with my knowledge, put any contracts abroad except in circumstances of a very special and peculiar character, or to break, or to prevent the formation of, a ring among the home producers.[2]

As early as the spring of 1911 the Standing Sub-Committee on strategic Imperial Defence had reported: "If the country does not move at once it may be placed in a disadvantageous position."

"What would be the position," the Prime Minister asked, "if the negotiations with Marconi broke down?"

"They ought not to do so," Samuel replied;[3] and there is no doubt this was his convinced opinion.

---

[2] Bowle, *Viscount Samuel*, 88.
[3] Bowie, *Viscount Samuel*, 89.

By the time Sir Rufus went to him and disclosed his dealings in American shares the two men were already being charged with using privileged knowledge to deal in the shares of the English Company, and by some people with having corruptly connived to favour Marconi in the placing of the contract.

Some doubt has been created about what happened next. In their account of the Marconi case the biographers of Asquith suggest that he was not informed of the dealings in American shares until six months after this, when the facts were made public in a libel action. Asquith himself seems to support this suggestion:

> In the debate on the appointment of the Select Committee, Sir Rufus Isaacs and Mr Lloyd George confined themselves to denying the suggestion that they had ever had any interest, direct or indirect, in the English Marconi Company: that being the whole gravamen of the accusations and insinuation that had up to that time been made against them. Neither of them thought it necessary or relevant to refer to the American transaction, *which was unknown both to their traducers and their friends.*[4]

Mr Samuel's account makes it clear, however, that Asquith was not merely informed at this time, but quickly appreciated the implications:

> In or about the month of June I was told of rumours . . . not long after I learned from the Attorney-General, Sir Rufus Isaacs, that he, together with Mr Lloyd George, Chancellor of the Exchequer, and the Master of Elibank, Patronage Secretary to the Treasury and Chief Government Whip, had in fact bought some shares . . . in the Marconi Company of America . . . I went at once . . . to inform the Prime Minister of what I had been told. He felt more concern than I did, and said that he thought "our colleagues could not have done a more foolish thing."[5]

---

[4] *Memories and Reflections*, 1, 209; my italics.
[5] *Memoirs*, 75.

4

On August 8, the day after he made his first statement on the contract in the House of Commons, Mr Samuel wrote to Sir Rufus Isaacs as follows:

As I was leaving King's Cross this morning I saw on a bookstall a copy of Belloc's paper, the *Eye–Witness*, with an article headed "The Marconi Scandal." I found it to be a gross and unrestrained libel on you and myself. I had just time before the train started to address an envelope to you at the House of Commons and to put the article into it with a scribbled note. I have since obtained your address by telegraph and this letter, enclosing another copy, will probably reach you before the first. One's natural inclination is, of course, at once to have an application made for a writ, and I am not at all sure that it is not the right course. There can be no possible doubt as to the result of the action. It is hardly necessary for me to say that during the long negotiations that preceded the conclusion of the contract there was no action of mine that I would wish withdrawn from any measure of publicity, whether in the courts or in parliament. The circumstances that deter me from at once coming to the conclusion that proceedings ought to be taken are the obvious ones: first, that this contemptible rag has a very small circulation; its pages are always full of personal abuse; its articles cannot influence any opinion which is worth having, and an action would give immense publicity to the libel . . . and one does not wish to soil one's hands with the thing. As there will in all probability be a Select Committee of the House of Commons in the autumn, to inquire into the wisdom of the contract, the report of that committee will supply a sufficient answer. On the other hand, it is a grave thing when ministers are directly accused of corrupt action by a newspaper, no matter how obscure and scurrilous, for them to do nothing. With your unrivalled experience of the law you are better able to judge than I what is best to do, and I will very gladly join you in proceedings if you think it is advisable, or do nothing, if you consider that the better course. If you are of opinion that a writ should be issued and will wire me to that effect, I will go to town and see a solicitor and start proceedings on behalf of both of us. . . . If you are in some doubt as to the proper course you might think it well to consult the Prime Minister, and in that case I should be glad if you would send on this letter to him.

Sir Rufus replied to this letter about a week later, although he had given an opinion by telegram more quickly. He said that, after taking time to consider it, he felt that Mr Samuel's reasons for not proceeding outweighed the immediate impulse to issue writs at once. He thought that "the rag" should be treated with contempt. "Itsmalevolence and prejudice were so marked that only the most blinded partisan could be led to believe the statements."[6] He had thought it right, nevertheless, to send the paper and Mr Samuel's letter to the Prime Minister, since as head of the Government he was entitled to give his opinion as to whether such a charge should be framed without public action being taken.

Sir Rufus then went on to reassure Mr Samuel that he had never held a share in the English Marconi Company or indeed in the American until after the signing of the "contract," and to remind him that they had never discussed the negotiations. He had, in fact, known nothing of them until a day or two before the execution of the tender. He said that Lloyd George, whom he had consulted, took the same view as he did, and so did Sir Charles Matthews, the Director of Public Prosecutions, to whom he had also put the case.

In due course Asquith replied:

I have read carefully the scurrilous rubbish, and I am clearly of opinion that you should take no notice of it. Samuel gives some excellent reasons in his letter. I suspect the *Eye–Witness* has a very meagre circulation. I notice only one page of advertisements and that occupied by books of Belloc's publishers. Prosecution would secure it notoriety, which might yield subscribers. We have broken weather, and but for Winston there would be nothing in the newspapers.

---

[6] Reading, *Rufus Isaacs,* 241.

These letters are the only record that the question of a libel-action against the *Eye–Witness* or any other paper was ever considered. They refer to the article of August 8, and there is no evidence that, when Cecil Chesterton continued week after week and ever more boldly to challenge the Ministers to proceed against him, it was ever thought necessary to reconsider the matter. There are no other letters, although it is difficult to believe there was no further discussion. Except that the Attorney-General made one public reference to him which is of some interest, there is no suggestion that anyone ever gave any thought to the almost equally insolent Lawson.

The *Eye–Witness* could not be dismissed with the ease that these letters suggest. It is true that its political pages were scurrilous and that they had continuously brought absurd charges against members of the Government, in particular Mr Samuel and Sir Rufus Isaacs. But it was a paper founded, edited and contributed to by Hilaire Belloc, and its literary pages were of a high quality. Among the contributors to the four numbers quoted here were Arthur Ran-some, Arthur Quiller-Couch, J. C. Squire, E. Nesbit, Desmond MacCarthy, John Phillimore and Hugh Dalton. At other times its contributors included Maurice Baring, H. G. Wells, Algernon Blackwood, Wilfrid Blunt, G. K. Chesterton, A. C. Benson, Edward Thomas and F. Y. Eccles. Its correspondence columns alone are evidence that it was read by people whose good opinion was not a matter for contempt. As one turns over its pages in the files, one's attention is continually startled by the distinction of the opening paragraph of some letter addressed to the editor, and, dropping one's eyes to the foot, one reads a famous name. There is no doubt that in a small but influential and important circle of intellectuals it was widely read.

But, even if this had not been the case, if it had been as unimportant as the Ministers protested, there is a point they overlooked. In reply to Mr Samuel, Sir Rufus says: "Its malevolence and prejudice were so marked that only the most blinded partisan could be led to believe the statements." In all but one circumstance this might have been true, because the political views of the editor were so extreme and so hostile, not merely to the Government but to all politicians. It could never be true, however, in default of any action by the persons slandered to give it the lie. No one would be likely to believe that men with nothing to hide would be content week after week to ignore public charges of the vilest corruption. Mr Samuel, here as throughout the whole course of this case, was free from all blame unless one attaches blame to loyalty, but Sir Rufus Isaacs gravely damaged the honour and dignity of public men by failing to restrain Cecil Chesterton. He also encouraged the rumours of corruption which were largely the cause of the failure to proceed with the wireless chain.

In defence of the Ministers, it must be remembered that this was a period when powerful invective was freely used in political life and in journalism. To readers of a time when the word "hack" used in the wrong context can bring large damages, it must already be apparent that in those days journalists were allowed very great licence. Apart from the scurrilous writings of Cecil Chesterton and Lawson, we have few journalists writing today who approach the freedom taken monthly by Maxse in the *National Review*.

Nevertheless, the silence of the Ministers was neither understood nor approved at the time. The *Spectator* remarked on 19 October 1912:

> The notion that such accusations as those made in the *Eye–Witness* against the Cabinet Ministers can be passed over as unworthy of notice is quite untenable. The paper in question is very ably written and is read by people in whose mind it is most undesirable that untrue suspicions should grow up. The *Eye–Witness*, whatever else it may have done, has not shown want of courage, . . . and it may fairly be claimed that it cannot be put aside as a voice too small to be listened to.

And so we come again to the great debate of October 11. In the light of knowledge of the American dealings, a knowledge the public were not to acquire for many months to come, it is natural to turn to the record to see in what terms the Ministers described the company whose shares they denied having bought. It can immediately be seen that Sir Rufus, instead of referring to the Marconi Company, as had nearly everyone else in the whole course of the debate, denied, on behalf of himself and his colleagues, ever having owned shares in "that company."[7] Mr Samuel made the same declaration about

---

[7] See p. 36.

"this company." They could not have said that no one had bought shares in "the Marconi Company," because it would not have been true; if they had spoken of "the English Company," there would have been a danger that in some agile brain on the other side of the House the thought might occur: "If not in the English Company, then in what other Company?"

The omission was carefully calculated. It ensured that for twelve months the Marconi case should exercise the minds of most of the leading men of the time, and that slander and truth, malice and honourable indignation should become so entwined that fifty years have failed to separate them. On the other hand, it may have saved the careers of the Attorney-General and the Chancellor of the Exchequer.

(5)

Behind the Scenes:
2. The Eye-Witness

1

The letter from Hilaire Belloc to Maurice Baring written after the debate of
October 11 and quoted on pages 35–6 appears in full in Mr Speaight's biography of Belloc and is introduced with the words:

> We can clearly read, beneath the bias and the banter, what it was
> that made so many people raise their eyebrows at the sudden popularity
> of the Marconi Company.[1]

We cannot clearly read it, because beneath the bias and the banter the
charge that Belloc is making against Mr Samuel and Sir Rufus Isaacs is not
the charge of speculating in Marconi shares, but that of corruption in the
placing of the contract. This charge was never believed except by people of

---

[1] Speaight, 309.

extraordinary prejudice who could not be convinced by the facts. It was dropped immediately at the Select Committee, where, once it became clear there was no evidence to support it, members of all parties regarded it as unworthy of examination, and all three of the reports of this Committee rejected it unequivocally. It is clear that Mr Speaight has no intention of re-stating it, however indirectly, because in a later paragraph he goes out of his way to clear the Ministers of the lesser charge of gambling in shares of the English Company. But the Marconi case is extremely complicated, and the enormities that were rumoured against Ministers have become so mixed with the impropriety they actually committed that biographers, studying it as a small part of a whole, constantly give an inaccurate picture.

For this Belloc was much to blame. Lawson was the first in the field with the charge of corruption, but Belloc and Cecil Chesterton spread it. In their day they all three gravely damaged the reputation of the two Ministers, because there are always people who, fundamentally uninterested in politics, do not read serious accounts of events, but take their views from the more readable if less accurate statements of writers of ability and wit. There are also people who, from some prejudice of their own, will, when offered two explanations of an occurrence, accept the more discreditable. In their day Lawson and Chesterton had some influence, but they are dead and their words died with them. Belloc was a man of genius, and genius has greater responsibilities.

He was a great and good man, brave and gay, lovable and devout, and there is already a considerable literature about him. It is all, however, written by his friends, and, although all the writers suggest there were difficult sides to his nature, for the love they bore him they have refrained from presenting these except in the gentlest and most forbearing way. In this incident of the Marconi scandal he played a considerable part, and, aside from a comic pugnacity in front of the Committee of Inquiry, there is little that seems to his credit.

It is difficult to be sure how much he was concerned. Publicly and privately he said he was in it with Cecil Chesterton all the way, and he said, too, that some of the articles in the *Eye–Witness* were written by him. He had resigned the editorship, however, before the campaign began, and he refused to say anything further on the grounds that unsigned articles are the responsibility of the editor of the paper, an honourable responsibility which he refused to limit. Nor is it possible to decide from the articles themselves by whom they were written. *The Party System* was written by both men, and Mr Speaight says of it:

Those who care for such games may try to determine which sections of *The Party System* were written by Cecil Chesterton and which by Belloc. The opening is clearly by Chesterton, and then, as the book proceeds, we have the impression that Belloc takes over. Yet there is no disunity: two pens are writing as one.

"Cecil Chesterton wrote one half and I wrote the other, just as the Hail Mary was written half by the Church and half by St Gabriel—a personal and individual author . . . Dual authorship is seldom a success, but the Hail Mary pulled it off all right."[2]

Almost everybody who has ever written about Belloc has found himself apologising. For no sooner has he decided on something he wishes to say than he discovers the opposite is almost equally true. Belloc was one of the most complex characters that ever lived. He was exuberant and highly talented, but, because the talent was of a kind that depended on no one but himself for expression, he never had to control the exuberance, as he would have if he had needed to make the best of that bad job, his fellow-men. He was a Roman Catholic and his friends are agreed that his faith was his life. He was honourable, affectionate and kind, but so un-shakably opinionated that he could be an implacable enemy. His biographer says: "It was very rarely, with him, a case of 'I think'; it was nearly always a case of 'this is so.' " This characteristic, although not unknown in other men, was with Belloc instinct in every aspect of his thought. In the letter to Maurice Baring he says:

Of this company Mr Marconi, his father an Italian Pantheist, his mother an Irish Protestant, was director.

There can be no doubt here that the inflexion is one of mockery, and part of the mockery is directed from the standpoint of one Roman Catholic writing to another. But at least half of it makes play with Marconi's mixed blood. Belloc's father was a Frenchman with Irish blood and his mother was an

---

[2] Speaight, 301.

56

Englishwoman. What in Marconi was a cause for amusement was in himself a source of pride. Belloc felt naturally in the right. This might not have mattered very much, for he had the charm and the wit to sustain the position, if he had not been inclined to think that opinions which differed from his own were corrupt, the men who held them base.

In Mr J. B. Morton's book, *Hilaire Belloc*, there is a passage that goes a long way to explain him.

> He was well aware of the risks he ran in his controversies, and of his frequent failures to restrain himself. In consequence, he brooded over these failures, and was saddened that the work he had to do so often led to quarrels and estrangements. I remember him saying as we passed a country house: "So-and-so lives there. I used to go there a great deal, but I can go there no more. There are so many houses where I'm no longer welcome." He saw the problem quite clearly. The work he had set his hand to must be done. It carried with it certain everyday disadvantages, but also the more serious dangers to the soul. The whole thing was his responsibility. If he damaged his soul, there was nobody to blame but himself.[3]

Most people will let an old friend go a long way before they turn him off completely. If there were really so many houses closed to Belloc there, must have been good reasons.

He was always active in search of the truth, but his prejudices impelled him to strange finds. He suffered too often from having a working hypothesis from which he was unable to depart. In an introduction to *The Cruise of the Nona*, Lord Stanley of Alderley tells of an occasion when he asked Belloc "what he thought of Galileo's Catholicism, and whether he placed it in the same category as that of Pasteur."

> He flared up at once and said "Certainly!. . ." Warming to his subject he roundly and loudly accused me of making an attack on the Jesuits, and of having used the word "Jesuitical" in a most improper sense (I

---

[3] Morton, 130.

had not used the word at all) and of a complete ignorance as to the meaning and nature of Jesuitry.

It is clear that, presented with a Protestant, Belloc expected and found an anti-Jesuit. In the same way, presented with a financier or a politician, he too easily found corruption. This was particularly so when the man happened also to be a Jew.

It is seldom seriously questioned that Belloc was *instinctively* anti-Jewish. This is an ugly and a stupid thing, and Belloc was far too intelligent and far too noble to be satisfied with the position himself. He often made statements in which intellectually he refuted the charge, and he no doubt strove to obtain objectivity. In the *Eye–Witness* there is a series of articles on this subject, very curious and turgid and difficult to understand. It is proposed that, as the Jews could neither be absorbed nor excluded, they should be privileged, and about the meaning attached to this word it is impossible to be precise. It may mean that they were to be privileged not to take part in such forms of national life as conscription to the army in countries that adopted this measure, but also privileged never to undertake public duties. The matter preyed on Belloc's mind in a way that inevitably suggests strong feelings. His biographer believes that this was a result of his French heritage, hardened during his period in the French army, and he makes the point that Belloc was not merely anti-Dreyfusard, but Anti-Dreyfus.

He was very astute in defence of himself. When accused of being anti-Jewish in the Marconi case, he said he could think of no one less Jewish than Mr Lloyd George. But neither he nor Chesterton originally knew anything about Lloyd George. They were conducting a campaign on the charge of corruption in the placing of the contract against Sir Rufus Isaacs and Mr Samuel, when suddenly, and no doubt to their joy and surprise, "our popular Welsh Chancellor" was thrown in for luck.

All might have been well if Belloc had kept out of politics. In the literary circles where he properly belonged his eccentricities were understood and could not have been seriously damaging (though there too he took up a militant position on behalf of the Roman Catholic Church). But his enthusiasm for politics was burning, although his principles are difficult to define. As a young man he believed himself a Radical and a Republican, and in some ways he was very progressive. He sat as a Liberal M.P. from 1906 to 1910, but his hatred of paternalism in government was so great that his views were in practice anarchic, and ensured that he would often be found pressing the Tory case. He shrieked like the poor housemaids at the introduction of the National Insurance Act.

He was incapable of that degree of compromise which is necessary if an enterprise such as government is to move in any direction, and he saw compromise in other people as a betrayal of principle. In consequence he became disillusioned early in life.

Nothing is so dangerous or so relentless as betrayed enthusiasm, and Belloc, proclaiming that truth is hard and necessarily hurts, became a self-appointed scourge for his fellow-men. Long before the Marconi scandal he and Cecil Chesterton had shown what they were capable of in the campaign against C. F. G. Masterman. Masterman had been a close friend of theirs, and, on his entry into politics in 1906, a critic of the Government on whose back benches he sat. Then he accepted office and his criticism ceased. In 1908 he voted for the Right to Work Bill, introduced by the Labour Party, and a year later, as a member of the Government, he voted against it. Belloc and Cecil Chesterton never forgave him. They castigated him in their book, *The Party System*, which is understandable, but not content they persecuted him in his constituency, organising attacks against him in two by-elections to secure his defeat.

It is often said that when it came to politics Belloc was unbalanced; given to obsessions. This is used as an excuse for his behaviour but it is not an explanation.

He had a powerful brain, capable of acute analysis. *The Party System* affords a complete example of the processes of his and Chesterton's thought. It is an analysis of the working of the two-party system, and of the procedure of Parliament. Two of the main points are more interesting than they have been generally thought, for, because of its exaggeration, *The Party System* has not been taken very seriously. The writers complain first of all of the discipline of the huge mass of back-benchers behind the two sets of leaders, which they postulate as both new and dangerous. (It is a source of much anxiety to the journalists of our own day, who also seem to think it new and perilous to the proper working of democracy.) Because of this loyalty to the Party, Belloc and

Chesterton go on to say, we are governed by an oligarchy and not by demo-
cratic representation of the people; the effective government is that of the two
Front Benches, who are self-elective and all-powerful. They then go on to
develop an important point. The two Front Benches are not in opposition, as
they are popularly supposed to be, except in unimportant matters, but in
league against Parliament and the people.

> The two Front Benches are close oligarchical corporations; or, to
> speak more accurately, one close oligarchical corporation, admission
> to which is only to be gained by the consent of those who have
> already secured places therein. . . .
> The greater number of the members of this close corporation enter
> by right of their relationship, whether of blood or marriage, to other
> members of the group, no matter of what social rank. They may be
> called the Relations. This family arrangement must not be confused
> with what was once the old aristocratic privileges of the Great Houses.
> There are still indeed certain wealthy political families whose
> members are regarded as having a prescriptive right to share in the
> government of the country. Their wealth is more and more important,
> their lineage less and less.[4]

Now what the writers are discussing here is something that has been
discussed ever since under one name or another, and today is known as the
Establishment. Many people believe that this thing does exist, has too much
power, achieves power through subterranean means, and uses it in subtle,
only half-conscious, but decisive ways.

So that Belloc's analysis was reasoned. What seems unbalanced is that
he saw in the movements and behaviour of society, which however regrettable are inherent in the life of a large community, deliberate, calculated
intention of a corrupt kind.

There has never been the smallest reason to suspect the Speaker or

---

[4] *The Party System*, 37–8.

Chairman of leaning unfairly to one or other side of the House. Why, indeed, should he, seeing that he at any rate knows the fight between them to be a sham one.[5]

This, then, was Belloc's view of human nature. He had the capacity to see evil everywhere, and he never lacked the zeal to ride out and trounce it.

Creative people are often a little unbalanced, and the egotism of genius does not leave much room for personal humour. If the mind can be made to jump right over some obvious facts in the foreground, there is often a tenable position in the middle distance. There was a case for saying that there was a good deal of mild corruption in politics, nor was it quite untrue that in the last resort the ruling class would always stand together as a ruling class regardless of their duty to the public. Belloc's mind simply jumped the fact that human nature is a compound of ideals and weaknesses. The ideals are often too easily reconciled to the weaknesses, but in a large community such as the House of Commons it is the vision of a distorted mind to see nothing but greed and the desire for self-advancement, all of it calculated, all unleavened by altruism.

In 1911 he launched the *Eye–Witness* himself as editor. The literary pages contained the work of many of the most distinguished writers of the day, and from its political pages the radical–republican–anarchist–Tory Belloc uttered tirades against the Insurance Act, ranted against the exclusion of young children from the pubs, and conducted a campaign against all politicians, financiers and international Jewry. Sometimes he revealed genuine scandals. He was among the first, if not the first, to draw attention to the sale of Honours. He listed the names of new peers and asked the simple question: Why? This would be more impressive if one did not feel that anyone swivelling a machine–gun in every direction is bound occasionally to hit a bull's–eye.

When, in June 1912, he resigned the editorship to Cecil Chesterton, he wrote a farewell letter to his readers:

> It was a difficult task because the telling of the truth in public affairs had ceased to be a habit of contemporary journalism, and because in

---

[5] *Ibid.*, 60.

the decline and cessation of that habit legal machinery for the suppression and punishment of free speech had grown strong. We have frequently been warned that this machinery had been put into action.

Five months later he published an article entitled "A Retrospect," which is interesting because it contains a sentence which seems very strong presumptive evidence that he wrote or at least collaborated in one of the strongly defamatory articles on the Marconi case.

> Now a certain measure of courage in the private citizen is necessary to the good conduct of the State. Otherwise men who have power through riches or intrigue or office or all three will administer the State at will and ultimately to their private advantage. . . . Let a society push those things just a little too far and it will be found to have taken the step beyond which there is no turning back.

It is the last sentence that is so suggestive. Writers of Belloc's prolificacy and talent often repeat a phrase or an idea again and again in different places, but they seldom lift their ideas or phraseology from other people's work. Consequently, there is good reason to believe that Belloc had some part in the writing of the second article, the one entitled "The Marconi Scandal Again" which appeared in the *Eye–Witness* on August 22.

Finally, in the *Oxford and Cambridge Review* of October 1912 Belloc wrote the following sentences which caused him later to be called before the Select Committee of Inquiry.

> As an example: I am myself acquainted with a small club of honest country folk which regularly invested its funds in Consols when they were at 110, and which is still investing them in Consols at 75. In other words its members have lost one-third of their savings because they knew nothing of the way in which our public affairs are conducted. Conversely one of those responsible for the conduct of public affairs has to my knowledge received information with regard to Marconis, and to the effect that this stock was about to receive a particular privilege. Through this information (given to him because he had a "pull," that is

could blackmail) he trebled his investment in six months.

2

Belloc will always be forgiven his faults by people who remember his wit and his charm, and because the qualities that made his behaviour so arrogant and so objectionable in the Marconi case assumed in ordinary life only the proportions of amusing quirks in an eccentric personality. And he will be forgiven by succeeding generations because he wrote well. But what of Cecil Chesterton?

He was, according to Belloc's biographer, one of the only two men who had any influence over Belloc. He is described by his friends as a man of great charm, with a smiling, chubby face and a youthful appearance. Here, however, is Sir Thomas Beecham's view of him:

> I must confess that the first sight of him was a distinct shock. I had pictured to myself a dashing and romantic knight of the pen, a champion of dangerous but righteous causes, and here was one of the most ill-favoured and unprepossessing individuals I had ever looked on. His method of speech—or, rather, delivery of it—was hardly better, for he stammered, stuttered, and spluttered and seemed to swallow his tongue as well as his words when he became carried away by enthusiasm or indignation.[6]

He was, in spite of this disadvantage, a brilliant debater and he wrote incisively. Where his brother Gilbert is hard to read today because of his florid and paradoxical style, and where Belloc's political tirades in the *Eye–Witness* are curiously heavy–handed and boring, Cecil Chesterton's invective remains lively and pungent. He was decidedly a good journalist and he was never happier than on the hustings.

If Belloc's feeling against the Jews was instinctive and under some control, Chesterton's was open and vicious, and he shared with Belloc the peculiarity that the Jews were never far from his thoughts. When Mr Samuel, speaking

---

[6]   *A Mingled Chime*, 140.

on a bill to prevent young children being taken into public houses, called it a much-needed change in the habits of our people, Chesterton asked immediately "Which people?"[7] If quips like this spring so readily to the tongue, it is useless to try to convince other people that your feeling on the subject of the Jews is the same as their own. When writing of Jews he fell instantly into such language as "the said Samuel," or "Isaacs No. 1 and Isaacs No. 2," and, shortly before the series of articles on the Marconi case, the *Eye-Witness* provoked the following remark in the correspondence addressed to the editor:

> May I point out that your habit of referring to the Postmaster-General and the Attorney-General as "Samuel" and "Isaacs," while designating other public men in the usual way, has somewhat lost its freshness, the full charm of this cheap appeal to prejudice being dependent on novelty.[8]

It seems to be generally agreed that Chesterton was a bad influence on Belloc.

It is always emphasised that Chesterton, in private life of a kindly nature, bore no personal ill-will towards the men whom he harried publicly. The bland impertinence of this particular tribute to him seems to have occurred to none of his friends. It reminds one of the Anarchists, who must learn to kill without hate.

Belloc said of him: "His courage was heroic, native, positive, and equal: always at the highest potential of courage."[9] And it was this quality which Belloc found most endearing.

Chesterton's conduct of the Marconi case can be better understood if it is realised that to the reckless courage, the dislike of Jews and politicians, the duty he shared with Belloc to clean up public life, was allied a passion for argument. He was good-tempered though relentless in argument, and he had the weakness of the born debater: he treated all men as equals, even those

---

[7] *The Chestertons*, 67.

[8] *Eye–Witness*, 11 July 1912.

[9] *New Witness*, 13 December 1918.

who were less robust and of inferior forensic talent. He hit hard, but he expected to be hit hard in return.

The intellectual curiosity, the belief in progress, the greater leisure and the mental vigour of that time made argument a natural pastime. All over London there were debating societies well attended not merely by people who wished to spend a social evening, but by professional writers, journalists and politicians. Men who were paid to lecture one night would be found doing the same thing freely the next. There were the Fabian Society, two or three mock parliaments, at which House of Commons procedure was followed and mock-bills prepared and introduced with as much attention to form as in the House itself, and innumerable debating societies. G. K. Chesterton was a regular attender, so were writers such as Bernard Shaw and the Webbs, some of the younger politicians and many journalists. In this society Cecil Chesterton shone.

In the *Eye–Witness* he and Belloc were accustomed to go to extreme lengths in invective and in their discussion of public events. It can be seen from Belloc's farewell letter that they were often threatened with libel. When Chesterton made the first attack in the Marconi case, there is no doubt it was a shot in the dark. He later admitted as much, and, although he said at the time he had evidence of corruption in the placing of the contract, this cannot have been true. He never produced any, nor did anyone else. Like all good fighters, he must have expected a counter-attack. When weeks went by, while he grew bolder and bolder and neither of the Ministers made any attempt to refute his statements, what could he have thought, except that his shot in the dark had hit a substantial target?

This is a vicious circle. When attacks on public men are so vituperative, so without charity, it becomes impossible to admit to any mistake. If Isaacs had not bought the American shares, he must inevitably have taken action to Chesterton: restrain because he had something to hide, the invective grew greater and greater.

In October 1912 the financial backer of the *Eye–Witness* went bankrupt. Cecil Chesterton immediately went to his father and borrowed money to finance a new start. In November he issued the first number of the *New Witness*, with no break in continuity, although he had to leave the premises of the *Eye–Witness* and make shift in inconvenient and ill-equipped offices.

Now there enters a strange but influential figure. This is Miss Ada Jones, who worked as a journalist under the pen-name of R. K. Prothero, and eventually became Mrs Cecil Chesterton. When Chesterton started the *New Witness* he made her assistant editor, but it seems not to have been generally realised that in the dramatic interventions of this paper she played a considerable part. Later she wrote her own account of the Marconi case in a book called *The Chestertons*, and from this it is clear she had no doubts of the righteousness and excitement of ranging herself with Belloc and Chesterton as a guardian of public morals. She had some reputation as a journalist and, in later life, in the field of social work, but her book is written in seedily romantic clichés and betrays vanity and malice. (One can only conjecture what Chesterton's highly talented but intensely loyal circle made of her, although she herself tells us that G. K. Chesterton, who took over the paper after the death of his brother, eventually dispensed with her services.) Her account of the Marconi case is inaccurate and its value lies only in the picture she gives of the fervour with which she and Chesterton approached their task.

During the course of the Marconi case Chesterton married her, and she must have had great influence on him. At least once she will be seen to have used it recklessly.

(6)

The Select Committee:
1. The Contract

A Select Committee of Inquiry is constituted on party lines and in accordance with the proportion of parties in the House of Commons. Of the fifteen men who met for the first time on 25 October 1912, Sir Albert Spicer, Mr Falconer, Mr Booth, Mr Gordon Harvey, Mr Primrose and Sir Herbert Roberts were Liberals, Mr William Redmond and Mr Mooney represented the Irish Party and Mr James Parker the Labour Party. This gave the Government a majority of three over the six Tories, Lord Robert Cecil, Mr Amery, Mr George Faber, Mr Harold Smith, Mr MacMaster and Mr Terrell. Nearly all these gentlemen were members of the legal profession. Of the exceptions, Sir Albert Spicer was chairman of a company, Mr Faber was a banker and Sir Frederick Banbury, who later replaced Mr Smith, was also a banker and Chairman of the Stock Exchange.

The choice of members should have ensured a judicial approach to the matters that were to be examined, but from the first the Tories prophesied that this body would seek to whitewash rather than to reveal the truth.

Sir Albert Spicer took the chair and at its first meetings the Committee deliberated procedure. It was agreed that all witnesses should be taken on oath and the following statement was publicised:

> This Committee wish it to be known that they are prepared to consider all evidence bearing on the negotiation and completion of the Marconi agreement, and invite any person in possession of such evidence to communicate with the Clerk.

It was decided to consider first the contract itself and to hear those witnesses concerned with the negotiation and those who wished to make criticisms of it; and secondly to hear those who had charged gambling and corruption, so that they might establish the case that Ministers would then be called to answer. There was a logic in this procedure which was inadequately appreciated when it became plain that the Inquiry, instead of reaching a conclusion in the course of a few weeks, was being conducted in such a way that the appearance of the Ministers would be indefinitely delayed.

The first witness to appear on October 29 was Sir Alexander King, Permanent Secretary to the Post Office. On January 8 of the following year the members of the Committee considered an interim report by Lord Robert Cecil. During the whole of the intervening period they had met regularly to examine witnesses whose evidence related to the contract. The interim report detailed the conclusions that had been reached as a result of this. Having said that the establishment of an Imperial Chain was a matter of urgency, the report concluded that either a particular company should be selected, or else the Government should leave themselves free to adopt or reject from time to time any system. In either case it was necessary to come to a conclusion as to the technical and scientific merits of the various systems.

> For this purpose the Committee believe that the best result will be reached by the immediate appointment of a highly qualified Technical Committee.

As a result, the body known as the Parker Committee met for the first time on 23 January 1913 under the chairmanship of Lord Parker of Waddington, and reported on April 30. Paragraph 24 of its report reads as follows:

We report, therefore, that according to our investigation the Marconi system is at present the only system of which it can be said with any certainty that it is capable of fulfilling the requirements of the Imperial Chain, but this must not be taken to imply that, in our opinion, the Marconi Company must necessarily be employed as contractors for all the work required for the Imperial Chain. Indeed in some respects it might, we think, be better for the Government themselves to undertake the construction and equipment of the necessary stations, acting for that purpose under the best technical and scientific advice which can be obtained, and employing the most suitable contractors for the various portions of the work or plant. On the other hand, it may be said, and is no doubt the fact, that at the present moment the Marconi Company alone has had practical experience of the sort of long-distance work required, including experience in putting down stations, in organising the traffic and staff, and in coping with the difficulties that arise in a new industry, and the value of such experience and organisation may well outweigh other considerations, if rapid installation and immediate and trustworthy communication be desired.

Although it is unnecessary and would be tedious to attempt any résumé of the interminable examination of witnesses that led to the appointment of the Parker Committee, some of the evidence given during this part of the Inquiry is relevant to that taken later from journalists and must be briefly mentioned.

At the beginning of the examination of Sir Alexander King, the Chairman asked him to give a short history of the negotiations. During his reply Sir Alexander made the following statement:

It was decided, however, to proceed with the negotiations with the Marconi Company on the ground that no other wireless company had practical experience of continuous long-distance working. . . . The only rival company with any practical experience in this direction is the Telefunken Company. There are two reasons for not inviting this company to compete: first, it is not a British Company, and secondly, it admittedly infringes the Lodge patent, which is now in the possession of

69

the Marconi Company, and it is stated by the Marconi Company also to infringe their own patents. The third possible course was to await demonstration by the Poulsen Company in long-distance wireless telegraphy or by some other yet untried system.

During the course of his examination on this statement the following exchanges occurred.

Q. But why did you, the Post Office, put yourselves into this position, that Marconi should be the only person to whom you could go, when the Telefunken system existed, and the Poulsen system existed, and the Lodge–Muirhead system?

A. None of the three have ever worked over the distance that is necessary for these long-distance stations.

Q. But at that time you had not gone into any details of those three systems?

A. But we knew.

Q. Then if you knew it all, why go into details afterwards with the Poulsen Syndicate?

A. For the information of the people who did not know.

Q. Then as far as you were concerned you knew it all and would never have referred it to the Imperial Wireless Committee to enter into negotiations with the Poulsen Syndicate at all; you were satisfied that Poulsen could not do it?

A. We were satisfied that Poulsen had not done it; we are not satisfied that they cannot do it this time next year. . . .

Q. But why had the Post Office as a Government Department put themselves into this position, that the only person they can accept is Marconi, and they never allowed a chance to any one of the other companies?

A. If I may say so, we did not put ourselves in that position at all. We were put in that position. The only company that has had the enterprise to undertake long-distance working, and to show that they can do the long-distance working is the Marconi Company. Our need was for a long-distance station. Naturally, we say that the people who have done the work are the people we must ask to tender. We could not go to an unknown firm who had never done any business of the sort and say: "Look here, will you take this business up and give us a tender?" It would have been a very reckless proceeding on the part of the Government to give any tender for a large sum of money to an unknown firm.

And later:

Q. I quite understand; and they [the Marconi Company] claimed that they had practically a monopoly of the knowledge on the subject?
A. Yes.
Q. And that was the opinion of the Post Office?
A. That is the opinion still.
Q. That is the opinion still? And the whole correspondence must be read in the light of that opinion?
A. Well, it is not only an opinion. It is a fact.
Q. Well, of course you think it is a fact or otherwise you could not hold it as an opinion.
A. It is a fact that there is only one company that has done the work over 2000 miles regularly.
Q. You tell me that is a fact?
A. It is a fact.

Every witness who appeared for the Government, all the men who had sat through those long months of conferences which preceded the acceptance of the tender, believed, as Sir Alexander King believed, that they had acted under the pressure of this one inescapable fact, and that every clause in the contract should be examined in the light of it. None of the critics believed it, nor could they be made to accept it. For this reason, more than any other, each section of the work of the Committee dragged on for months, while hour after hour was spent going through the same interminable question and answer, the same explanations and the same objections. All the Liberal members of the Committee framed their questions to elicit this one answer, while the Opposition members covered the same ground in an

71

attempt to get it denied. All the Government witnesses withstood days of cross-examination directed to shaking them on the point, while all the Opposition witnesses were prepared to continue indefinitely giving indirect answers rather than admit it. Later, when the Inquiry passed to matters not concerned with the contract, this irreducible difference of opinion still lay between question and answer, so that witnesses always seemed to be replying to questions they had not been asked or evading the ones they had.

Many of the critics of the contract were well-grounded in the technicalities of the new science of wireless telegraphy and after months of discussion and arguments they had a vested interest. It would have been as easy to convince them that no company but the Marconi could undertake the work as it would to convince the ordinary member of one political party that, in some particular controversy, the other had an unanswerable case. When men have upheld one side of an argument at dinner-parties or with their business colleagues, in buses or at the local pub for long enough, it takes more than facts to change their views.

Memory, too, plays odd tricks when history has proved a man in the wrong. Lord Robert Cecil attended on twenty-six of the twenty-seven days' discussion of the contract and asked ten per cent of over 13,000 questions. After nearly three months he drafted the report that brought the Parker Committee into being. In July 1913 he opposed the second Marconi contract in the House of Commons. In his memoirs, in an account of the Marconi case, he says this:

> Accordingly they [the Government] negotiated with various undertakings, and rightly arrived at the conclusion that the Marconi system would be the best for the purpose . . . we early investigated the contract which we approved.[1]

Many of the witnesses were honest men who seriously believed the Marconi Company had been unjustly favoured and that the Poulsen System was superior. It was a simpler system, and there was some reason to think

---

[1] *All the Way*, 121.

that, if the company could find the capital and be given time to develop it, it might supersede the Marconi system. Sir Alexander King admitted in evidence that some of the Post Office engineers had been attracted to it, although he qualified this by saying they were attracted to anything new. If it could have been proved that there was no great urgency to establish an Imperial Chain, then, at the existing stage of development of wireless telegraphy, there was a good deal to be said for allowing Poulsen to improve and demonstrate their apparatus. But no witness was prepared seriously to adopt this attitude.

Secondly, Poulsen had offered much lower terms than the Marconi Company, both for the initial capital required and because they were willing to accept a comparatively small capitalised royalty against Marconi's ten per cent. Thirdly, they had recently had great successes in working over shorter distances and by night, while they offered a higher speed of transmission than the Marconi Company had yet achieved. Against all these points, they had no staff or experience comparable with the Marconi Company's, and the Marconi Company were suing them for infringement of patents.

One odd and possibly sinister fact emerged from the cross-examination of Sir Alexander King. Clause 16 of the final contract gave the Post Office the right to discontinue the royalty to the Marconi Company if they ceased to use any Marconi patents. From the file of the negotiations sent to the Select Committee by the Post Office, it transpired that when this clause had been first discussed Godfrey Isaacs had said that, although in principle he was prepared to agree to it and thought it unimportant because valuable discoveries were more likely to be made by his company than by anyone else, he would be unwilling to have it made public. No member of the Post Office thought it possible to keep the clause a secret, and it was finally incorporated in the contract. But the circular setting out the terms of the contract sent by the Marconi Company to its shareholders, which for so long had been the only source of information to Members of Parliament as well as everyone else, had suppressed it. Naturally this caused much excited and adverse comment.

Sir Alexander King was examined for five days. During the latter part of his evidence Mr Terrell questioned him in a manner which suggested that he was personally on a charge of corruption and finally drew the reply: "May I say that I do not like to be addressed as if I were an Old Bailey prisoner; it makes me very cross and I do not give my answers so well as I ought." A Tory member therefore set the precedent for the bullying of witnesses, later to be so marked and disagreeable a feature of the Liberal conduct of the case.

Other witnesses included many of the civil servants who had been connected in one way or other with the contract, and those Members of Parliament who had conducted the case for the Opposition in the House of Commons, among whom Major Archer-Shee was always to the fore.

After the appointment of the Parker Committee an important document reached the Select Committee. This was from the managing director of the Marconi Company. Godfrey Isaacs complained that "much of the evidence which has been given, standing alone and without opportunity of refutation being afforded to my Company, has resulted in erroneous statements, technical and otherwise, being reproduced in the Press of nearly every country in the world to the serious detriment of my Company," and said that while in principle he would welcome this sub-committee, providing proper facilities were afforded for testing evidence, he regretted it had not been appointed three months before, "as the necessity for such an inquiry, if it existed, is not more apparent now than it was then." He then went on to say that the expense to his Company in keeping idle the staff of engineers prepared for the Imperial Chain was considerable, and that the cost of material had risen and might rise further. "It is, I submit, inequitable that my Company should remain bound whilst investigations never contemplated should be continued over an indefinite period." Mr Marconi and the staff of engineers must be freed to attend to other important work.

For all these reasons he asked the Government to agree to treat the contract as no longer binding upon either party. The Post Office were advised that, although the contract was binding on the Marconi Company, an action for damages against them for breaking it was unlikely to be successful, and there was no other course than to let it go by default.

(7)

The Select Committee:
2. The Journalists

1

When, on January 22, Wilfred Ramage Lawson appeared as a witness it was a surprise for all but the initiated. His easy handling of the English language, the intricacies of the contract and the reputations of the Ministers had suggested a young man, one who still found life explicable by confident criticisms and conclusive judgments. But Lawson was over seventy, his hair, beard and moustache, which turned unexpectedly downwards at the corners, were white. He had a broad face, which at first sight suggested strength, and large, suffering eyes.

Nevertheless, once his appearance had been assimilated, he was for an hour or two easily recognisable as the clever and ruthless journalist who for months had piled criticism upon criticism of the contract and had been the first to draw attention to the possibility of mysterious circumstances surrounding the negotiations. He had prepared, as had every other witness, a précis of his evidence, and, as a preliminary to his examination, he was taken through this by Douglas Hogg, who was there to watch his interests. As Hogg courteously put to him one question after another he answered in the manner journalists have of being immune to the weaknesses of other men. He had no wish to be merely destructive, and in his précis he indicated not only in what respects the Post Office had failed, but what, if they had been cleverer, they might have done. If Lawson had fed month after month on his critical task and become a little elated, it was not yet apparent. His was the studied and equable wisdom of the leader-writer.

When Lord Robert Cecil and other Conservatives began to question Lawson, they wished to clear up certain matters relating to the issue of the Marconi shares. Lawson was by profession a financial expert and he elucidated the points for them, gently and in the manner of one who, having come to instruct, is determined to do it thoroughly and pleasantly. When all these points had been dealt with, Falconer began to question him for the Liberals.

His first point was really a question of grammar. Lawson, in the privacy and comfort of his daily task, may have become a little careless. In the précis of his evidence there occurred a sentence, referring to the monopoly that had allegedly been given to the Marconi Company, in which it is quite clear that he had meant that the general terms of the contract must inevitably give Marconi a monopoly of wireless telegraphy. What he had succeeded in saying was that they had been given an indefinite monopoly to *build* wireless stations for the Government, and this was clearly untrue. With this first question Falconer and Lawson gave a demonstration of the course they were to pursue for days of agony, agonised boredom for the rest of the Committee, agonised retreat on the part of Lawson. Falconer's method was to isolate a sentence of Lawson's and question him on it interminably, relentlessly, repetitively, until he forced him to withdraw it. Lawson's method was not to answer the question he had been asked, but to dilate at length on some other matter. Falconer can be said to have based his questions on the letter of Lawson's single sentences, while Lawson based his replies on the spirit of his general criticisms of the contract. Lawson, the acute and humorous, critical Lawson had been a little disingenuous, and often with the first of Falconer's questions one can see that he is done for. He was not a stupid man, and he could see it too. He followed in defence of himself two methods, both of which seem instinctive to witnesses in a like case. The first, and the most natural to Lawson, is to talk volubly and propitiatingly about anything but the question asked. The second is, with a certain airiness, to refuse to admit that black is black or white white.

Poor Lawson was a very weak character. Falconer was endlessly, endlessly strong. For one thing he had no sense of time. He soon made it plain that he intended to take each sentence that Lawson had ever written in criticism of the contract and examine him separately on it until he forced him to withdraw it. Lawson, in a petulant, ineffective, womanish way, was on each occasion originally equally determined not to withdraw. It became clear after a while that he was dreadfully frightened of what might happen if he did. Perhaps he would lose his job, or have to leave the country to save his face. Perhaps there might be some terrible libel action in which he would be fined a great sum of money he could not pay. He soon quite lost touch with that other figure, that omnipotent journalist who week after week had sat in judgment on his fellow-men.

In the middle of the second day of Falconer's examination Lord Robert Cecil made the first of many interventions of the same kind.

> I do not know whether you think it right, Mr Chairman, to suggest to the witness that we should get on much quicker if he would answer the questions asked.

As question followed question, hour followed hour, day followed day, Lord Robert was often to plead, sometimes with the Chairman, sometimes with the witness, occasionally with Falconer himself, that some halt might be drawn to the proceedings, but after a while these interventions began to resemble groans emitted by someone in pain. He had no hope of achieving any result; he merely relieved the aching desperation of his boredom.

Falconer had an expression "walk the plank." Each time he persuaded Lawson to withdraw a sentence, he said: "So this one, too, walks the plank." When he said this all the people in the room, many of whom one can be sure had enjoyed Lawson's articles for months, and shared his light-hearted contempt for the Post Office, roared with laughter. They became a kind of chorus for Falconer, driving his points home with a timed and heedless stupidity.

Sometimes, by telling a quick, nervous lie, Lawson stumped Falconer. Ultimately this did not pay him. Falconer would drop the matter at the time, but next day or the day after, fortified by re-reading, he would return to it.

77

Lawson never quite gave in. Although he eventually withdrew practically every sentence he had written, one feels that he never changed his opinion about the contract, and that this was a victory of force. Between the question and the answer there was still the great gap described in an earlier chapter, and often his awareness of it made Falconer's questions as evasive as Lawson's answers. On one occasion Lawson suggested that the original offer the Marconi Company made to undertake the work was absurd because they had not the finance necessary for it. The point here is perfectly clear. Once the Government had accepted their tender they were in a position to raise the finance. If they were the only company with the necessary knowledge and experience, if they had spent years of hard work and taken all the risk, expending very large sums of money on research, then it was equitable that they should receive the reward. But if this was not admitted, if it could be suggested that there were other companies in the same position, then, whether corruptly or not, they had received a singular advantage over the others. Since this matter was still *sub judice,* Falconer could not frame his questions on the open assumption that the finances of the Marconi Company before the contract were irrelevant, because the whole purpose of his cross-examination was to show that they had not received this advantage. At this point he displayed a mind as disingenuous, as incapable of distinguishing between black and white as Lawson's own, and there seemed no reason to hope that these two tortuous individuals would ever conclude that round of the battle.

Lawson had devoted the first ten pages of the précis of his evidence to criticisms of the contract, and it was on these that Falconer examined him. It was a great surprise that, when they reached the far more interesting, far more important matter of the slanders of Ministers, Falconer suddenly turned the witness over to Lord Robert Cecil.

A contemporary writer said of Lord Robert Cecil:

> The Member for Hitchin has a certain definite faith which sustains him amid all adversity. It is that Radicals constitute the criminal class, and that the only question is how many of them can be found out.[1]

---

[1] *Truth,* 25 June 1913.

Nevertheless, he came of a great political family, interested in the honour of public men, and he showed here no political bias. On the question of the contract, there was still room for difference of opinion. On the insinuations against the Ministers there was none. Either Lawson had some evidence on which he had founded his iniquitous suggestions, or he had not. Lord Robert framed his questions to get at the truth.

Q. Will you look at the fourth paragraph in the first article beginning: "The Marconi Company has from its birth been a child of darkness. Its finances have been of a most chequered and erratic sort. Its relations with certain Ministers have not always been purely official or political." What does that mean?

A. Well, there is the relationship between the managing director and the Attorney-General.

Q. You say it in the plural. It is "certain Ministers." What had you in mind.

A. That was the principal thing I had in mind.

And in answer to a further question, Lawson said: "Well, the suggestion of being personally interested should not have been made." Then Lord Robert continued:

Q. I want to know what are the mysterious relations to which you refer. . . . Tell us quite frankly what was in your mind or what you heard?

A. What took place in New York did have a great influence on my mind. I admit too much influence, and it may have been in my mind when I was writing that.

Q. What do you mean by "what took place in New York"—the telegram sent by the Attorney-General to his brother?

A. Yes.

Q. Was that the only thing you had in mind?

A. That was the basis of it all.

Later the strain began to tell. Lawson, who all along had refused an explicit answer to any question and had been so obviously guarding himself against unknown terrors, began to babble.

Q. Had you any foundation whatever for the charge that mysterious relations did obtain between certain members of the Government and the Marconi Company except market rumours?

A. Might I explain this. These articles were written under very strong provocation with regard to the agreement. What we wanted to do was to get this agreement stopped, to have it further inquired into and to have a committee appointed. I wrote strongly from that point of view.

Q. In your own interest, I ask you to be very careful what you are saying now.

A. Yes, of course, I wrote strongly.

Q. Just think what that sentence really means. . . . You thought this a bad agreement and you wanted to get it stopped?

A. Yes.

Q. And you therefore suggested that certain members of the Government had mysterious relations with the Marconi Company? . . .

A. No, in the first place . . .

Q. Do you think that was a procedure that was either in the public interest or fair to the Ministers concerned?

A. The writing was in the public interest but these passages were not. The general effect of the article was in the public interest. I maintain that still.

Q. Do you think it is in the public interest to charge Ministers of the Crown with something like corruption?

A. If Ministers of the Crown will allow lying rumours to go about for months at a time, how can they expect other people to take more care of their characters than they do themselves? I stand beside the *Spectator* and I consider we are both right and that we had a right to call on the Ministers to deny those rumours. They did not choose to deny them. I have gone further and I admit I have incurred legal liability in putting them in that way, but I am quite prepared to take the risk of it. We expected when these articles were published that they would do what they immediately threatened to do, but never did. They should have taken these articles into Court at once.

Lawson was questioned for some time, but he refused to explain what he had meant by "we." Later Gordon Harvey questioned him.

Q. What I want to ask you is this: before putting the articles into cold print and circulating them up and down the country under your authority, did you or did you not take any steps to see that these rumours had any foundation?

A. How could I go to a Minister and ask him whether he had been gambling in Marconi shares?

Asked whether it was not the practice in honest journalism to try to verify rumours before putting them into print, Lawson replied: "But the Liberal press knew them just as well as I did."

Later the members of the Committee tried to get him to agree that, even if he had not invented the rumours, he had in the article in the *Outlook* of July 20 been the first person to put them in print, and now he became incoherent. He constantly referred them to an article in the *Daily Herald* of July 30 and one in the *Spectator* of the following September. But he did admit again and again that he had no foundation for the charges of corruption and gambling, no evidence of any kind.

Lawson was followed by the Hon. Walter Guinness, a Member of Parliament and the proprietor of the *Outlook*. Guinness was in a difficult position. He was a Tory and a gentleman, and a greater nicety was required to sustain his opinion of himself than was necessary for journalists, and yet he was the owner of a newspaper which had just been shown to have based a series of scurrilous articles on no evidence whatever. He was greatly assisted by the members of the Committee, who were never in doubt that the manners adopted towards journalists could not be used to Members of Parliament, and, taking full advantage of the deference he received, he adopted two lines of defence. One, that he had been abroad during most of the period when the articles appeared and afterwards ill; and two, that the articles had gone no further than fair comment on public men, or that, if they had, this had not been intended. Some sympathy was due to him, because a more manly regret for error would have involved disloyalty to his employees. He escaped without being mauled and without serious loss of face, but he cannot have enjoyed it.

He was followed by Mr Edwin Oliver, the editor of the *Outlook*, a pugilistic gentleman, who raised a spontaneous laugh when, after commenting that he was much impressed by the standards of reticence that appeared to be demanded of journalists, he went on to say: "If one makes a statement one must prove the fact. That simply makes political comment impossible." Both he and his employer were forced to admit that they knew of no foundation for the charges of corruption and gambling, and both refused to give the names of persons who had spoken to them of these matters. They said, as most witnesses did, that they could not remember.

During Lawson's evidence there had been several interruptions. On January 23 Lord Robert Cecil addressed the Chairman:

In a well-known provincial paper . . . it is stated, referring to Mr Cecil Chesterton, "According to the latest account, as confirmed by Mr Chesterton himself, it is now doubtful if the Committee will call him at all. If they do his evidence is to be taken in private, not publicly, as in the case of previous witnesses." Is there any doubt at all that we shall call Mr Chesterton?

The Chairman replied that there was no doubt that Mr Chesterton would be called, and no truth in the suggestion that his evidence would be taken privately. Then on January 27 he stated that Mr Chesterton had again asked when he would be called, that journalists were being called in order, and that Mr Chesterton would be called as soon as possible.

2

On February 12 Leonard James Maxse was called to the witness-stand and the atmosphere changed immediately. Maxse was the editor and proprietor of the *National Review*, and he was there to answer for Lawson's articles in that paper and also because he wished to make a statement of his own. He was a very well-known and colourful figure, and he must have been on terms of close acquaintance with at least two members of the Committee. His sister had married a Cecil and later became Lady Milner. He was a diehard Tory closely connected with political circles at home and abroad. He was also familiar to the public because, in his *Review*, under the title "Episodes of the Month," he regularly voiced very strong opinions in a kind of schoolboy invective which was often extremely funny. There are two successful kinds of humor—theunexpected, and the often repeated and therefore expected. Maxse was adept at both. When Mr Samuel denied that he had bought Marconi shares and then made the same disclaimer on behalf of every member of the Cabinet, Maxse remarked: "When Mr Samuel states in so clear and categorical a manner that he has never made a penny out of Marconi speculation . . . we believe him, though it is a very large order to ask us to accept a similar statement on behalf of a large body containing several very enterprising gentlemen." The adjective "enterprising" here is extremely well chosen, because it says everything it is possible to say while stopping far short of the kind of insolent, underdog invective employed by Lawson and Cecil Chesterton. Maxse regularly invented nicknames for his political targets, and, although these were often in the first place rather brash, by repetition in otherwise grave sentences they finally became a joy to the reader.

He was not taken very seriously by his contemporaries, because his strongly-held views were too often unbalanced and uncontrolled,[2] although in after years he could claim that he had always predicted trouble with Germany. For posterity he has the distinction of having said that votes for women would be a calamity second only to a German invasion, and of having ridiculed with almost monthly regularity the man who won the first war and the man who won the second under the respective nicknames of the Artful Dodger of the Carnarvon Boroughs and the Windbag of Dundee. In the later stages of the Marconi case he always referred to the debate of October 11 as the Festival of Truth.

He was a very original and independent character and he often conducted a campaign against some member of his own party. He initiated the slogan

---

[2] Lady Astor is reputed to have said to him: "Ah! Leo. You are all heart and hate."

"Balfour Must Go," and Balfour, when he did resign, remarked: "I really think I must ask Leo Maxse to dinner to-night, for we are probably the two happiest men in London."[3] Maxse was strong and disrespectful, not easily frightened by Cabinet Ministers or members of a Select Committee.

Very early in his evidence he made the following statement:

> Several people drew my attention to it [the Marconi scandal]— Members of Parliament and others. I cannot remember who the first person was, and I may as well say—as it may save a great deal of trouble—that, of course, an editor depends entirely for his efficiency as an editor on the confidence he inspires in other people, and he cannot give away confidential communications under any circumstances. I have taken a great deal of trouble to collect what evidence or information I could on this question. I have received a good deal of evidence confidentially, and I have to exercise my judgment upon it, and I am not able to give the names of people.
>
> *Mr William Redmond.* No names at all?
>
> A. No.

Maxse maintained that he had collected information the purport of which he was prepared to give and he stated that he had not relied on Lawson when he published his articles, because the statements he made "coincided made with statements I had heard otherwise." When asked the question: "You do not suggest that Mr Lawson was any less honourable because when closely questioned he saw fit to withdraw most of what he had stated?" he replied: "I think Mr Lawson is by temperament unfitted to be a witness."

He then withstood all attempts to induce him either to divulge the names of people who had given him evidence or to produce any papers or letters in his possession. At one time the room was cleared so that the Committee could consider the matter. It was put to him that the Committee had powers and could, if he continued to refuse, report his refusal to the House of Commons to take any action they liked. To this he replied: "I am quite aware of that."

---

[3]   Dugdale, *Arthur James Balfour*, ii, 86.

It was then suggested to him that the Committee were sitting in an attempt to arrive at the truth, and that, if a precedent were to be set that witnesses could refuse to give names, they might as well resign their task. He remained unmoved and finally the Committee were forced to relinquish their attempts and later to report him to the House of Commons.[4]

During the time that Maxse was in the room he managed to say most of the things that he wanted to say, however. Speaking of the debate, he said:

> To make things worse, the Chancellor of the Exchequer got up a perfectly gratuitous row with an old friend, Mr George Lansbury, and in his excitement Mr Lloyd George unfortunately omitted to deny that he had had any dealings in Marconi shares. If significance be attached to the denials of other Ministers, which we are invited to regard as final, some significance must surely be attached to Mr Lloyd George's omission, which may have been an oversight.

When Mr Parker said to him: "We are searching for the facts, and the only way to obtain those facts is from witnesses who come here before us," he replied: "Or to get Ministers here."

And he made one statement which suggests that, if the Committee had been willing to agree that he should give them the purport of his information without mentioning names, it might have been profitable. There is no doubt, too, that with the same statement he provoked an event from which the Marconi case erupted into a new and more sensational phase. He said:

> I confess to sharing the general uneasiness as matters stand at present. Over four months have elapsed since the discussion in the House of Commons, but Ministers have done nothing whatsoever to dispel the mist of suspicion overhanging the affair. Mr Samuel stated

---

[4] This happened immediately before the recess, and Asquith suggested it would be best to take time to reflect on it. The matter was not referred to again and seems to have been dropped, although one press report says that Maxse was hanging round the lobbies of the House of Commons waiting to be called.

that Ministers "will be most ready to appear before"—I am quoting him—"the Committee." One might have conceived that they would have appeared at its first sitting clamouring to state in the most categorical and emphatic manner that neither directly nor indirectly, in their own names or in other people's names, have they had any transactions whatsoever, either in London, Dublin, New York, Brussels, Amsterdam, Paris, or any other financial centre in any shares in *any* Marconi Company throughout the negotiations with the Government.

(8)

Le Matin

1

On February 13, the morning after Maxse appeared before the Inquiry, the newspapers were full of the stand he had taken and of the fact that he would probably be called before the House of Commons. In the excitement this had caused no journalist had noticed, and none reported, the significant sentence quoted at the end of the last chapter. In the room at the time, however, there were at least two people who understood exactly what Maxse had intended to convey, and it is probable that the events which immediately occurred were a result of this understanding.

On February 14 a French newspaper called *Le Matin* seriously misquoted some words of Maxse's and gave a version of his evidence which contained a gross libel. Here is a literal translation of what it said:

A FINANCIAL SCANDAL IN ENGLAND

London. Feb. 13.A very grave scandal occupies the English Press. Some little time ago the English Government signed a contract with the

Marconi Company by which that company bound itself in consideration of a large sum—too large, they tell me—to connect by wireless telegraphy all the British possessions with the Mother Country. Mr Leo Maxse, the eminent Editor of the *National Review,* protested vehemently against the way in which this agreement had been concluded. He imputed that Mr Herbert Samuel, the Postmaster-General, whose idea it was to enter into negotiations with the company, had entered into an arrangement with Sir Rufus Isaacs, the Attorney-General, also a member of the Government and brother of Mr Godfrey Isaacs, managing director of the Marconi Company.

All three had bought shares in the company at an average price of about 50 francs, at which these shares were quoted before the opening of the negotiations with the Government, and had resold them at a profit rising to as much as 200 francs per share according as the negotiations enabled it to be foreseen that the contract would be concluded.

Mr Maxse attacked at the same time the fact that the contract had been signed in haste on March 7, without having been brought before Parliament as it ought to have been.

On the day this article appeared Sir Rufus Isaacs went to see the London editor of *Le Matin,* who after some conversation expressed his regret and agreed to publish a withdrawal and an apology. On February 18 the apology appeared, and this is again a literal translation.

A FINANCIAL SCANDAL IN ENGLAND
What the Official Documents Say.
Special Telegram of the *Matin.*

London. Feb. 17. Under the heading "A Financial Scandal in England," I sent you on Thursday last an abstract of the rumours which had been current with regard to accusations brought by Mr Leo Maxse, Editor of the *National Review,* against Mr Herbert Samuel, Sir Rufus Isaacs the Attorney-General, and his brother, Mr Godfrey Isaacs, managing director of the Marconi Company. The official documents of the Parliamentary

Inquiry which I have just read in no way confirm these rumours: far from it. It appears therefrom that Mr Maxse simply said in answer to his questioners that he had repeated rumours which were floating about, and that he could in no case give the source of his information.

Under these circumstances and pending publication of the discussions, I take the earliest opportunity of sending you this correction with an expression of regret that I should, in perfect good faith, by communicating current rumours to you, possibly have done an injury of any sort to three men of quite unimpeachable honour.

In spite of the apology "this opportunity for a full statement could not be allowed to pass,"[1] and on the 19th Sir George Lewis issued writs for libel on behalf of both Mr Samuel and Sir Rufus Isaacs. The Prime Minister, who had been consulted, had on this occasion, if rather half-heartedly, agreed. On February 24 he wrote:

I return the enclosed. The statements are so specific and personal that you were probably bound to take proceedings, though it is a little unfortunate that the peccant journal should be a French and not an English newspaper.[2]

On March 19 therefore Mr Herbert Samuel and Sir Rufus Isaacs, who had found it possible to ignore the *Eye–Witness*, the *Outlook* and the *National Review* for more than six months, appeared before Mr Justice Darling in a libel action against a French newspaper which had apologised in print, proceeded to apologise again in Court, did not defend the case and accepted the costs of the action. Mr F. E. Smith appeared for Mr Samuel and Sir Edward Carson for Sir Rufus Isaacs. Mr Schwabe and Mr Raymond Asquith were the Juniors. Mr Campbell appeared for the *Matin*. The Marconi case held the headlines again.

---

[1] Reading, *Rufus Isaacs*, 256.
[2] Bowle, *Viscount Samuel*, 95.

Sir Edward Carson opened the case for the plaintiffs. After saying that there had for some considerable time been rumours of impropriety in the entry into and the execution of the contract, he said:

But the first real crystallization of these rumours into an averment of actual facts as to the alleged delinquencies of members of the Government is contained, as far as my two clients are concerned, in this paper the *Matin*, and they were naturally desirous at the earliest possible moment of taking the opportunity of coming here to refute them.

After describing the events that led up to the action and explaining that the newspaper did not intend to enter a defence and was prepared to pay a full indemnity against all costs, he continued:

That, my Lord, the plaintiffs have accepted; but I am bound to say that they have accepted it without damages solely because this was a French paper circulating in France, though with some circulation in England, and because it is quite clear that what was sent over was merely sent as gossip with reference to a scandal and one does not impute any motive of malice either political or otherwise against the defendants. But whatever the position of the parties, such a course would not be taken if this had been an English journal making deliberate causeless accusations against members of the Government under whose rule that paper was conducted.

He then discussed the negotiations for the contract, making the same explanation about the number of committees that had sat to consider it as Mr Samuel had made in the House of Commons. He denied that part of the libel that alleged the plaintiffs had bought and sold Marconi shares at a profit. Then he said:

There were other Marconi Companies. There were the Canadian and the Spanish Companies, and, although what I have said on this point entirely completes the matter as regards the truth or falsity of the libel, I must, in regard to one transaction in one of the companies by the

Attorney-General which it is necessary to explain, ask your indulgence, although it is a little outside the libel. . . .

Up to March 7, the date when the contract was accepted, the Attorney-General had never had any dealings with any of them.

Sir Edward then explained the issue of American shares, saying that this company was entirely independent and had no interest in the contract at all.

Six weeks after the tender had been made public, the Attorney-General, having heard of this American Company, I think, for the first time a few days before, bought 10,000 of its shares at a premium, which was the market price. . . . As there is a suggestion that in some way or other these gentlemen or either of them were dealing with shares when they were low at 50 francs and then sold them at 200 francs, I ought to say that at the time when the Attorney-General bought these shares the British Company's shares were at the very highest figure to which they have risen.

With regard to this purchase of 10,000 shares, in reality it turned out to be a loss. He sold some of the shares, and amongst others 1000 to Mr Lloyd George and another 1000 to the Master of Elibank, who is now Lord Murray. They were intimate friends of his. Though at the time neither of them knew of the shares and probably never would have heard of them, it is right to say that he offered them the shares believing them to be a good investment, having nothing whatever to do with the shares in the English Company. They were offered and bought 1000 each of these shares, and I am afraid it also turned out to be a loss for them. At all events, as regards the Attorney-General, the net result is that, having sold these and some other shares, some of them at a profit, he still has 6400 of the shares, and, taking the whole, is a loser of £1000 to £1500 at present prices.

After introducing this red herring to create sympathy (he can hardly have believed that speculation is less questionable if it is unsuccessful)[3] Sir Edward

---

[3] See also Max Beerbohm's contemporary drawing opposite.

went on to say that there had been no secrecy of any kind in the dealings over the shares and added:

> I only go into it at all . . . on account of the position of the Attorney-General and because he wishes to . . . state everything and keep nothing back. That is the whole matter.

In this way the dealings in the American shares were, after so long, made public.

Mr Samuel thought, correctly, that the statement of his position would be complete and satisfactory. That evening he wrote in a letter:

> The case went very well in all respects, as we anticipated, and the newspaper apology could not have been more ample. . . . The statement about Rufus's and Lloyd George's American shares was received with equanimity, and, although most of the posters of the evening papers are devoted to the case, only one, the *Star*, refers to that aspect of it, with a placard "Marconi Lloyd George Sensation." They will have to pass through a somewhat unpleasant time for a few days and it will then be forgotten.[4]

He was wrong. On the following morning (March 20) *The Times* certainly took the new revelation calmly. In a second leader it said:

> We are of the opinion that more delicacy might have been shown by Ministers involved in the selection of investments. But mere lack of judgment is a very different thing from the monstrous offences that have been imputed to them.

Lord Reading, commenting on *The Times* leader, says: "This detached attitude did not, however, find an echo in the rest of the Conservative press."[5]

---

[4] Bowle, *Viscount Samuel*, 96.
[5] Reading, *Rufus Isaacs*, 260.

The Times was as detached as this: when it was decided that Sir Edward Carson should use the occasion of the libel action to make the first public statement of the Ministers' dealings in American Marconis, Mr Winston Churchill immediately telephoned Lord Northcliffe and asked to see him. Soon after this telephone call he arrived in the newspaper proprietor's bedroom, where he told him the whole story, explained that the revelation would be made, and captured Lord Northcliffe's sympathy.[6]

Bonar Law also had prior information. Campbell, who appeared for *Le Matin*, was a member of the Conservative Party (as were both Counsel for the plaintiffs), and he sought Law's advice before accepting the brief. He had been informed by Sir Edward Carson that the statement was to be made and he was authorised to confide the news to Bonar Law. The confidence reposed in the latter did not prevent his friend, Mr Max Aitken, from hurrying round to see Lord Northcliffe, only to learn that Mr Churchill had been there before him.

On March 21, two days after the case, Mr Lloyd George wrote to Lord Northcliffe as follows:

11 Downing Street, Whitehall, S.W.

Dear Lord Northcliffe,

I feel I must thank you for the chivalrous manner in which you have treated the Attorney-General and myself over the Marconi case. Had we done anything of which men of honour ought to feel ashamed we could not have approached you on this subject. But although the transaction was in itself a straight-forward one, we were only too conscious that it was capable of exciting unpleasant comment. The atmosphere is now a morbid one owing to the controversy that gathers round Marconi enterprises. I therefore appreciate deeply the generosity

---

[6] Lord Rothermere, Lord Northcliffe's brother, also wrote to him on behalf of the "Marconi Ministers." In the account given in *The History of The Times* (iv, 1056) it is said that Northcliffe re-wrote an intended leader himself. When read to him the leader was disapproved as seeming libellous, and Northcliffe "patched one together" himself; and "a very poor patch it was." (Northcliffe to Dawson, 20 March 1913). It is also made plain that this was not the only occasion during the Marconi case on which Northcliffe restrained the Editor's comments.

and largeness of view which have distinguished your treatment of the matter. I firmly believe that time, and a short time, will justify your foresight. None the less I do feel grateful for a great kindness done to me, for I know the power you wield.

Ever sincerely, D. Lloyd George.[7]

The Liberal papers made very light of the new disclosure (with the honourable exception of the *Nation*, where Massing-ham, the editor, expressed genuine distress), but the Conservative press, apart from *The Times*, were hostile from the start. The public took a little while to under-stand exactly what they had been told and to assess this new knowledge in the light of the facts they already knew. The opinion of most unprejudiced people when it finally formed seems to have accepted that, although the dealings in American shares were very rum, they were probably innocent. An entirely different view was taken of the Ministers' subsequent behaviour. Cecil Chesterton concluded a critical comment in the *New Witness* with the words:

> We have not got to the bottom or anywhere near the bottom of it yet. But, so far as we have gone, we have at least discovered one thing, and that is that we can place no reliance in future on the assurances of these politicians, unless we examine every word they say with a microscope. We know that they say indignantly that they have never dealt in the shares of the Marconi Company when they have dealt largely in the shares of asso-ciated companies. We must be prepared to find that when they say they did not "see" a man they mean they spoke to him on the telephone. In a word, we must take it for granted that truth is not expected of them as truth is understood by common men of honour.

For once this seemed fair comment. The editor's brother, G. K. Chesterton, in the same issue of the paper drew attention even more effectively to the

---

[7] Owen, *Tempestuous Journey*, 231. Sir Rufus Isaacs also wrote to thank Lord Northcliffe.

other strange aspect of the case in a poem called *A Song of Cosmopolitan Courage*. In each verse of this some (imaginary) continental paper makes amends for a statement published in London—a Polish paper apologising for the *Morning Post*, a journal in Alsace retracting for the *Nation*, while the *Frankfurt Frank* withdraws a charge the *Outlook* has not made.[8]

2

When in the debate of October 11 the Ministers had said they had not bought shares in "that" company, there was more than one interpretation that might have been put on their words. The ordinary man, the non-partisan, the indifferently charitable, the normally credulous, took them to mean that they had not bought shares on the Stock Exchange or anywhere else in any Marconi Company. He was not merely shocked at the subsequent disclosures—he felt fooled.

Maxse took advantage of the atmosphere to make the following suggestion, which cannot be altogether discounted. The journalists had been called first before the Select Committee to make the case which Ministers would then be called to answer. Supposing that they had failed entirely to do this, and without Maxse himself they might have, then it would have been possible, even reasonable, for the Coalition majority on the Committee to rule that the Ministers could not be called, since no case had been made out against them. Whether or not this calculation was ever made, it is difficult to believe that in such a case the Ministers would have felt it necessary to insist on appearing and placing the facts of the American deals before the House of Commons and the nation.

In any case, the announcement had now been made, and this had been done, partly with the aid of *The Times*, without so seriously weakening the position of the Ministers that any immediate action was contemplated. What had really happened was never known except by the handful of people concerned. It has always been accepted that Maxse flushed the quarry into

---

[8] I have been refused permission to publish this poem, but it can be found in Ward's *Gilbert Keith Chesterton*, page 293.

the open, and it is almost certain that he did this not by accident but from knowledge he had somehow acquired. He never claimed the credit nor disclosed the source of his information, but the word "any" before Marconi Company was underlined in the précis of his evidence sent to the Committee.

Out of the case against the *Matin* there arose a new source of controversy. F. E. Smith and Sir Edward Carson were both prominent members of the Conservative Party in Parliament. It was very strongly felt that by appearing for their colleague at the Bar they had forgone their opportunity to attack their opponents in the House of Commons, and this was much resented by their fellow-Conservatives. The two men were to repeat the offence in the case against Cecil Chesterton which forms the subject of a later chapter of this book, and as a result they were effectively silenced in debate during the whole of the final months of the Marconi case. The argument concerning the propriety of their action was conducted with heat, and finally, in June, found a place in the columns of *The Times*.

This began with a report of a luncheon of the Scottish Constitutional Club, where Sir John Stirling-Maxwell accused Sir Edward Carson of carrying chivalry too far when he lent "the assistance of the leader of the Ulster Party to those Marconi knaves or fools or both—i do not know which they are."[9]

Sir Edward replied: "We are given a monopoly of advocacy not for this person or that person, or this side or that side,"[9] but on the following day a *Times* leader remarked:

> To the man of ordinary intelligence there is something inexpedient, if not impossible, in the attempt to fulfil two irreconcilable parts, and no appeal to the rules of etiquette will convince him of the contrary.[9]

To this F. E. Smith replied with his accustomed pith:

> I invite our critics to indicate with precision the grounds upon which it is suggested that it was our duty to refuse these retainers. Were we to

---

[9] *The Times*, 13 June 1913.

say "We cannot accept because the plaintiffs are Liberals and we are Conservatives, and therefore, the issue being political, the circumstances are special?" I would recommend those who take this view to examine with some care the certain consequences of such an action. Political issues constantly present themselves for decision in the Law Courts. In the overwhelming majority of cases juries have done their duty indifferently between the parties, treating their own views upon politics as immaterial. How long do you think this state of things will endure if every Conservative case is to be presented by Conservative advocates and resisted by Liberal advocates? . . . How long do you think it would be before our Law Courts reproduced the grotesque travesty of judicial procedure which has disfigured the record of the Marconi Committee? . . . You speak of the ordinary man. I do not in this connexion recognise such a tribunal. May I without incivility add that, if upon a matter requiring some degree of enlightenment and cultivation for its adequate comprehension, the "ordinary man" is uninstructed upon the function which every civilised country in the world has assigned to the advocate, *The Times* would be better employed informing his mind than appealing to his judgment.[10]

And to him a Mr Hay ward replied:

The answer is to be found in the proposition that no advocate with deep political convictions can honourably to himself accept a brief which compels him to defend a cause which he loathes and despises. . . . The idea is grotesque and no one knows it better than that "Brutus of the Bar" Mr Smith. If his views are correct the Government can easily dispose of Sir Edward Carson by briefing him in a Treasury prosecution on the eve of the Battle of the Boyne.[11]

The solution of the point seems to lie in the converse proposition: The

[10] *The Times*, 17 June 1913.
[11] *The Times*, 20 June 1913.

advocate should believe his cause just and true. If he does not he writes himself down a hired mercenary. This may be applied with equal force to the Member of Parliament pleading a case in the House of Commons. It seems likely that F. E. Smith and Sir Edward Carson had no wish to take part in a debate where their position as leading members of the Unionist Party would bring them into action against Sir Rufus, who was not merely a colleague but also a friend. They were both men of vigorous ambition and remarkable intellect and they were personally concerned with the major events of the time. They were not interested in small points, probably not even in small moral points. It may have seemed to them that, while a friend and colleague was being persecuted with vile and false charges, they had a greater duty as advocates to defend him against these, than as politicians to press others, which, however true, they personally felt unimportant. In any case, if, consciously or unconsciously, they felt reluctant to speak against him in the House of Commons, they could not more effectually have muzzled themselves or done so with less publicity for views that must have been unpopular in their own party. Presented with a choice, men will always behave as thinking feeling human beings, and it is right that they should. It is only when, for instance as Attorney-General, a man is unequivocally bound by his public duty that he can adequately present a case personally repugnant to him.

(9)

The Select Committee:
3. Sir Rufus Isaacs

1

Immediately after the *Matin* case the Select Committee departed from intended procedure and called the Ministers. On March 25 Sir Rufus Isaacs appeared on the witness-stand.

About three weeks later Asquith had an audience with King George V at which he expressed himself very freely, and of which an account has been given us by Sir Harold Nicolson.[1] He said that in the previous January Lord Murray of Elibank,[2] Sir Rufus Isaacs and Mr Lloyd George had "confessed to him" that "although they had had no dealings in the shares of the British Marconi Company, they had in fact bought some shares in its American counterpart." Asquith told the King that he considered their conduct "lamentable" and "so difficult to defend," but he added that they had said they feared

---

[1] *George V,* 210.
[2] The Master of Elibank had resigned the office of Chief Whip the previous August and had been created Baron Murray of Elibank.

they might be placed "in a terribly awkward position" and had offered their resignations, which he had refused to accept.

This is the only published record that the Ministers ever considered resignation, and by now it was too late. The opportunity passed with October 11. After nine months of rumour and slander the resignation of three Ministers would inevitably have been treated as an admission, not merely of indiscretion, but of the whole case which reckless and malicious imagination had contrived. It could only have been followed by the fall of the Government. Throughout his political career Asquith was remarkable for his loyalty to his colleagues; on this occasion he had no choice but to support them, and when he rejected their resignations it amounted to a tacit if enforced agreement that he would stand behind them.

Sir Harold Nicolson's is also the only published record of the Prime Minister's feelings about the Marconi case and of the curious slip which allowed him to tell the King the Ministers had confessed something in January of which in fact he had been informed six months before.

2

For the understanding of all the evidence that is to follow it is necessary to have some knowledge of the issue of the new shares in the American Marconi Company.

The capital of the company was at the time one million, six hundred thousand dollars, divided into sixty-four thousand shares of twenty-five dollars, standing at a heavy discount. Isaacs suggested an increase of the capital to ten million dollars—one million four hundred thousand to be spent on acquiring assets of the United Wireless Company (making, with the issued capital, three million dollars), the balance of seven million dollars to be used for the expansion of the Marconi system in America. To raise the capital he suggested that the existing shares of twenty-five dollars should be divided into five shares of five dollars each, carrying the right to apply for five new shares of five dollars.[3]

---

[3] The capital sum thus raised would be nine million, six hundred thousand dollars, not ten million. It was Godfrey Isaacs's habit to take all sums to the nearest round

Under the laws of New Jersey the opportunity to subscribe new capital had first to be offered to existing shareholders, although as these were scattered all over America holding the shares in small parcels, it was not expected that many of them would apply.

After Marconi and Godfrey Isaacs between them had guaranteed the subscription of the whole of the new capital it was arranged that the new issue should be formally agreed by the directors of the company at a meeting to take place on April 18, after which the shares would be introduced on the markets of London and New York.

Then Isaacs went on to negotiate the agreement with the Western Union Cable Company, by the terms of which the American Marconi Company were to receive preferential treatment for messages passing over land-lines of the cable company, making it unnecessary to set up competing stations and equipment. The Western Union Cable Company stipulated, and this is important in view of the evidence which is to follow, that the agreement should not be made public until after the directors of the Marconi Company had formally agreed the new issue of shares, that is until after April 18.

When Sir Rufus took the witness-stand, he began, as had other witnesses, by making a statement on which he was afterwards to be examined. He described to the Committee how at luncheon that day his brother Godfrey had told him and his brother Harry of the arrangements that had been made in New York, and had then gone on to offer them the opportunity of buying American Marconi shares at £1.

His description of what took place did not differ in any way from that which has already been given, nor from the accounts his two brothers were later to give. He said that Godfrey had assured him that "it did not make one halfpence of difference to the American Company" whether the contract with the British Government went through or not. The English Company was a shareholder in the American Company, but the American Company had nothing whatever to do with the English.

Sir Rufus said, and Lloyd George was also to make a great point of this,

---

figure, and in the Marconi case this method was adopted by everyone else.

101

that at that time the name "Marconi" meant to him wireless telegraphy. "I knew of no other." And he added that it had not occurred to him there could be any difficulty about the contract. "I never thought there was any question about it or of its ratification."

Describing how he had bought 10,000 shares at 163;2 from his brother, Harry, and sold 2000 of these to the Master of Eli-bank and Lloyd George, Sir Rufus added that there had been an agreement between the three of them that if the shares rose they would sell half to reduce the price of the other half, which, he said, they intended to hold as an investment.

Previously he had made an agreement with his brother Harry, which he called a *pro rata* agreement, that their shares should be dealt with together. "I did not want to get an advantage over him in the price that I might obtain, or he over me in the price that he might obtain—whatever it was, the proportion of sales was to be the same at an average price."

These two overlapping agreements made for some difficulty when Sir Rufus tried to explain his existing holding in Marconi shares. He and his brother had sold between them some 8000 odd shares at varying prices. The Attorney-General's proportion of sales was 3570 shares averaging £3. 6s. 6d. a share. That left him with 6430 shares, and applying the profit he had made on the shares sold to reduce the loss on those he still held, the latter stood at an average cost of £1. 5s. 3d., or in other words on that day he sustained a loss of £1607. 10s. (the shares being at approximately £1). But of that sum Lloyd George and Lord Murray of Elibank owed him one-tenth each, or together £320, leaving him with a net loss in round figures of £1300.

Many of these facts were new to the Committee. During the *Matin* case it had been announced that the Attorney-General had bought 10,000 shares in the American Marconi Company and sold 1000 each to Lloyd George and the Master of Elibank, but only the bare facts had been stated. The Committee, like the general public, learned now for the first time of the circumstances in which the transactions took place. They were naturally very much interested and for three days they asked Sir Rufus questions in an attempt to get at all the facts behind the transactions. How, for instance, had Godfrey Isaacs been in a position to offer his brothers the shares? If the new issue had, by the New Jersey law, to be offered in the first place to the holders of old shares, how was it possible for Isaacs to dispose of such a large quantity of new shares before the public issue?

This question and many more of the kind were to be asked again and again of later witnesses, Godfrey Isaacs himself and Mr Heybourn, who were in a better position to answer them. It is therefore only necessary to deal here with that part of Sir Rufus's evidence which was concerned with his own transactions and the further matters which arose as a result of it. It emerges from the examination of this witness that there were four main points on which the Committee must try to arrive at an opinion.

(1) Had Sir Rufus and the other Ministers bought shares in a company associated with a company in contractual relations with the Government?

(2) Had they received a favour from the managing director of a company in contractual relations with the Government? Had they, for instance, been given an opportunity to buy the shares before they were available to the general public, or on information not known to the general public?

(3) Had they on October 11 dealt fairly with the House of Commons?

(4) Had they done anything which, while not actually improper, might give an appearance of impropriety, or, if accepted as a precedent, might lead to impropriety on the part of public men less scrupulous than themselves? In connection with this last question the case of Mr Taylor must be referred to, because it was so often quoted at the time.

Mr Taylor was a subordinate Post Office official who bought thirty shares in the English Marconi Company which he paid for in cash out of his savings. When he bought them he was under the impression that the contract with the Company would not go through. Then he learned that the tender would, after all, be signed, and, realising that he might be called upon to advise on the specifications, he sold his shares and explained to his superiors what had occurred. He was reduced in rank and in salary, and the Postmaster-General stated that, but for the obvious innocence of his intention, it would have been impossible to retain him in the public service. Amery, in a speech made some months after these events, said:

But why was he punished at all? Because, as Mr Samuel told him, with perfect justice though with rather superfluous unction in view of what he knew about his colleagues, "in his position he ought to have

103

realised that such investments were not permissible" and that "action such as his is wholly contrary to the tradition and practice of the civil service, and could not fail, if it became usual, profoundly to impair public confidence in its integrity."[4]

Sir Rufus was questioned for the whole of two days and for part of a third. It is exceedingly difficult to summarise the proceedings for several reasons. Sir Rufus, who was for the most part affable, was extremely loquacious. He seldom said anything without repeating it in different terms, and he was much addicted to parentheses. To an onlooker he might at first have seemed propitiatory. He soon made it plain, however, that the loquacity was merely habitual, the affability conditional.

A second difficulty arises out of the constitution and procedure of the Select Committee. Because the Inquiry took the form of question and answer, the temptation is to compare it to a court of law. But this comparison is not just, and if it is taken further it can be seen that there is no charge made and no defence entered, nor are there any advocates. It is much more as though the jury left the box in turn to question the witnesses. Even here the comparison breaks down, because these were not all good men and true; too many of them were political partisans determined to establish such points as told in their favour, to suppress all others. The Liberals had long before discredited the proceedings by adopting unhesitatingly the position that their duty was to their Party rather than to the truth. In the cross-examination of Sir Rufus they showed how far they were prepared to go. Mr Falconer, who had the merit of being a clever man, intervened very little, though effectively, allowing his talented chief to speak for himself; but Mr Booth behaved like an obsequious nanny, and provoked at times the impatience of Sir Rufus himself.

The greatest difficulty the Tories encountered, however, was that, as had occurred before in this Inquiry, it was impossible to get any agreed data on which to pose their questions. In the final resort they were trying

---

[4] Speech delivered by L. S. Amery at a meeting in Finsbury Town Hall on 9 July 1913 and reproduced in full in the *National Review* of August 1913.

not merely to establish the facts of some matter fought out between two disputants, but to arrive at an opinion on such large and abstract concepts as propriety or impropriety and the standards of behaviour required of public men. In order to frame questions designed to elicit information sufficient to base an opinion upon, they had to establish or take for granted that there were certain matters of fact. Sir Rufus continually destroyed the foundation of their questions by arguing the premises. Moreover, since it is nearly impossible to ask a question that does not carry some implication, he put them again and again in the position of making a charge. It was not part of their duty to make charges; he was a respected colleague; and he was a man who for months had borne the burden of atrocious public attacks on matters of which he was completely innocent. The task of the Tory members of the Committee, which had never been easy, became exceedingly unpleasant.

They had grown used to the conduct of witnesses who are in an uneasy position, but, if Sir Rufus's methods may be seen to have much in common with those of the witnesses heard during the discussion of the contract and even with those of Lawson, he was exceptionally acute and quite unusually formidable.

It was the habit of this Committee to question the witnesses in turn. In this way they covered the same ground again and again. If one of them failed to get a satisfactory answer, another took over where his colleague had left off. In the earlier part of the examination of Sir Rufus the questioner was constantly driven off by the manner in which he struck out in reply to any question which suggested so much as comment on any action of his. Again and again he showed an instinctive understanding, faster than the speed of thought, for the line of reasoning behind an apparently innocent opening question, and he made it very clear that only a brave man would proceed with this part of his examination. He never allowed the little patronising but suggestive jokes irresistible to the legal profession which this Committee inclined to indulge nor did he let pass any assumption of agreement on a matter of fact. Once when he had denied that he had retained half the shares in the expectation they would go higher, and said on the contrary his advice had been that they were above their market value, Mr Faber remarked: "That was very public-spirited of you."

"I do not," Sir Rufus replied, "quite understand what you mean by saying 'very public-spirited'" and Mr Faber was forced to make a fumbling retreat.

"The parent company," Mr Faber said on another occasion, "that is the English Company—has a number of associated companies. There are the American, the Spanish, the Argentine, and so forth?"

"Yes," Sir Rufus replied. "But why do you say associated?"

As his examination proceeded his examiners became more and more stubborn. That part of his evidence quoted here is chosen because it gives most completely the points the Committee (or part of it) was trying to establish, and the replies Sir Rufus made. But it should be remembered that, during the course of the proceedings, these matters were argued again and again, and while the form of the questions varied, Sir Rufus's replies never did.

3

It was the habit of the Chairman, Sir Albert Spicer, to ask a few preliminary questions himself. He was a good and gentle man, but an ineffective chairman. In a memoir written by one of his children, which has the unusual distinction for this type of work of being both candid and sincere, it is stated that he had great doubts, when he was asked to occupy the chair, of his ability to undertake the task.

He conducted the inquiry [the writer states] with unremitting zeal and absolute integrity. He spared no personal effort to study the subject and all its ramifications, but he failed to dominate the Committee as a stronger Chairman might have done. His task was exceptionally hard, for the Prime Minister himself failed to back his own nominee and allowed the Liberals on the Committee to turn it into a mere white-washing expedient. Against that attitude my father's integrity was not enough. He was already slightly deaf and did not always hear remarks when they were not addressed directly to him. Distinguished witnesses called upon to give evidence sometimes treated the Committee with scant courtesy, and in the absence of a strong line by the Chairman were allowed to do so with impunity.[5]

Sir Albert Spicer belonged to the Liberal Party, and it cannot therefore be suggested that he was actuated by anti-Government bias. He drew Sir Rufus's fire quite quickly, however, and in answer to a question of his the witness made it plain to what end, in his opinion, the efforts of the Committee should be directed. The Chairman asked:

> When you were making your speech in the House of Commons on October 11 did the thought occur to you that you might get rid of some of these rumours if you mentioned your investment in American Marconis, because both being Marconis you could easily understand one might get confused with the other?

And to this Sir Rufus replied:

> It did not occur to me and it does not occur to me now.

He found it very difficult, he continued, to understand how any person who had information—"I will assume he had information, I do not know whether he had or not, but there were books and entries in books with my name, and contract notes and accounts"—could have written the lies that were published on such a foundation. "That is what I want to know and what I am entitled to know."

Pressed as to why he had not revealed the purchase of American shares on October 11, he made a very long statement, a statement he was to make again and again in different places.

> I confined my speech entirely, I think you will find by reference to it, to dealing with the four specific charges which were made, which I formulated. I did not want to confuse any questions which were being raised on other matters with these charges.

---

[5] *Albert Spicer*, 40.

And he said that he had always regarded the Select Committee as the right place to tell the whole story and had expected to come almost immediately before it.

If anyone had said in October when I made that speech that it would be some six months before I should be called before the Committee he would have been laughed at and ridiculed.

When Mr Faber began to question the Attorney-General on his reasons for buying the shares from Harry when he had refused them from Godfrey the peculiar difficulties in the examination of this witness first became plain. Sir Rufus explained that he had seen no objection to his buying shares from Godfrey, "but I had the feeling that I did not want to have any dealings with the company, that is with the English company."

Q. Why not?
A. Because I preferred not.
Q. Because you did not think it quite right?
A. No, it was not a question of it not being quite right.
Q. Because you did not think it quite right that in the circumstances of your position you should, on your brother's request, he being Managing Director of the Marconi Company here, take shares in the American Marconi Company. Is that what you mean?
A. I thought it was liable possibly to misconception.
Q. Do you not think so still?
A. I thought so then.
Q. Why did you alter your mind later?
A. I did not. I never altered my mind.
Q. Perhaps my mind is not marching so quickly as yours, but at first, when Mr Godfrey Isaacs made this proposal to you and your brother Harry, that you should take the shares, you said no, you thought you had better not.
A. Yes.
Q. But later on you altered your mind and then took the shares?
A. That is right. I altered my mind and the difference is

important . . . I dealt direct with my brother who had nothing to do with the Marconi Company. That was the difference.

Q. That is with your brother Harry?

A. Yes.

Q. Did you know then, or do you know now, where your brother Harry got his American Marconi shares?

A. Of course I did.

Q. From where?

A. Undoubtedly he took some of the shares that were offered by the company; that is by my brother Godfrey.

Q. Then does it not really come to the same thing?

A. It seems to me to be very materially different.

Q. You agree to take shares from your brother Harry, your brother Harry in his turn gets them either from Mr. Godfrey Isaacs, the Managing Director of the Marconi Company, or direct from the Marconi Company.

A. Forgive me, is not the order just exactly the opposite.

Q. Will you tell me the order?

A. He takes shares from the company or from Mr Godfrey Isaacs. He has bought the shares . . .

As each of the Tory members finished his examination either Mr Falconer or Mr Booth took the witness through the same points, framing the questions in such a way as to ensure the reply most favourable to Sir Rufus. Their interpolations seemed quite irrelevant, but they secured these interpretations for the record and thus confused the issue.

Lord Robert Cecil succeeded Mr Faber and in the following question he was referring to the fact that Godfrey Isaacs had told his brothers of the agreement with the Western Union Cable Company which was not made public until April 19.

Q. In other words you were in a rather more favourable position than the ordinary public when you bought these shares?

A. Oh, no. Let me point out why, because I think it is important. I would not have bought those shares in the market—going in buying them of a stranger—for the reason that I should have been going in knowing something that the other person did not know. When I bought them of my brother Harry I was knowing nothing but what he knew, and of course the 1,400,000 shares had to be distributed and had been placed.

Q. I quite understand that. That was not the meaning of my question.

A. But I was a little anxious to make that plain.

Q. I mean that at the time you bought you knew of these contracts. If the public had known of those contracts in the same way, what you have called the market price would have been a great deal higher. It was, in fact, a great deal higher when they did become known.

A. It would mean that I should have paid my brother so much more.

On the morning of the second day of Sir Rufus's evidence, Douglas Hogg appeared before the Committee and asked permission to cross-examine the Attorney-General on behalf of four witnesses for whom he had earlier appeared. These witnesses, he said, and in particular Mr Lawson, had been very strongly attacked for referring to rumours. He did not complain of the attacks, but he thought it only fair that he should be allowed to question Sir Rufus on those parts of his evidence which related to the evidence given and the articles written by his clients. He was cut short by the Chairman, who refused his request, as Hogg must have known he would, but he too had succeeded in getting it on the record.

Lord Robert Cecil then resumed the examination of the Attorney-General, and after he had covered many of the points already put by Mr Faber the following interchange occurred:

Q. I am very anxious to avoid expressing or indicating any opinion of my own during the questions I am putting to you, and I do not propose to do so. That will be a matter for us to consider afterwards when we have arrived at the facts.

A. I am not quite sure I understand what that means, and I would like it made very clear. If that means that in anything you are putting to me you are imputing to me any want of personal honour or integrity, then it is news to me. I did not understand Mr Faber's

110

questions to be framed with that object.

Q. I am not imputing anything to you at all. I am here to investigate this matter on behalf of the House of Commons, and I am doing my best to do so, and it is not at all an agreeable task for any of us.

A. I object very strongly to it being left there, and will you allow me to say this: if . . . it is meant that either you or Mr Faber, or any member of this Committee is imputing to me anything of a nature which affects my personal honour or integrity, then I demand that it be put to me . . . in perfectly plain language.

Q. Certainly.

The Attorney-General then repeated his request several times in different words, and Lord Robert Cecil continued to agree. Then Lord Robert said:

Q. Now about the connection between the two companies; after what you have said to me I wish to be perfectly frank with you . . . It is quite obvious that the questions I have asked you up to now deal with this difficulty: that on a certain view of the facts you may be held to have received an advantage indirectly from the managing director of a company that was in negotiation with the Government. Do you see what I mean?

A. I confess I do not. I did not understand any question you have put to me to suggest that.

Q. Your brother, Mr Godfrey Isaacs, was the managing director of the English Marconi Company?

A. Yes.

Q. And the English Company was still in negotiation over this contract?

A. I did not think so, and I do not think so now.

Some time was now taken up while Lord Robert Cecil attempted—by quotation from State papers—to convince Sir Rufus that at that time the contract was not ratified, and various Departments of State were still in nego-tiation about it. Unable to reach any agreement with the witness as to the meaning of words, he tried afresh and from a slightly different angle.

Q. The managing director offers you shares on very favourable terms in another company, and let us take it for the moment that they have no connection at all?

A. Yes.

Q. And you refuse at first?

A. No, I refused absolutely.

Q. To take them from him. The same shares are then offered to you by his the brother—by the brother of both of you. That is right?

A. Yes. That is to say the shares which he had purchased on the 9th he offered me on the 17th—Part of them.

Q. Still on favourable terms to you, because that is why he offered them and why you accepted them.

A. No, on market terms.

Q. But on market terms in the sense we arrived at at the beginning of my questions today?

A. At market terms in the only sense in which I understand the Word: that is to say the price that would be fixed between a willing buyer and a willing seller.

Q. But not at a price at which any ordinary member of the public could have got them?

A. I do not agree in that. Any ordinary member of the public could give his orders to his broker and he could buy the shares.

Q. [After several more questions.] I think you and I can carry it no further.

Later:

Q. You ask me to say what is the criticism which occurs to me provisionally in reference to that transaction. Do you not think that a transaction of that kind is just such a transaction as might have been— accepting fully, as I personally do, and I wish to say so, that in your case it was due to no corrupt motive at all—entered into with a corrupt motive?

112

A. No, it certainly does not seem to me so, because I should have thought if a person wanted to enter into a corrupt transaction the last thing he would have done would have been what I did—to have bought the shares at the market price.

Presently Lord Robert asked the witness whether he did not think in conceivable circumstances his interests might have conflicted with his duty, and Sir Rufus replied:

Not in the remotest degree. After all the consideration and after all the views that you have put, if I may say so, very fairly to me, it does not alter my opinion in the slightest degree. Never in any circumstances should I have been in regard to this contract in any position which would bring me in conflict with my duty, that is as I view it.

Lord Robert gave this up and turned to something else:

Q. The point is this rather, is it not: There were rumours?
A. Yes.
Q. And rumours which at any rate according to some evidence we have had before us began long before any of the articles were published? . . . And it was with a view to the disposal of those rumours that this debate took place?
A. I did not think so. I thought that it offered an opportunity for me to get up and deny in the House of Commons, the first time that I had the opportunity, the stories which so far as I knew were in circulation. If there was any other surely someone would have stated it in the House of Commons to me at the time to have given me the opportunity of denying it.
Q. Surely it is not a question of denying the particular rumours. The question which really the House was discussing—or so I gather from reading the debate—was what was the foundation, if any, for this kind of general rumours of corruption, suspicion or what not?
A. I thought that was what the Committee was to inquire into.
Q. But the House was talking about it too, and it was directed to that

subject, as I read it, that the debate took place?

A. That is not quite my view. . . . The debate upon it was, or so it appeared to me, the opportunity to me of denying the statements which had been made . . .

Q. But surely the debate was also with the view of calming and disabusing the public mind. That was the real purpose?

A. Certainly; and in so far as there were statements of this character made, I thought I had disabused it. . . .

Q. Do you not think now, looking back, it would have been wiser and better if you had then and there told them all this story?

Sir Rufus made again, and at equal length, the statement that he regarded the Committee of Inquiry as the right place to tell the whole story.

Lord Robert then referred to a question asked of the Prime Minister in the House of Commons,[6] and Sir Rufus stated that the Master of Elibank had told Asquith of the purchase of American shares and that he himself had told Mr Samuel.

Speaking of the correspondence between himself, Mr Samuel and the Prime Minister on the publication of the first Marconi article in the *Eye–Witness*, Sir Rufus said that the letter he wrote Asquith had unfortunately been destroyed, but that in it he had referred again to the purchase by himself, the Master of Elibank and Mr Lloyd George of the American shares. He read

---

[6] On March 26 Major Archer-Shee asked the Prime Minister in the House of Commons whether he was informed by the Attorney-General and the Chancellor of the Exchequer that they had been dealing in the shares of the American Marconi Company *before the debate on October 11*. The Prime Minister replied: "I was informed by the Master of Elibank at the end of July or the beginning of August that he and the Attorney-General and the Chancellor of the Exchequer had purchased shares in an American Marconi Company. At a later date in August the Attorney-General repeated the statement to me, and I believe added that they had sold some of the shares but retained the bulk of them. Both assured me that the purchase was made after the publication of the contract between the Post Office and the English Marconi Company and that the American Company had no interest direct or indirect in that contract. That was the whole extent of my information at the date of the debate in October."

to the Committee the reply the Prime Minister had made to his letter—
quoted here on page 51—and Lord Robert Cecil asked:

Q. You then did decide to sue the *Le Matin* this year, as we know?
A. Yes.
Q. Have you considered the desirability of suing any of these other
newspapers?
A. Yes. Every one.
Q. Have you been advised about it, or have you relied on your own
judgment on the matter?

Sir Rufus replied that he never felt too confident of his own judgment
where personal matters were concerned, and, although he had not taken
formal legal advice, he had consulted colleagues and friends.

With regard to the *Eye–Witness* I certainly did not come to the
conclusion that a prosecution might not lie. I thought that there might
be difficulties, undoubtedly. I mean difficulties because of attacks on
Ministers of public position and so forth—but with regard to the others,
I could not find anything definite; it was mere insinuation and suggestion. I thought that the *Eye–Witness* went rather further than that.

4

When Mr MacMaster took over the examination he returned to the debate of
October 11, but he elicited only one new piece of information. In answer to a
question whether he had felt no obligation to disclose his purchase of
American shares, Sir Rufus replied: "It was not a question of making a disclosure. I had no objection to anybody knowing about the American shares."
And when MacMaster asked whether he had gone to the Chairman on the
appointment of the Committee to ask for urgency to be heard on an important communication, he said: "I do not look upon it as an important
communication."

Following this MacMaster precipitated an unexpected scene. He asked Sir
Rufus whether he had mentioned to any member of the Committee his

115

transaction in American Marconi shares, and Sir Rufus replied: "Certainly."
Immediately Falconer objected to the question.

There was nothing unusual in the objection itself, but on this occasion it took the form of a long speech that was completely unintelligible to everyone in the room. Falconer appeared either to be fighting for time or trying to find a debating point to make his objection arguable. The only point he succeeded in making was that the last question was a breach of an agreement "that it was not only the right, but the duty of any member of the Committee to receive any communication which any person might wish to make to him."

At the end of this speech no member of the Committee had the slightest idea what Falconer had said or why he had intervened, until during the course of a long conversation Harold Smith suddenly said: "I think Mr Falconer's objection, or the point he raised, referred to a question which was asked in the House."

Mr Falconer replied: "In a supplementary question of which I had no notice, so I could not be there, a suggestion was made as to whether some inquiry had not been made of me by the Prime Minister."

In the House of Commons on March 26 the Prime Minister had been asked whether he had known of the purchase of American shares and in a Supplementary Major Archer-Shee inquired whether Mr Falconer and Mr Booth were also in possession of the information. To the first question the Prime Minister replied that he had been told, but to the second he replied: "No, sir, certainly not."

The Chairman, still unable to follow the discussion, now ruled that it should be continued in private. On the following morning MacMaster opened the proceedings by telling Sir Rufus he was about to ask him a question.

"But," he said, "I wish to tell you in advance that you are not to answer it. There has been a ruling by a majority of the Committee that you are not to answer the question."

He then again asked whether Sir Rufus had communicated to any member of the Committee the purchase of American Marconi shares, and, if so, when and to whom. Sir Rufus replied:

"Of course, all I have to do now is to bow to your ruling, but for myself I may say that I raise no objection to this or any other question that has been put to me."

116

Five days after this interchange a letter addressed by Harold Smith to Sir Albert Spicer was published in *The Times*. Having stated that the writer could no longer attend the meetings of the Committee, it continued:

> Two members have been publicly charged with having received and withheld from the Committee most vital information, which, had it been communicated to their colleagues, must have very much shortened, and, I submit, materially altered our proceedings. These two members have not denied this charge, and one of them has publicly objected to a question which was put to a witness with the object of testing its accuracy. This objection was upheld by a majority of the Committee, which is thereby precluded from obtaining information to which, in my judgment, it is entitled. I desire for the present to refrain from all comment. I can only draw my own conclusion, with the result that I cannot see my way to attend further meetings of the Committee.

It had been the custom for many months for hecklers at political meetings and even in the House of Commons to interrupt Liberal speakers with cries of "Marconi! Marconi!" The cry was now changed to "Gag! Gag!"

Maxse and the other journalists concerned with the case were thrown into paroxysms of delight. It enabled them to say, and it has constantly been repeated, that, when he was examining the journalists, Falconer had steered them away from any line of argument that might have developed into a discussion of the American Marconi Company.[7] In fact, this is not clear in the record, and, although it would be an injustice to Falconer to suggest that he was not ready and willing for such an eventuality, the truth seems to be that it had never occurred to anyone that the Ministers might have had dealings with some company other than the English, until Maxse, who undoubtedly had definite information, was called.

The press was cut short in its frenzy of speculation and comment by the

---

[7] Lord Reading in his book says rather ingenuously that his father had told Mr Falconer and Mr Booth in order that they might be forearmed when the journalists came to give evidence.

necessity to deal with even more sensational matters that immediately followed.

5

When L. S. Amery took up the questioning he began to discuss the *"pro rata"* agreement and suggested that it might have been the basis of the rumours. He pointed out that, as a result of it, Sir Rufus had sold in his own name 8000 shares for £27,000, and that between them the two brothers had sold 17,850 shares at a profit which covered the original cost by some £6000 and left them 32,150 shares in hand. If, he postulated, some person or persons had acquired this knowledge and assumed that the shares were not merely sold as a common pool but paid for on the same basis, might not this account for the whole of the rumours?

During the time that Amery took to explain his theory the Attorney-General grew more and more restive and interrupted constantly. The suggestion had no value, he maintained, unless it was meant offensively. At the end of a long altercation he showed signs of being very angry indeed.

> In my view that is impossible. Any person who knew I had sold 8000 shares in my name, or that Mr Lloyd George had sold 1000 shares in his name, which he did, any person who knew those things, and who relied upon them in any way as basing these rumours, was undoubtedly guilty of as wicked an act as possible.

At this moment Amery's attention was entirely engrossed by the attempt to explain his point. Sir Rufus and Falconer, who quickly came to his aid, insisted on behaving as though his questions were directed to finding a defence for the journalists. Amery persisted and the conversation became more and more acrimonious, until Lord Robert Cecil intervened.

> *Lord Robert Cecil.* I do not wish to intervene. . . .
> *Witness.* Let me finish what I was going to say. I will not be stopped. I am being charged with something; and all I am saying with regard to it is this—and if I appear heated, I am sorry, but it is not very easy, all

I mean to say is we cannot have—at least, I ask you, sir, and I ask the Committee to say that we cannot have a confusion between a charge of corruption and a charge of impropriety. One concerns the honour and the other the judgment of a man.

Lord Robert Cecil. Everybody admits that. That is quite plain and there is no dispute about it.

Witness. That is all I meant.

Lord Robert Cecil. We are not trying the journalists. That is not the point.

Witness. But are you trying me?

Lord Robert Cecil. We are not trying anybody; we are inquiring into the facts.

The following morning when Sir Rufus was recalled he asked permission to ask a question. He said that on looking through the notes of his evidence he noticed that he had misunderstood a question of Mr Faber's and given an answer which might create a wrong impression. He asked that at the end of his examination he might be allowed to correct this.

Sir Rufus's mind had worked at its accustomed speed, but no faster than Amery's, who began immediately by asking the witness to look at his evidence of the day before. He then quoted the passage in which Sir Rufus had said: "Any person who knew that I had sold 8000 shares in my name, or that Mr Lloyd George had sold 1000 in his . . ."

"Have you anything," he asked, "to say on that?"

"Nothing," the witness replied, "except that it is correct."

"It was news to some members of the Committee," Lord Robert Cecil remarked, "that Mr Lloyd George had sold 1000 shares in his name."

Sir Rufus now returned to his earlier statement that there were certain questions of Mr Faber's which he had misunderstood.

It is Questions 214 and 215. I understood the question as relating to April 19 and I made the note that I thought that without stating something that I knew of on April 20 it might not convey the complete answer, and therefore I was going to call Mr Faber's attention to it so that he could put any further questions he desired.

There are several columns of elliptical speech on the record before anything further emerges, and it is never clear whether this great lawyer, accustomed to framing pointed questions, was unable to construct a plain sentence, or merely had an overwhelming resistance to instructing this Committee. Eventually it was apparent that Mr Lloyd George, under pressure from his broker (who thought, as Sir Rufus's had, that the shares were much too high), had asked Sir Rufus's permission to sell the second 1000 shares belonging to himself and the Master of Elibank, and receiving permission had done so on April 20. But by June 20, when the special settlement was made, he and the Master of Elibank had bought a further 3000 shares at something like £2. 3s. 0d., which they still held. Questions 214 and 215 were as follows:

Q. Did you know, aye or no, whether they had sold any of their 1000 shares on April 19. Do you know what they have done with their shares?

A. They did nothing on April 19.

Q. How did you know they had done nothing, because they had the right to do what they pleased?

A. I know that they did not. I told them exactly what I was proposing to do, and what my idea was—that if the shares went up certainly above three, I should sell some of them in order to reduce the price of the balance which I intended to keep, and in what I was doing I quite understood it was left to me to do the same for them. I really was doing the whole transaction.

Sir Rufus had to explain not merely his answers to these two questions, but how it was that in all the hours the Committee had spent on mental arithmetic he had always treated one-tenth of the shares he retained as belonging to Mr Lloyd George, one-tenth to the Master of Elibank, and how it was that he had also said more than once that they still owed him for them. It was a complex matter, and again it was some time before it was cleared up.

If, after the sale of the 1000 shares, nothing further had been done, the position would have been that Sir Rufus had to deliver their shares to the broker, who would have paid for them. After they had paid Sir Rufus £2 a share, the difference would have been their profit. But four or five weeks later they bought a further 3000 shares at £2. 3s. 0d. So that on June 20, when the account came, they took from their broker, not 3000 shares, but 2000 and paid not for 3000 shares at £2. 3s. 0d., but for 2000 shares at that price less the profit they had made on the sale of 1000 shares at £3. 3s. 0d. The result was that the purchase price was reduced by something like £1000, and that Sir Rufus retained on their behalf the 1000 shares he had originally sold them.

He said now:

> As regards myself, it left me in exactly the position that I had been in with them throughout, and that is why I said in answer to your question when you put it: "Is that the result?" "That is right." And that is my answer now—"That is right."

The members of the Committee were not so easily satisfied. Mr Faber began:

> Q. I put to you Questions 214 and 215. At the end of your answer to my question 215 you say "I really was doing the whole transaction."
>
> A. That is quite right.
>
> Q. Then, in the light of our present knowledge, when you said "I really was doing the whole transaction," that meant your 10,000 shares, including their 2000.
>
> A. Yes, I think it appears so if you will read it.
>
> Q. And you did not intend in any way then to refer to the 3500 shares which they apparently bought subsequently on their own account?
>
> A. The 3000, no; I was not referring to that at all.
>
> Q. You were not extending your answer to the other shares which you knew, when you made that answer, that they had had on their own account.
>
> A. I am not quite sure what you mean by that. Are you suggesting that I was not telling you purposely?
>
> Q. No, no; I only want to get at the fact.

A. I agree with you in the fact.

Q. I do not want to have any heat. I only want the information.

Sir Rufus replied that his great anxiety had always been to state the facts.

The question that was to exercise people's minds for some time to come was none of the questions Mr Faber had put to Sir Rufus, but the question Sir Rufus put to Mr Faber: "Are you suggesting that I was not telling you purposely?"

If Sir Rufus had said: "I did not tell you that Mr Lloyd George had sold and then bought shares because, as far as I am concerned, it is hearsay, and Mr Lloyd George is to appear before you and will have an opportunity of telling you himself," it would have been an attitude that from a barrister might have been credible. But as he said, in effect, "I did not tell you that he had sold shares on April 20 because you asked me if he had sold shares on April 19," it was widely believed that he had lost his temper and made a slip. The manner in which he gave this information made it possible for Mr F. J. Sheed, in a chapter written in his wife's biography of G. K. Chesterton thirty years later, to say:

> There may, of course, have been far heavier purchases than we know about: the piece-by-piece emergence of what we do know gives us no confidence that all the pieces ever emerged. We have only the word of the two brothers for most of the story and one comes to feel that on this particular matter their word has no great meaning.[8]

In the light of the whole of the evidence given in the case this suggestion is almost certainly unfounded: nevertheless, it is not necessary to draw so hostile an inference to feel that the logic exhibited in Sir Rufus's account of Lloyd George's transactions was a worthy production of the mind that considered "that company" a sufficient description of the company with which Ministers had not had dealings.

One person who was made very angry by Sir Rufus's evidence was

---

[8] Ward, 306.

Lord Northcliffe. He had been persuaded by Mr Churchill to express a lenient view in *The Times* of the evidence given in the *Matin* case, but he had not been told that Lloyd George subsequently bought further shares. Mr Churchill had not known it. Now Lord Northcliffe wrote to him: "Your Marconi friends stage-manage their affairs most damnably,"[9] and in future the leaders in *The Times* were considerably less "detached."

At the end of his examination Sir Rufus handed the Committee all his passbooks, including those of accounts held jointly with his wife.

---

[9] *History of The Times*, IV, 1056.

(10)

The Select Committee:
4. Mr Lloyd George and
Mr Herbert Samuel

1

In a life of her husband Mrs Charles Masterman gives the following account
of an event that took place during the week-end after Sir Rufus Isaacs had
given his evidence to the Committee and before Lloyd George gave his.

There was a really very comic, though somewhat alarming, scene
between Rufus and George on the following Sunday. George had to
give evidence on the Monday—the following day—and Rufus discovered that George was still in a perfect fog as to what his transaction
really had been, and began talking about "buying a bear." I have
never seen Rufus so nearly lose his temper, and George got extremely
sulky, while Rufus patiently reminded him what he had paid, what he
still owed, when he had paid it, who to, and what for. It was on that
occasion also that Charlie and Rufus tried to impress upon him with

all the force in their power to avoid technical terms and to stick as closely as possible to the plainest and most ordinary language. As is well known, George made a great success of his evidence.[1]

Obviously someone had been explaining to Lloyd George the workings of the Stock Exchange, for, when he sold shares that he had not got and had not paid for at a little over three, and later delivered shares that he had subsequently bought at a little over two, there is no doubt that, however inadvertently, he had gone near to bearing the market.[2]

This passage has been quoted in criticism of Lloyd George and Sir Rufus Isaacs. Viewed in a kindly light, it can be seen as a rather endearing revelation that, when the Chancellor of the Exchequer was first pursued by unfounded rumours and later charged with a real indiscretion, he was in a "perfect fog" as to what it was all about.

It is a curious view that he made a great success of his evidence, but he was for the most part pleasant and relaxed, and, although he never gave formal agreement to any point that might have told against him, and was at least as adept as his predecessor in the witness-stand at blocking argument prejudicial to his own view of what had occurred, he did not give the same impression of strain, of acute, defensive watching and waiting.

He made a long opening statement, much of which was concerned with the Treasury's connection with the contract. When he passed to more personal matters he said, as Sir Rufus had, that in April 1912 Marconi had meant to him wireless telegraphy. He had had no idea that there were other companies or that the contract could be seriously opposed. He then gave a rather piteous picture of his financial affairs.

It was true, he said, that when a man became a Minister he received a substantial salary, but his was not larger than his predecessors. "There is always the suggestion that I am the first Chancellor of the Exchequer to be

---

[1] Masterman, *C. F. G. Masterman*, 255.

[2] To "bear the market" is to sell shares that have not yet been bought in the hope of buying them at a lower price before settlement day—in other words to gamble on a falling market. Lloyd George had bought his shares, although he had not paid for them.

paid £5000 a year." Every Minister had, nevertheless, to look forward to the day when another would fill his post and to save and invest a little against this day. He had done this and his total investments brought him in £400 a year. "That is my great fortune." He added that the only other property he owned was a small house in Wales that had cost £2000. The house at Walton Heath, where he lived, and which the press photographers had made look like a palace, belonged to someone else.

The Chancellor then said that he did not wish to be cross-examined about his personal and private affairs, but he would do as Sir Rufus had and submit his passbooks. He concluded:

> I entered into this transaction because I thought it was a good invest-ment. I may or may not have been right in that respect—time will show that. I entered into the transaction feeling convinced that it was not inconsistent with my duty as a Minister of the Crown. I did consider—of course, I had taken part in debates of that kind—that it was not inconsistent with any principle which I had laid down myself when I was criticising; and you naturally put it at its highest when you are criti-cising. I wish to say further that I then thought it was a perfectly straightforward transaction, a perfectly clean transaction. I still say so today. I am very glad to be given an opportunity of making this statement.

2

The innocent Chairman, who had been the first to provoke Sir Rufus, quickly got into trouble with Lloyd George.

> Q. May I refer to one matter which you have referred to partly. . . . It is going back a long time, I admit, but I think possibly you would like me to refer to it. In 1900, when you were a member of the Opposition, there was a question arose in debate in the House with regard to the association of the Chamberlain family with regard to contracts. . . . You stated your view as to what the action of Ministers should be. . . . And, of course, it has been criticised lately that you laid

down certain principles, and the question is, are you, so to speak, living up to them?

Twelve years before Lloyd George had had much to say on the financial standards required of Ministers. In the Khaki election of 1900 Henry Labouchere had advised: "Go for Joe"—Joseph Chamberlain. Lloyd George had gone for Joe by suggesting that the Boer War ensured a dividend for the Small Arms Factory, a Chamberlain interest. Chamberlain, on becoming a Minister, had sold out all his shares in the Small Arms Factory and also in Kynoch's, a company which came under fire as having received advantages when competing for a Government tender. He had an investment in the Birmingham Trust Company, however, and through this, without his knowledge, a small holding in a company contracting with the Admiralty, and also a few shares in the Colombo Commercial Company, which, formed to act as commission agents, had in the exigencies of the Boer War undertaken a government contract, although again without Chamberlain's knowledge. It was believed it had taken employees of the Liberal Party months of research at Somerset House to discover these facts, and this added considerably to the passionate anger aroused when Lloyd George proceeded, in an Amendment to the Address, to move that Ministers or Members of either House of Parliament, holding subordinate office in any public department, ought to have no interest in firms competing for contracts with the Crown, unless the nature and extent of such being first declared should also have been sanctioned.

Chamberlain had cleared himself of the insinuated charge in a speech in which he said: "I think it hard that after twenty-five years of Parliamentary service in the full light of day I should have to stand up here and explain to my colleagues that I am not a thief or a scoundrel," and, if in principle Lloyd George had been right, he had not persuaded his opponents that his motives were pure. Throughout the course of the Marconi case he had to combat a tendency on the part of critics to quote his own moralisings on the subject of the standard of behaviour required of Ministers of the Crown. He now replied to the Chairman:

I am perfectly prepared to be judged by the principles which I laid

127

down myself for application to other Ministers—absolutely. Of course, I must say this: If I am examined about the Kynoch's Debate the responsibility must be upon those who put the question to me. I shall have to refer to the facts in order to show the distinction, and if I do I shall do it very reluctantly. . . . I want it to be clearly understood that if I do so the responsibility is not mine; otherwise it will be said that I am reviving old, personal, painful controversies, and I am the last man to do that.

Sir Albert Spicer, who had apparently believed that this was the time, and Lloyd George the man, for a candid discussion of principle, retreated immediately in shame.

During all Lloyd George's evidence Sir Rufus Isaacs sat in the room and intervened when he felt it necessary. There occurred a scene which is typical of the methods used to reduce the inquiries of the Committee to a stale and static passage at arms on nebulous and irrelevant topics.

Early in Lord Robert Cecil's examination he asked Lloyd George whether Sir Rufus Isaacs had spoken to him about the conversation he had with his brother, Godfrey, on Godfrey's return from America, and Lloyd George replied that he could not recall it. "I heard Sir Rufus say it and I have no doubt it is correct." Lord Robert later asked him whether he thought it desirable that Ministers should take advice about their investments from the managing director of a company in contractual relations with the Government. To this Lloyd George replied:

> I took no advice of the managing director of the Company. I did not even see him. I had no communication of any sort with him.
>
> Q. You will remember that the Attorney-General told us that his opinion was conveyed to you, and you said no doubt that was quite true, although you did not remember it?
>
> A. His opinion?
>
> Q. Mr Godfrey Isaacs's opinion was conveyed to you between the 9th and the 17th.
>
> *Sir Rufus Isaacs.* I think you are putting it a little too high. I am speaking from recollection. I think you are right in saying that between the 9th and the 17th I did see Mr Lloyd George and the Master of Elibank

128

and tell them some part of the conversation I had had with my brother Godfrey on the 9th.

Lord Robert Cecil. That is what I wanted to convey. It is much better that we should try to find the exact phrases that were used.

Mr George Faber. It is on page 5, I think, when Sir Rufus was being examined in chief: "If I may proceed, in order of date, which is probably the most convenient for the Committee, when I had done this I saw Mr Lloyd George and the Master of Elibank."

Sir Rufus Isaacs. That is the 17th.

Mr George Faber. Pardon me, let me read on: "I do not think I should be right in saying that I had never mentioned American shares to them before. I probably had told them something of the conversation I had had with my brother earlier not as a matter of business, but in discussing what happened."

Witness. But you are asking about the opinion of Mr Godfrey Isaacs. I do not remember him saying anything about an opinion.

Sir Rufus Isaacs. There is a little confusion between the two periods, and perhaps I may clear it up. . . . I did say I told them substantially what had passed between my brother and myself on the 17th—that was my impression—that was the conversation I had with my brother Harry.

Now the clue had been found. The exchange continued, but the day was once more lost for Lord Robert. "My brother Harry" had become brother the date of the conversation was in doubt. Some minutes later Lord Robert asked the following question:

> Then your recollection is that you were not told what Mr Godfrey Isaacs's opinion or judgment in the matter was, or that it was a desirable investment, or anything of the kind?
> A. No, I do not remember anything of that kind being said.

In any sphere where truth or reality is being considered this conversation would seem nearly insane. In the first place, could any disinterested person believe that, when the Attorney-General offered his friends a proportion of "a perfectly straightforward, perfectly clean" transaction in the shares of a company "not in association with the British Company," which "did not stand to gain a single halfpenny" through the contract with the British Government, he omitted to mention that his brother Godfrey, who had negotiated the agreements for that company and was chiefly responsible for the issue of capital, thought it a reasonably good thing? But, in any case, outside the Committee room, in the real world, all this begs the question. Supposing that in truth Sir Rufus never did use his brother Godfrey's name, what difference would it make? Where was Lloyd George supposed to think he got his information? Sir Rufus advised his friend, with whom he was on intimate terms and who was not a rich man, to invest £1000 in American Marconi shares, and Lloyd George took his advice. In all the circumstances of the case, how could anyone suggest that it made the slightest difference to Lloyd George's understanding of the matter, whether Sir Rufus actually gave his brother's opinion or not?

Again, no one seems here to be aware that to the ordinary non-political mind all the anxiety on this point is a tacit agreement that, if Lloyd George had received information from Godfrey Isaacs (which Sir Rufus admittedly had), it would have been improper.

But this conversation was not concerned with reality: it was for the record. Eventually the battle was to be won, the Ministers saved by the majority and in terms of the record. No newspaper would ever now be able to preface a statement with the sentence: "We have Mr Lloyd George's word for it that. . . ." Of even more importance, something that had previously been accepted as a matter of fact had become a matter of opinion; a matter on which Liberal opinion, however incredible, was decisive.

3

Throughout the whole course of his examination Lloyd George was very definite that he had bought the shares as an investment. The following is an exchange between him and Lord Robert Cecil.

Q. You said just now that you had never speculated. I wish to be quite sure that you and I understand the word in the same way.

A. I know it is a word which is capable of all sorts of meanings—I meant gambled.

Q. Tell me if we are agreed about this: I understand an investment to be buying either shares or any other security for the purpose of receiving dividends?

A. Yes.

Q. A permanent investment?

A. Yes, that was my view of this transaction, certainly.

Q. I understand a speculation to be buying in order to sell again.

A. I have never done that—never in my life.

Lloyd George explained that "if you put money into a concern intending it to be an investment and something happens which you never expected and your broker advises you to sell, that does not mean that you did not buy them originally for an investment."

Mr Faber asked the witness when he had paid for the shares and Lloyd George replied that the broker had received £3131 from the sale of shares—that is half—and a cheque for one-third of the balance on October 21. The remainder was still owed. There followed a long wrangle in which Lloyd George said that he would pay his broker "tomorrow, if the Master of Elibank was in town," and then became extremely angry because Mr Faber maintained that shares which are not paid for cannot be termed "taken up."

In all other matters his views coincided very closely with those of the Attorney-General. Asked why he had not made a statement on October 11, he replied: "It has taken me now about a day and a half to make this statement. I could not make a full explanation before the House as to figures and transactions and submit myself to examination."

On the second day of Lloyd George's evidence Lord Robert Cecil introduced something new. He said that the *Daily Herald* had suggested—"I will read the passage if you like, but it is a very offensive one and I do not want to read it if I can help it"—that the *Matin* action was a put-up job, not a real proceeding at all.

> *Sir Rufus Isaacs.* Ought not that to be put to me?
> *Lord Robert Cecil.* I think it ought.

Sir Rufus said that it was absolutely untrue, and that he could not imagine how anyone could invent "that I should have done this, for some purpose which I do not appreciate."

> *Witness.* I think it is really the limit to quote the *Daily Herald*.
> *Lord Robert Cecil.* I only do it to call attention to any rumours which had been published.
> *Witness.* You know the *Daily Herald* and its position?
> *Lord Robert Cecil.* I do not.
> *Witness.* A paper with absolutely no position at all.

The Ministers were at that time on oath. Sir Rufus Isaacs's statement was direct and quite unequivocal: "It is absolutely untrue." And yet this curious theory—which would require extraordinary trust on Sir Rufus's part and much complacence on the part of the Editor of the *Matin*—has always had its adherents. Lord Robert Cecil, after nearly forty years for reflection, says:

> During the recess it was arranged, presumably by Ministers, that the French newspaper the *Matin* should publish an extreme version of the charges.[3]

At the time the Editor of *The Times* apparently believed it, because Lord Northcliffe wrote reproving him for the suggestion. Maxse speculated upon it in print, advancing as evidence to support it the fact that the *Matin*, a paper with a perfectly competent London office, took two days to produce a garbled version of his evidence and several more to arrive at the truth. But Maxse was by now thoroughly over-excited and he seems to have jumped to a conclusion not supported by the facts. The *Matin* appears to have been summarising, not his evidence, but the London press reports of it, so that its account would naturally appear one day later than these. February 14, the date of the libel, was a Friday. The apology was sent from London the following Monday and published on the Tuesday. With a week-end intervening, it is hard to see how the matter could have been more speedily arranged.

---

[3] *All the Way*, 121.

Maxse had become a little unbalanced about the Marconi case. Up to the time that he gave his evidence to the Committee he had always given it plenty of space in the *National Review*, but although he discussed it with his accustomed vehemence he was not personally engaged. Later it became an obsession. After he gave his evidence and before the *Matin* disclosures he came in for a terrible drubbing from the Liberal press, who treated him, along with Lawson, as the scum of the journalistic world. Maxse was a man of good birth and, because he was an exceedingly amusing companion, he had all his life been a figure in high society both at home and abroad. He cannot have enjoyed being named in the daily press as the contemptible writer of scurrilous articles, the content of which he had entirely failed to substantiate.[4]

---

[4] The whole of the Liberal press had much to say about Maxse. What must have stung most were the words of the *Manchester Guardian*, a thoroughly reputable paper, edited by C. P. Scott.

Since the wretched Pigott broke down under cross-examination during the Parnell Commission, no public offender against honour and decency in public controversy has suffered so prolonged and terrible an exposure of his offences, and of the degradation of character which made them possible, as the unfortunate man Lawson. The spectacle of this poor wretch raking together the dirtiest garbage of City gossip, all the foul tittle-tattle of party spite and cunningly invented rumours of dishonest financial gamblers, and imposing the stuff on the ready credulity of the rancorous editors or owners of the Outlook, the Eye–Witness and the National Review—the loathsomeness of this glimpse of an underworld of financial and journalistic baseness has appalled every reader of the Press.

And again:

Like his contributor Lawson he [Maxse] seems to have based some very scurrilous and quite untrue imputations of corruption on the ordinary tattle of the lower kind of gossiping partisan. Some remnant of decency led Lawson, when challenged, to own his offence, admit that his informant was rumour, and acknowledge that those whom he had defamed were, as far as he knew, perfectly blameless. Even this modicum of courage and decency must have failed Mr Maxse; when questioned by the Marconi Committee he shirked the manly course of admitting his offence, attempted to insinuate that rumour was not a lying jade after all, and adopted a histrionic pose as the editor who will not give away his private informants. . . . That course is both swaggering and cowardly, a boast and

133

Possibly for this reason, he was from now on to show an interest in the case so intense and so unflagging it is a wonder he held his readers. Month after month he gave up a large part of his journal to reports and repetitive comments, and a year later, when the Marconi case had long passed out of the news, he was still discussing small details with a deadly and malicious relish. Only the 1914 war diverted him from what had become a passion.

Lloyd George's evidence met much ironic comment. In particular, his allusions to the pathetic state of his finances were hard-heartedly received. His salary, it was pointed out, was adequate for his immediate needs, while, if he wished to put something by, there was still no need to select a highly speculative investment in the middle of a wild gamble in its shares. Again, need the future have held such terrors for him? The spectacle of an ex-Cabinet Minister begging his bread had yet to be witnessed.

Could his transactions correctly be described as investment of savings? A rise had always been contemplated, and, while a man considering an investment usually concerns himself with the expectation of dividends, this question seemed not to have been discussed between the three friends. Nor could savings which have to be borrowed from a stock-broker at five and later at seven per cent truly be said to be burning a hole in the pocket.

The Chancellor of the Exchequer looked unexpectedly silly. He and the Master of Elibank had done what every tyro indulging in a half-guilty flutter does. They had bought half-way up a boom and sold excitedly at a profit. Then at the first serious drop they had bought again in larger quantities, on this occasion half-way down a slump.

---

a running away. It would not have profited Mylius, the man who defamed the King, and it should as little profit Mr Maxse, an equally reckless traducer.

On which, after the Matin case, Maxse commented:

In those happy far-off days to accuse pure and immaculate Ministers of Marconi speculations was comparable to accusing the King of bigamy.

And in fairness to Maxse it must be said that the Manchester Guardian made no expression of regret for the Matin disclosures as did the Nation edited by H. W. Massingham.

The Chancellor of the Exchequer is, in a sense, the ex-officio head of the City of London; for he is the highest financial officer of the British Empire. City opinion is therefore affronted by the disclosure of this sublime functionary behaving for all the world like the poor, greedy, excited Mr Juggins of ordinary life.[5]

4

When on March 31 Mr Herbert Samuel was called, it was stated that he would not be examined on the contract at that time, but only on matters arising out of the *Matin* case. Mac-Master did, however, introduce the famous Clause 16 which had been suppressed in the Marconi circular.

He pressed Mr Samuel as to the importance of the clause, and secured his agreement that Isaacs had asked that it might be kept secret. This did nothing to remove suspicions as to Isaacs's motives; nor were fears about the efficiency of the Post Office much allayed when Mr Samuel said that he had not attempted to correct the impression created by the Marconi circular because his attention had never been drawn to it. "In fact, I never noticed it until a long time afterwards."

Some interest was created when Mr Samuel was reading to the Committee the letter he had sent the Attorney-General about the *Eye–Witness*. He interrupted himself as follows:

> "As I was leaving King's Cross this morning I saw on a bookstall a copy of Belloc's paper, the *Eye–Witness*"—in justice to Mr Belloc, I should say I have since been told—I do not know whether correctly or not—that he had nothing to do with the *Eye–Witness* at that time, the editor of which was a Mr Granville, who is now awaiting trial on charges of fraud, embezzlement and bigamy.

Lord Robert Cecil asked Mr Samuel about a matter on which his conduct had been criticised. Immediately before the recess of 1912, finding the

---

[5] *Round Table*, June 1913, 45–34.

opposition to the contract very strong, the Postmaster-General had spoken to one of the chief opponents, Major Archer-Shee, and asked him to withdraw his opposition. He had not mentioned the Ministers' purchase of shares.

He explained now that he had hoped to persuade Major Archer-Shee to allow the contract to be ratified "in order that the Empire could get these wireless stations," and, asked whether his knowledge of the Ministers' transactions did not affect his view, he replied that he could not see the smallest reason.

> I put it to him that the strategic importance was regarded by the Government as being very great, and I think I said to him . . . that if we were involved in war and had not got any long-range wireless stations at all, and if our cables were cut, it would be very greatly to the discredit of the Empire generally, and that the Government could not take the responsibility or words to that effect.[6]

Lord Robert Cecil's final questions concerned Lord Murray of Elibank. The late Chief Whip could not be called because in the previous summer he had resigned his position, and, now in the employ of Lord Cowdray, had left the country two months earlier to investigate large business interests in South America. He was at this time in Bogota, a place which Maxse described as "fourteen days' hard mule-riding from the nearest wireless office."[7] When this became known hecklers at Liberal meetings abandoned cries of "Marconi!" and "Gag!" and took to yelling "Bo-go-ta!"

---

[6] Five days before this, on March 26, the First Lord of the Admiralty, Mr Winston Churchill, had made the following statement in the House of Commons: "In one respect, however, Admiralty interests have suffered a grave and to some extent irreparable loss to which I am bound to draw the attention of the House. The delay in ratifying the Marconi agreement and the consequent prevention of all progress in the Imperial Chain of wireless stations has deprived us of the advantages in regard to wavelength and priority which we hoped to gain through being first in the field. . . . No step which will now be taken can put us back in the position which has been lost."

[7] *National Review*, September 1913.

(11)

The Select Committee:
5. Godfrey and Harry Isaacs

1

In January 1913 Cecil Chesterton got tired of attacking the unresisting Ministers and turned his attention to the managing director of the Marconi Company. He made some intensive research into Godfrey Isaacs's past, and in the first January issue of the *New Witness* he published the first of four articles with the title "Ghastly Record." This gave the names and records of companies Isaacs had previously been connected with. Chesterton printed a long list—twenty-one companies, none of which had had any success. In reality there were two main enterprises, most of the companies being connected with one or other of these.

Chesterton brought off a coup with these articles, not merely by drawing attention to the impressive lack of success that had attended Godfrey Isaacs, but because of the droll and romantic character, reminiscent of the *Boys' Own Paper*, of the undertakings. Isaacs believed, figuratively and actually, in the possibility of gold everywhere, and he had searched for it in the most unlikely places. The St David's Mining Development Company, formed in 1898 to adopt an agreement between Mr Isaacs and another for the purchase of eleven mining claims, later sold them to the Glyn Mines (Merioneth) and Voel Mines (Merioneth), of both of which Isaacs was a director. The St David's Gold and Copper Mines Ltd bought claims from the Mining Machinery Co. Ltd and was later reorganised as the St David's Gold Mines (1903). These companies and others sought gold in Wales, silver in Ireland, minerals in Somerset, granite from Carnarvon. None of them was successful. One paid dividends from 1900 to 1904. Two were dissolved by the Registrar of Joint Stock Companies, four went into voluntary liquidation, and one was reconstructed and absorbed into one of the others. At the time of Chesterton's articles two were still in existence, neither quoted on the Stock Exchange. In addition, two companies had been formed for mining and prospecting in the Transvaal, neither of which now survived.

The second of Godfrey Isaacs's main interests, less improbable but no more successful, was taxi-cabs. There had been three London, one provincial and one Australian taxi-cab companies of which he was director. By January 1913 only one was quoted on the Stock Exchange, the £4 shares standing at 3s.

Chesterton allowed Isaacs's magnificent optimism to speak for itself. In these four articles his comment concentrated on the implications to be drawn from the unexpected picture of the managing director of the Marconi Company. Was he a fit person to be given one of the largest government contracts ever placed? How reconcile, without corruption, this child in arms with the "iron front" that had forced Mr Samuel to agree to such favourable terms? He then went on to use his own not negligible imagination in many black suggestions.

> The files at Somerset House of the Isaacs Companies . . . cry out for vengeance on the man who created them, . . . who filled them with his own creatures, who worked them solely for his own ends, and who sought to get rid of some of them when they had served his purpose by casting the expenses of their burial on to the public purse.

He charged that, had not the Attorney-General been his brother, Isaacs would have been prosecuted. "This is not the first time in the Marconi affair we find these two gentlemen swindling." He called on Sir Rufus to do his duty "irrespective of blood relationship."

It is possible that Godfrey Isaacs might have taken his brother's view that the *New Witness* was a scurrilous paper of no importance, but for one thing. Men with sandwich-boards were sent to patrol the streets outside the House of Commons and outside the Marconi offices in the Strand. As each of the brothers entered and left his place of business he was confronted with *New Witness* placards bearing in large letters the legend: "GODFREY ISAACS' GHASTLY RECORD."

On January 27 Godfrey Isaacs's solicitor wrote to Cecil Chesterton. In this letter he said:

> He [Godfrey Isaacs] has no desire in any way to prejudice the hearing of your evidence before the Parliamentary Committee but has instructed us to request that you will in the course of tomorrow send us a definite written undertaking that you will not publish any further statements attacking our client's honour until after you have completed your evidence before the Parliamentary Committee. Unless we receive that undertaking within the time stated our client will forthwith take proceedings against you in respect of the articles already published by you.[1]

To which Cecil Chesterton replied that he was "pleased to hear that your client, Mr Godfrey Isaacs, proposes to bring an action against me."

On February 27 a magistrate at Bow Street committed Chesterton for trial on a charge of criminal libel.

All these facts were known to members of the Select Committee and to the public when evidence was taken from the City in connection with the American flotation and Godfrey and Harry Isaacs appeared as witnesses.

The members of the Committee had now to try to get the answers to the following questions:

(1) On April 17, when Sir Rufus bought his shares, could the general

---

[1] *New Witness*, 31 January 1913.

public have bought at all, at the same price, with the same knowledge? In this respect, was knowledge of the agreement with the Western Union Cable Company withheld in order to raise the profits of the intermediaries when it became known on April 19?

(2) Was the market rigged? If so, by whom?

(3) As all the shares had to be offered to holders of existing shares, where did Godfrey Isaacs get the large number of shares he took responsibility for?

The American issue had excited criticism, not merely because of the gamble, but also because the shares had been privately placed. In fact, they had to be because of the New Jersey law that they must first be offered to existing shareholders, but it was a method the Marconi Company had used in other flotations. In 1912 the law requiring a prospectus did not apply to private issues, nor to an issue of a company such as the American Marconi, incorporated abroad.[2]

The system of a private issue is for the intermediaries to take shares from the company at one price with the intention of selling them to the general public through the Stock Exchange at a higher price. Without a prospectus the public had no basis for appraising the value of the shares and it was to the advantage of the people fixing it to put the price as high as they could. Regarded by the public as a real market valuation it was in reality nothing but a basis for opening transactions. Without going into the devices by which the market could subsequently be "rigged" to higher price-levels, it is obvious that this system lent itself to the establishment of an entirely fictitious level from the beginning of the dealings. Equally it is obvious that when shares are being unloaded on the market for as much as they will fetch, every prospective additional holder tends to raise the price.

The Committee took evidence on these matters for nine days, and the

---

[2] Under the Companies Act of 1929 companies placing an issue privately must nevertheless publish a prospectus. In the case of companies incorporated abroad no prospectus is required if the shares are quoted on the Stock Exchange of the country concerned. In other cases all particulars must be thoroughly advertised in the leading newspapers before the issue is placed.

140

questions and answers during this time would fill an ordinary book of about 600 pages. At the end of this time a good deal of confusion had been created. It would have been difficult enough in any case because these were all highly complex matters and as usual witnesses gave contradictory accounts. It was made impossible by the Liberal majority who steadily overruled every question that might have resulted in an answer they preferred not to hear. The proceedings resembled one of those interminable American trials where the jury cannot remember the significant facts from among the mass of verbiage which, day after day, week after week, dulls the mind and bears the particulars away on a stream of inconsequent thought.

The first question: Could the public have bought when Sir Rufus did? might seem to many people one of those points which exercise only the academic mind, the answer being obvious to all general observers. But, owing to the assiduity of Mr Booth, who spent three weeks trying to get into the evidence a certificate showing that in one case 5000 shares had been bought by a member of the public before the official introduction on April 19, the word "public" had to be defined to include everyone not currently and professionally occupied with the Stock Market. Mr Booth achieved very little in real terms. Later evidence showed that this certificate represented the only record given to the Committee of a large parcel of shares bought before the opening, and that it was in fulfilment of an order placed through an arbitrage firm in America for 10,000 shares.

Mr Heybourn, of Heybourn & Croft, had control until opening day of all the shares except those placed by Godfrey Isaacs himself and those that came through arbitrage houses from America.[3]

The leading jobbers and brokers had agreed not to deal in the shares before they came into existence on April 19, and by then the applications were so numerous that Heybourn allotted only fifteen per cent of the amount of any order. There were small unofficial dealings on the Street in shares from

---

[3] By the rules of the Stock Exchange a jobber cannot deal with an outside member of the public without the intervention of a broker, and the business must be put through a broker. Mr Heybourn dealt directly with Godfrey Isaacs in America and later in England because Mr Campbell of Messrs Billett, Campbell and Grenfell, the brokers to the Marconi Company, authorised him to do so.

arbitrage houses in America, but these dealings would not be authorised by the Stock Exchange and were necessarily largely confined to professional operators. A member of the public might have instructed his broker to buy direct from America, but this again would have required knowledge outside the range of the ordinary man, and the shares would have been subject to the same disadvantage as those bought on the Street.[4]

The answer for all practical purposes to the first question was that Sir Rufus did buy at a time when it would have been difficult for the general public to buy, probably impossible on the scale of his purchase, and certainly impossible without specialised knowledge.[5] In addition, on opening day no member of the public dealing officially through a broker received more than fifteen per cent of his application. Thirdly, knowledge of the agreement with the Western Union Company was withheld from the public until April 19. There was no direct evidence, however, that this was done with the object of suddenly raising the price, and it would be impossible to have an opinion on this matter without an answer to the second main point on which the Committee sought evidence: Was the market rigged?

An enormous and sudden rise in the price of shares is not evidence that there was any previous intention to rig the market. A witness before the Committee made the following remarks about the behaviour of the general public on these occasions, which, taken in conjunction with the interest in

---

[4] Normally the Stock Exchange has a settlement day every six weeks. On the occasion of a new issue a "special settlement" is granted, that is a date for the first settlement. This may be withheld if there are any circumstances connected with the issue which are unsatisfactory. Official dealings—that is dealings recognised by the Stock Exchange—must be for special settlement, and these cannot take place before the shares are in existence. All Street dealings and dealings through arbitrage firms in America were in shares not yet in existence and were for "coming out settlement." They would not have been recognised by the London Stock Exchange.

[5] The shares bought by Sir Rufus were for special settlement for this reason. Holders of shares were in reality dealing in these and their conversion rights, not in the new shares which did not yet exist. Technically Godfrey sold Harry, and Harry Rufus, shares in the Company as constituted before the new issue and the rights these carried. The shares were treated as belonging to Godfrey or the Marconi Company until after opening day, when they were delivered by Godfrey to Harry.

Marconis on account of the contract with the British Government, the sinking of the *Titanic* and the arrangements known to have been made in America, account quite sufficiently for the boom. "It is a well-known fact," he said, "that the public will not buy at bottom prices. They only come in and buy as a share rises, and the higher the share rises the more anxious the public are to buy the shares, and the more the American shares went up the keener were the applications."

It may have been true that the boom in American shares was due to nothing more than the fact that the shares were introduced at a propitious moment, and the public, as more than one witness was to say, "went off their heads."

But, if there was any manipulation of the market, then by whom—Godfrey Isaacs himself in connection with Heybourn, or Heybourn alone? To this question the Committee in their confused way also sought an answer. Such facts as emerged were summed up by Lord Robert Cecil in the minority report of the Committee, which is quoted in Chapter 15 and given in full as an Appendix. Here only the evidence necessary to understand his conclusions, or which has bearing on larger issues, or is interesting for its own sake, will be discussed.

2

Mr Campbell, of Messrs Billet, Campbell and Grenfell, the official brokers to the Marconi Company, early defined the situation that confronted Godfrey Isaacs when he decided on the new issue of capital.

At that time the American Marconi shares in the then existing Company were 25-dollar shares which were standing at a very heavy discount: they were at about 10 dollars per share. It was therefore not an easy job for the Marconi Company to raise one and a quarter million or more of money with the shares of their company standing at a discount. They could not issue them at a discount in America; that is against the law. The shareholders in the American Company would not be likely to take shares of twenty-five when they were standing at ten dollars in the market, and therefore it had to be a bold stroke to agree to take over £1,000,000 worth of shares at par when the shares were standing at less than half.

And a later exchange between Sir Frederick Banbury and Godfrey Isaacs makes it clear that the "bold stroke" could not have been undertaken without the enormous interest the British public had already shown in Marconi shares.

Q. At the time when you made the plan, you felt that in spite of these good agreements having been made, the spring of American money in that direction was dry?

A. Absolutely.

Q. I presume that arose because the American public had just realised that they had lost in wireless between twelve millions and fifteen millions sterling?

A. They had realised it some little while before, yes.

Mr George Faber. Therefore you had, I was going to say, to appeal from Philip sober to Philip drunk?

A. That is not very complimentary to England.

Mr George Faber. One of the witnesses who has been in the box, Mr Schiff, stated the public over here had gone absolutely mad, so that there is only the difference between drunk and mad.

When Heybourn took the witness-stand to answer questions on the methods he had used to secure the issue in London it became clear that the Liberal majority would prevent the details of his transactions ever being made public. Heybourn was accompanied by Counsel, Mr Schwabe, and from the beginning he was taciturn and cautious. Then Amery asked the question:

How many of the 250,000 did you place among your friends before the 19th at £1. 10s. 0d.?

Heybourn replied: "That is a question I am afraid I cannot answer. That is entirely my own firm's business. It is not anything material to this Inquiry," and the battle was joined.

144

There are pages of heated argument on the record as a result of this answer. Mr Schwabe for Heybourn explained that the reason he would not give the information was that he had sold a considerable number of shares and he did not wish to get into trouble with his friends because some might say: "If you were selling as many as that I ought to have had more and he less." The room was twice cleared so that the Committee could deliberate in private, but the upshot of the discussion was this: Mr Heybourn agreed to give the Committee for their private information—that is, it was not to be published or discussed—a list of names of people to whom he had sold shares at £1.5s. 0d. or £1.10s. 0d. before the 19th, but he refused all other information and he refused to produce his books.

When the Liberals upheld him in this decision, the Tories made it the occasion of a long public protest in which they stated that it was impossible for them to do their duty if they were prevented from investigating the facts by the majority vote of their colleagues.

The relationship between the two parties had all along been strained and their behaviour towards each other undignified. From now on a high proportion of the questions asked were framed in sarcastic terms and were in reality addressed through the witness to some other member of the Committee. In this exercise of petulance both sides were equally uncontrolled and the proceedings became a scandal as well as a farce. One cannot, nevertheless, refuse all sympathy to the Tory members, because, as they lamely took up the task of questioning Heybourn, they found that every opening eventually led to the same *impasse* where, now openly insolent, he refused the information asked.

Heybourn was a very tough gentleman, and he had nothing to lose by offending Tory Members of Parliament or by a public refusal to co-operate with the minority of the Committee. He had made a killing in Marconi shares, a coup for which he himself said he had been waiting for fourteen years. But there is nothing in his refusal to answer questions which is in itself evidence that there was anything unorthodox in his conduct. He might, as he said, simply have been determined to protect himself from inquiry into his private business, or from the kind of public comment which would have made him unpopular with his associates.

He denied that there had been a syndicate.

There was no syndicate at all. I noticed in his evidence that Mr Campbell used the word "syndicate," but the syndicate was my firm and no one else.

No evidence was ever produced to prove that this statement was untrue. One new fact emerged as a result of his examination. Having agreed that he received 250,000 shares from Godfrey Isaacs while they were in America, he told the Committee that on two different occasions he received 50,000 more—100,000 in all. On the morning of April 18 he telephoned Isaacs and told him that the shares were going very fast and bid him for 50,000 at a higher price—£2. 2s. 6d.—and Isaacs accepted his offer. Later on the same day Heybourn again telephoned and this time bought a further 50,000 at £2.8s. gd.

Earlier than this, as soon as it became plain the issue would be successful, Heybourn had asked Isaacs's permission to place his remaining shares at £1. 10s. 0d. instead of the £1.5s. 0d. originally arranged, and Isaacs agreed on the condition the profit went to the Marconi Company. When the shares were finally issued to the public on April 19 Heybourn fixed the price at £3. 5s. 0d. without consulting Isaacs, because the shares were already at that price in America and in all unofficial dealings.

3

Godfrey Isaacs followed Heybourn. In appearance he had a strong family likeness to Sir Rufus, although perhaps less handsome, less polished. When he first confronted the Committee he spoke in a friendly way and with some enthusiasm. He seemed to feel that now, given his opportunity, he would soon put everything right. He often addressed the questioner by name, "Yes, Lord Robert," "No, Lord Robert," in a manner which suggested, if not complicity, at least equality and identity of purpose.

On the first day of his evidence he was asked if he had heard rumours, and he replied vigorously that yes, he had heard rumours. Immediately on his return from America he had heard that a great attack was to be made on the Marconi contract by a syndicate endeavouring to promote the Poulsen Company, strongly supported by influential people, among them Members of

146

Parliament, who would attempt to prevent the contract going through. He suggested the Committee might find it profitable to try a new line and inquire into the methods of the group hostile to the Marconi Company.

He then handed the Committee the prospectus of the Poulsen Radio Telegraph and Telephone System. There were, he said, two names on this document and one of them was the expert engineer who reported on the system, Mr A. A. Campbell Swinton, "a name which was so warmly recommended to the Committee by Sir Henry Norman as being one of those expert engineers who would be best able to advise the Committee as to which was the best system for the Government to adopt."

Isaacs then said that the rumours he had heard had at first been only word of mouth, but that he had now received a letter "which I think will help the Committee," and he would read it and then hand it in. This letter was from a Mr Hawkings. It related how at dinner one night the writer had listened to a gentleman explaining to the people present the worthlessness of the Marconi system in comparison with the Poulsen. After dinner Mr Hawkings had spoken to this gentleman who had then said that he was confident the Marconi shares (English) would fall to thirty shillings, and that he had several clients who, on his advice, were bears. He said there was going to be a great outcry in the House of Commons against the Marconi Company and he mentioned the names of two Members of Parliament who would take part in it. The letter continued:

"One of the Members whose names he mentioned has, in fact, been very much in evidence in the discussions which have subsequently taken place, and the impression left on my mind is that a certain section of people interested in the Poulsen Syndicate have been devoting their attention to preventing the ratification of the Marconi Company's contract with the Government to serve their own ends. The gentleman who gave me this information is a stockbroker. I have listened for nearly a year to the wildest rumours against the Marconi Company and against the contract, and these rumours have almost invariably come from people who were personally interested in the Poulsen Syndicate, or from people whose interest it was to see a fall in Marconi shares. I have written to you on this subject because it seems so apparent that most of this outcry against the Marconi Company's contract originates with those who are trying to run another system."

Chairman. The Members of Parliament are not mentioned?

A. He does not mention them.

Godfrey Isaacs's evidence was interesting. There had been many signs of energy on the part of the Poulsen Company. When the proceedings were adjourned that evening it was amid some excitement, and the following morning the Marconi Committee was featured in several newspapers under the headline "MR ISAACS COUNTER-ATTACKS."

At the resumed hearing Lord Robert Cecil, without any heat or emphasis, drove some questions to the heart of Isaacs's new evidence and shattered not merely his argument but his standing as a serious witness. He began slowly, but under questioning Isaacs immediately adopted the position that he made no charge, he merely repeated what he had been told and suggested a possible line of inquiry.

Q. Then you suggest that there is some ground for thinking that this informal syndicate proceeded by way of blackening the character of Ministers?

A. I think there is some ground for thinking so.

Q. That is indeed a very serious matter?

A. Very.

Q. Probably criminal and certainly very villainous?

A. Yes.

Lord Robert then put some strong pressure on Isaacs to reveal the names of the two Members of Parliament said to be involved, which he reluctantly did. Of these Major Archer-Shee had already declared in evidence a certain interest in the Poulsen Company but one that was completely disinterested and quite unobjectionable, while the other, Mr Norton Griffiths, had had no connection with the contract or the Poulsen Company except to ask a question of the Postmaster-General in the House. Lord Robert Cecil now asked the witness.

Do you wish the Committee to believe that these gentlemen then formed the design of blackening Ministers' characters in order to prevent the ratification of the contract?

With this question the tone of the investigation dropped from the high, adventurous altitude in which Godfrey Isaacs lived back to humdrum probability. Neither Isaacs nor Mr Hawkings, who was called to explain his letter, had any definite evidence of any sort. By the time the two Members of Parliament had made a hurried appearance to deny on oath the allegations, it could be seen that the counter-attack was based on exactly the kind of assumption that had inspired journalists on the other side.[6]

Lord Robert Cecil now turned to the Poulsen Company prospectus which Isaacs had handed in, but before questioning the witness he read to him a passage from Sir Henry Norman's evidence to the Committee. This made it plain that Sir Henry Norman had mentioned Mr Campbell Swinton's connection with the Poulsen Syndicate, and had suggested a long list of names to the Committee, one of whom, Sir Oliver Lodge, was at that time employed by the Marconi Company, and all of whom had a standing in the scientific world which would prevent their judgment being biased by fees paid for consultant opinions.

This passage had been available to Isaacs from the published reports. Indeed he must have consulted it, since he knew that Sir Henry (who was known to be an amateur of wireless and a Liberal and who had no connection with any company) had recommended Campbell Swinton. The slightest thought must have convinced him that the examining Committee would turn up the evidence before questioning him. In all his recorded actions he showed the most curious mixture of the highly intelligent and the unintelligent. He gives the impression of an impetuous and rather brash character. The most complex matters lost for him their subtleties because of a conviction that right was right and on his side. This led him in blinkers to a resolution of any problem, and led him, too, to an imputation of motive reminiscent of Cecil

---

[6] A later witness was to suggest that Godfrey Isaacs himself was responsible for the rumours that Ministers had bought Marconis, and that his motive was to bolster the market.

Chesterton. He had not, however, the hunting instinct, the moral superiority. He merely felt that people whose opinions did not coincide with his were conspiring against him. On this occasion his over-simple view harmed no one but himself.

During his evidence he was continuously amiable, and showed every desire to help the Committee. Sometimes when asked to give some evidence he said he preferred not to, but he never refused, instead leaving it to the Committee to decide whether they did not think it was a personal or business matter irrelevant to their proceedings.

One of the first things on which the Committee desired information was the arrangement by which Isaacs had made himself responsible for 500,000 shares. Asked whether there had been a bargain in writing, he replied that there had been nothing but a verbal agreement between Marconi and himself. He did not regard this as the least unusual. Questioned as to whether the Company could have sued him for half a million if he had failed, he replied that they could, but he did not think they would have. He could only have failed, he explained, if something so unforeseen had happened that the whole deal had fallen through. But he said: "From the moment two people are agreed I think that is an actual binding contract, although nothing is written." He said that the arrangement was on the minute-book in America and minuted again in England on the date he reported it on his return. Asked by Lord Robert Cecil if he would produce this minute-book, he agreed to do so. Several times during the course of his examination Lord Robert asked again for the minute-book and each time he agreed to produce it.[7]

Godfrey Isaacs was often asked how many of these shares he kept for himself, and he always replied 2500. He always said, too, that he never speculated in shares of a company he was connected with, holding only a small number of shares as an investment.

Sir Frederick Banbury asked the witness:

---

[7] When the minute-book was finally handed to the Committee there was no record of the arrangement in it. Lord Robert attached great importance to this—see p. 275—and wished to recall Isaacs. Nevertheless, Marconi always confirmed Isaacs's version of the agreement.

Q. Supposing the American shareholders had voted the increase in capital, and supposing then that instead of being able to place the 500,000 shares, there were no buyers or very few buyers and the shares went to a little discount, in what position then would the English Company have been?

A. That is a hypothesis I would not like to answer.

Q. But it was rather serious from the English Company's point of view?

A. It amounts to this, that, if you put it to me that I had given my undertaking to the chairman of the Company in a very important matter and stated that I was confident of being able to fulfil that undertaking, and then I had failed to do so, I should think that the English Company would have been in a position of no longer having faith in their managing director, and they would have looked for another.

Q. Yes, but they might have been left with 500,000 shares?

A. That is possible, assuming I failed in my undertakings, just as they might be left in a more serious position if I did a number of other extraordinary things.

Isaacs's mind worked quickly, if instinctively, and on one matter he availed himself of a chance coincidence which he was lucky to have been offered. He was anxious to conceal the terms agreed between the English Marconi Company and the United Wireless Company for the purchase of the assets of the latter, and also the sum received by the English Company on re-sale to the American. Both purchases had been paid for in shares of the American Company, and the law of New Jersey allowed shares to be issued for this purpose without their being first offered to shareholders. The Committee were extremely anxious to know the figures of these agreements because they wanted to discover whether the total issue had been sufficiently under the control of Hey-bourn in London for him to have been able to rig the market. Obviously, if there had been a large number of shares that could have been thrown on the market from America, Hey-bourn had no real control.

The Committee pressed Isaacs again and again for the two agreements, but he withstood their efforts, although at one point he wrote something on

151

paper which he said would convince the Committee that his reasons were sound and did not concern them. He also made a statement of the number of shares that had come to the English Company, and he agreed to an approximate figure of what that must leave in America.

When, in the middle of these proceedings, the *Financial News* suddenly published two agreements of sale—allegedly the one between the English Marconi Company and the United Wireless Company and the other between the two Marconi Companies—Isaacs was involved in some disagreeable explanations.

He had previously said that the English Company had had by right of conversion of 35,000 old shares, 175,000 new; secondly, 875,000 shares to which they had been entitled on the ratio of five new shares for every old one: and further they had acquired 119,000 shares after the expiry of the date on which holders of old shares must have applied for new, that is 119,000 shares not taken up by the American public. In answer to further questioning he admitted that something like 30,000 further shares had come to the English Company, a balance acquired from the American Company during the purchase and re-sale of the United Wireless Company, which he said was for services rendered by the English Company.

When the Committee examined the contracts published by the *Financial News* the discrepancy between the terms of these and Godfrey Isaacs's statements was too gross for the Liberal majority to rule the matter out of order. In answer to questions put by Sir Frederick Banbury, the witness admitted that the English Company had paid 750,000 dollars for the assets of the United Wireless Company and received 1,400,000 from the American Company, leaving a balance in favour of the English Company of 650,000 dollars, although Isaacs insisted that this sum could not be regarded simply as a profit, since it was paid "in conjunction with a general agreement for other services for which they received one sum."

Sir Frederick then reminded Isaacs that he had said the objection to making these figures public would be apparent to the Committee and he had written it down.

That was the answer we all read and which, of course, I cannot mention in public beyond this that it was more or less a legal objection.

There now appears to be another reason, and a very good reason, a profit of 650,000 dollars.

Isaacs naturally denied the imputation and explained again there had been other considerations. He did not convince anyone that, if these considerations had been genuine and straightforward, he would have felt it necessary to keep the two agreements secret and refuse to divulge the figures until forced to by the *Financial News*.

Nor did this finish the matter. Sir Frederick now returned to the discussion of two days before. Isaacs had told the Committee that the English Company's holding had been made up of three figures: 175,000 by conversion, 875,000 by rights to the new issue and 119,000 being the balance not taken up by the American shareholders.

> Q. Those added together came to 1,169,000 shares?
> A. Yes.
> Q. Now I ascertain that there were a further 130,000 shares. . . . What I want to know is why you did not tell us that there were the further 130,000 shares? That is the first question.
> A. My reply to that question in the first instance is because I was not asked. You asked me how many shares we were entitled to and I told you. . . . You asked me how many shares we had sold and I told you.
> Q. Your answer is that you did not tell us because you were not asked?
> A. That is so. That is my answer to your last question.
> Q. I do not agree with that answer. . . .

Isaacs now had to go through all the figures again, and several hours were spent on it. None of the Committee was very agile at mental arithmetic or skilled in the understanding of figures, and each one asked Isaacs to explain what he had already explained to the last. The gist of his explanations was this.

He said that he had given the correct number of the total holding of the English Company, but he had made a mistake in the figures it comprised. The conversion of shares, he explained, had not been exactly 5–1 as had always been understood. It was in reality 4 and a fraction to 1. In order that they should not have to deal in fractions of a share, it had been arranged that the shareholders should receive exactly five new shares for every old one and that the Marconi Companies should take in conversion of their own shares the slightly reduced number this arrangement would leave. This reduced the figure he had given as 875,000 to 723,000. In reading to the Committee from the paper prepared for him by the secretary of the Company he had given the correct total, but he had followed the argument with regard to the breakdown from memory and without referring to the paper. The discrepancy between the figures 875,000 and 723,000 was so nearly exactly 130,000 that the total number of shares owned by the English Company was the same he had originally given.

Mr Amery. These figures work out perfectly correctly, but on those figures of yours the American old shareholders would have taken up 558,000, and you did tell us they took up 406,000?

Witness. I quite see your point.

After the next session Isaacs addressed the Chairman.

Witness. Mr Chairman, before we pass away from the figures with which we were dealing just now, I think it would be fair for me to be told that the Committee is satisfied that there is no attempt at concealment of any figures such as was suggested by the question put to me. I have given you full particulars of those figures. I have given the notes from which I quoted. . . . I would like to know that they are clear to the Committee.

Chairman. I think it would be better for you to put that question to Sir Frederick Banbury when he is there.

Lord Robert Cecil. I think it would be an improper question to put.

Isaacs had not created a good impression, but it seems likely that, if he wished to conceal something, it was the profit he had made out of the American Company, rather than the allocation of shares, since the second set of figures left more rather than less shares outside Heybourn's control. His final replies might have been made with no great impact but for one thing. They were oddly reminiscent.

A thought eludes and then invades the mind. This particular explanation of a discrepancy in figures—that an agreed total is correct and has misled the witness into a mistake in the breakdown—bears a family relationship to something that has been heard before. The words of the Attorney-General return to the mind—answering questions about Lloyd George's dealings in shares and demanding, far more belligerently it is true, for an assurance that the Committee believe there has been no deliberate attempt at concealment.

The only other matter of importance that came out in Isaacs's evidence he introduced himself. He asked whether he might refer to a question that had been put to Mr Campbell but not to him—the question of the suppression of Clause 16 from the circular issued by the Marconi Company to its shareholders. He said that he had not included this clause—which allowed the Government to cease payment of royalty if they ceased using Marconi patents—because it was not a material fact. Asked to explain this statement, he said that, if the Government should use some system entirely independent of the Marconi system, they "would have to use some system other than the transmission of signals by ethereal waves." Therefore, he later concluded, "I wanted to point out to you that there was nothing suppressed—or wilfully suppressed—there as being of material importance to the shareholders."

4

Godfrey Isaacs was followed by his brother Harry. Harry Isaacs had nothing to hide, nothing to save. He had no great political career in jeopardy, he was not in contractual relationship with the Government. He can be judged in the simple fashion of the judgments of everyday life. We do not know, nor do we attempt to assess, the potential of men pushed to the furthest extremity; we are not concerned with the subtlest distinctions of courage, of honour or intelligence; we admire what seems attractive, and are often attracted to qualities that are brave rather than noble, human and not necessarily great. Considered in this way, he seemed a splendid, jolly fellow. His brain worked faster than the speed at which questions were put to him, and he often offered to help a member of the Committee by breaking through his ponderous opening to tell him what he so obviously wanted to know. He agreed to his brothers' version of all that had taken place at the Savoy and at his subsequent meeting with Sir Rufus, and he endorsed the explanation of the *pro rata* arrangement between himself and the latter as to the selling of shares. He agreed, too, that as a result of his own dealings he had acquired 30,000 American Marconi shares for nothing, in addition to some liquid cash. But he allowed no familiarities. In answer to the question: "Your business is not that of dealing in stocks and shares?" he replied: "My business is what I like to do." Asked whether he did not think 56,000 shares at £1. 1s. 3d. a pretty large commitment, he answered: "It depends." But when the questioner went on: "To a person like myself it seems a large commitment," he replied: "That is your business. It did not occur to me."

Harry Isaacs made one new contribution, of which the Liberals were to take every advantage. Asked when he had first heard that Ministers had gambled in Marconi shares, he replied in December (1911) or January (1912). No other witnesses had ever suggested that the rumours had been in circulation before April, and this answer was clearly designed to imply that they could not have arisen as a direct result of the purchase of American shares. It seems certain that what he said was untrue, for this reason: if he had really heard the rumours in December or January, then he persuaded his brother in April to do something that had been reported in criticism of him for three months.

(12)

The Select Committee:
6. Four Important Witnesses

1

During the next few weeks witnesses flocked to the Committee—
stockbrokers, City journalists and the like. A great many insinuations were
made, all tending towards one of two suggestions. The first was that, a large
number of shares of the Marconi Companies having been bought by
foreign banks and syndicates, it was perfectly possible that blocks of these
shares had been transferred back to London. The implication here was
always that the Ministers might have bought far more shares than they
admitted, through nominees or in some such way. Secondly, many witnesses
believed that there was a great syndicate in London itself operating in the
Marconi market, and that the Committee would do well to inquire into the
accounts held by certain banks. The Committee laboriously called witness
after witness in an attempt to get evidence of the truth of these suggestions,
to which it is clear some of its members were themselves attracted. Amery
in particular was extremely interested in the *pro rata* agreement between
Rufus and Harry Isaacs, which he found difficult to explain unless the shares

were held in this way to control the market.

There were times when the Committee appeared to be hot on a trail that might lead to annihilating revelations, but they never succeeded in exposing more than some oddity of human behaviour quite unconnected with the issues they were investigating. From first to last there was no real evidence of a foreign syndicate buying for London or of a London syndicate operating to rig the market. No Minister's name was ever properly connected with any transaction other than those at one time or another disclosed to the Committee, and no one could ever prove that the *pro rata* agreement was anything but a family arrangement.

Suggestions of this kind continued to be made, however—for which the Ministers had to thank the continual blocking of inquiry into them— although no one ever attempted to answer one simple question. If the three men—or any one of them—had held shares in a syndicate, then the intention could not have been innocent. But if they were not innocent, they were not fools. Why should they have endangered a concerted plan to fleece the public, by buying and selling £20,000 worth of shares openly and in their own names?

During this period four witnesses were called who, serious in themselves and earnest in their purpose, provided the public with some entertainment.

The first of these appeared because a Mr Powell, Editor of the *Financial News*, said that three Ministers had been mentioned in the original rumours, two who were now known to have dealt in Marconi shares, and one other. Hard pressed to reveal the third name, he finally and unwillingly replied:

> Well then, sir, in obedience to your ruling, and with the reservation that I believe the statement to be absolutely false, the name is that of Mr Winston Churchill.

As a result the First Lord of the Admiralty was called.

Mr Churchill bounced in in a formidable temper. His rage was disconcertingly directed not against the witness who had mentioned his name, but against the Committee themselves. He addressed the Chairman as follows:

> This is a very insulting charge that you have thought proper to ask

me to come here to answer. I am bound to point out that it is a most insulting charge. The charge which your Committee, Sir Albert, have thought proper to summon me at a moment's notice to answer, is nothing else than that, having had dealings in Marconi shares, I sat silent while friends and colleagues came forward and voluntarily disclosed their exact position—that I sat silent while they were subjected to gross ill-usage and covered with every species of calumny and insult—that all the time I skulked in the background, keeping my guilty knowledge to myself and desiring to conceal it from your Committee. I say it is a very insulting charge, a most grave and insulting charge, and I do think before I am asked to answer it I am entitled in all common fairness of English life to ask what is the foundation—what is the evidence and foundation—upon which your Committee have summoned me before them this afternoon.

Sir Albert with some timidity endeavoured to explain how the charge had come to be made, and also that the Committee had thought it right to give him the opportunity to deny it. Not in the least placated, Mr Churchill continued to protest against the "ill-usage" to which Members of the House of Commons were subjected when a Committee of their fellow-Members thought it right to summon a Minister of the Crown "upon mere unsupported tittle-tattle" to answer a charge "which obviously affects his honour"; and he repeated "a charge of skulking in the background."

I am grieved beyond words that a Committee of my fellow-Members of the House of Commons should have thought it right to lend their sanction to the putting of such a question to me. Having said so much, I will proceed to answer your question. I have never at any time, in any circumstances, had any investment or any interest of any kind, however vaguely it may be described, in Marconi telegraphic shares or any other shares of that description in this or any other country of the inhabited globe—never. And if anybody at any time has said so, that person is a liar and a slanderer; and if anybody has repeated this statement and said he had no evidence and believed it to be false, but there it was, the only difference between that person

159

and a liar and a slanderer is that he is a coward in addition.

Several members of the Committee now strove to soothe Mr Churchill, but without success. Having asked: "What public man is there about whom lies are not in circulation?" and declared: "If I were to contradict every lying statement brought against me since I have been a Minister, I could not get through my daily work," he added: "I have made my protest. May I assume that your examination of me is finished?" and strode out.

2

When Marconi appeared before the Committee he was also exceedingly put out. In an effort to convince his audience of the unworthiness of the treatment his Company had received, he read out a list of every honour and honorary degree presented to him by the universities and countries of the world, a list which must have occupied nearly half an hour of the Committee's time. He followed this with a narrative history of his work in wireless telegraphy which included details of almost every scientific advance he had ever made.

Then he dealt explicitly and ably with the criticisms that had been urged. Today his evidence has lost its interest because, owing to the subsequent advance in wireless telegraphy, all the systems then employed are out of date. Two points in his evidence contribute to this narrative.

Speaking of the Poulsen System, he said that it would be more correct to refer to it as the Poulsen "arc," since its "only important particular feature consists in the use of the arc in place of the spark or high-frequency alternator, all other essential parts of the system being identical with those used in other and particularly in my system." Having claimed that there were in fact a dozen or so different Marconi systems, he continued:

> I may perhaps make this point more clear. I have now at Clifden a
> system utilising continuous waves[1] and employing no spark whatever in
> the transmission of messages, and I am right in saying that it is still a

---

[1] The Poulsen method.

Marconi system, but more often than I care to mention during this Inquiry has it been stated that the Marconi system is a spark system and so-and-so's system is not.

He then gave a lucid explanation of why, for commercial purposes, he preferred the spark system to the arc.

The other statement he made which seems interesting today was that, if the Government had made a contract with any company other than the Marconi, they would have had to alter the apparatus on all the ships of the British navy, since these had installations of the Marconi system.

When he had finished replying to criticisms, Marconi addressed the Committee:

> I do not wish to conclude without expressing my resentment at the reflections that have been made upon my Company and upon me for having innocently entered into a contract with His Majesty's Government. I resent the inquiry into the affairs of my Company which have no relation whatsoever with the contract entered into with His Majesty's Government, and in this respect I would particularly refer to the business carried out by Mr Isaacs and me in America, as related by Mr Isaacs in his evidence, which I fully endorse and confirm, and I regret that the services which my Company and I have for so many years rendered to the Post Office, the Admiralty and the Mercantile Marine, and in fact the whole nation, should not have been deemed worthy of higher consideration.

3

On April 23 Mr Charles Granville was sworn and examined. Mr Granville was the sole proprietor of a firm called Stephen Swift & Co., printers and publishers, which had at one time or another owned or published the *Oxford and Cambridge Review*, *Rhythm*, the *Onlooker*, the *Free Woman* and the *Eye–Witness* He was at this time on bail on a charge of fraudulently converting a cheque for £1500 from Mr Richard Johnson Walker, editor of the *Oxford and Cambridge Review*, and on a second charge of bigamy. There was a further charge against him of obtaining £2000 by false pretences from Mr J. E. Terry of York.[2] Mr Terry and another had entered into negotiations with him in connection with the *Onlooker.* Mr Terry bought 2000 £1 shares and became Literary Editor at a salary of £8 a week. Mr Granville, an undischarged bankrupt, then absconded to Tangier with the £2000.[3]

Under cross-examination Mr Granville said that he had been editor of the *Eye–Witness* from June to September 1912—that is during the period after Belloc left and until the paper went bankrupt. He had been unable to prepare a written statement owing to "the unfortunate position" in which he found himself. He said that he had not written the Marconi articles but had supervised them.

> I had in my employ at that time Mr Cecil Chesterton, who was sub-editor but practically editor, and two other persons in my office to whom I delegated work in connection with the supervision of the matter that went to the press.
>
> Q. Who were those two?
>
> A. Mr Edward Terry and Mr Jack Collings Squire.[4]

---

[2] The police later dropped the two money charges and proceeded only on the charge of bigamy.

[3] In *Edward Marsh* (pp. 216–7) Mr Christopher Hassall quotes a letter from John Middleton Murry in which, referring to himself and Katherine Mansfield, he says:

> However, at that particular moment, we were not badly off; in fact, we were living in a fool's paradise concerning the financial position of Rhythm . . . a rising and apparently prosperous publisher who traded as Stephen Swift was taking over the financial responsibility for the magazine and giving us a joint salary of two pounds a week for editing it. That, we thought, gave us the opportunity of escaping from London. We promptly took a little house at Runcton, between Chichester and Selsey. . . . Our fool's paradise quickly collapsed. Stephen Swift went bankrupt; and then we discovered to our complete dismay that though he had taken over all the assets of Rhythm he had not taken over the liabilities. The printer's bill had been left in my name. In short, I owed them something over £400.

[4] At the Magistrates' Court at Bow Street, Edward Terry, appearing as a witness when Granville was charged, said that proof-sheets for the *Eye–Witness* were brought

Mr Granville, who was slightly incoherent, then explained that he had had to take a certain nominal editorship because an attitude was taken up by the previous editor which he objected to.

> Q. Who was the previous editor?
> A. Mr Hilaire Belloc. That previous attitude was in connection with his antipathy to Jews.

And asked by Lord Robert Cecil what was the real motive of the Marconi articles, Granville replied that the real motive was an attack on the Jews as Jews, and that the instigators were Messrs Belloc and Chesterton.

He then said that after some of the articles had appeared a gentleman "whom I do not know" had called at the offices of the *Eye–Witness* asking for information. Mr Chesterton had been sent for. In reply to questions put by the caller "it transpired that there were no data."

> Q. You mean to say that he could not give any facts?
> A. He could not give any facts.
> Q. Did he say "I have no facts to support those statements"?
> A. Yes.
> Q. No facts—merely his own surmises?
> A. Merely his own surmises.

In reply to a question about the Chancellor of the Exchequer, Granville said:

> I do not think the attacks on Mr Lloyd George were either racial or personal but they were connected probably with his having initiated the insurance scheme. This has nothing to do with that, but a certain animosity had existed on account of the attitude Mr Lloyd George had taken in the matter.

---

to him to read for libel. He stated that the prisoner had been drinking and drugging.

Granville then said that he had ceased to have any connection with the paper at the end of September because "finding that the finances were failing, they ran away with the paper, and put another name upon it."

Mr George Faber. What do you mean by "ran away with the paper"?
A. They took it away from my office.

4

On April 24 Hilaire Belloc himself took the oath. His evidence had been long awaited. In the article in the *Oxford and Cambridge Review* he had said that "to my knowledge" one of those responsible for public affairs, having received information with regard to Marconis because he had a pull—"that is, could blackmail"—had trebled his investment in six months. In addition, the *Eye–Witness* had said in one of its earlier articles and after openly accusing Ministers of corruption:

> Meanwhile what we have written remains; and our readers may be assured that it was not written without a full sense of responsibility or without an intimate acquaintance with the facts which are not only notorious in political life, but which we happen to be in a position to substantiate.

No other newspaper or journal had ever explicitly claimed knowledge of the facts, and, although there was no evidence to suggest that the sentence in the *Eye–Witness* had been written by Belloc, he was known to be on terms of intimate friendship with Cecil Chesterton, and claimed to have helped him in his campaign against the Marconi contract.

When the Chairman began to question him Belloc asked whether he could first read a statement he had written.

Mr Booth. May I ask whether the witness was not invited to send us a précis of his statement, and he declined?
Chairman. That is so.
Witness. I had not the time. The fact that I had to appear before the

Committee today was forwarded to me in London from my country address.

Chairman. You were asked some weeks ago for your précis, and I think you were not prepared to send a précis but you would answer questions?

Witness. Yes. Is there a prejudice against my reading this statement?

Belloc was then allowed to proceed. He said that he was an intimate friend of, and had often worked for, Mr Cecil Chesterton, "the editor and the man responsible for, and the only man responsible for the *New Witness,* or as it was then the *Eye–Witness,* which I myself edited for a year previously."

While necessarily dissenting from many points in an editorship which was not mine, I was Mr Chesterton's friend, and I am proud and glad to be his friend, and to have my name associated with his in an effort which, I think, he has successfully conducted. I desire to state that the point upon which that effort turned was this: that one Minister of the Crown, the Postmaster-General, gave to the brother of another Minister of the Crown, the Attorney-General—or rather promised him—certain public advantages, including the payment of public money or the equiv-alent thereof, which promises, could they have been carried out, would have multiplied shares which were 14*s.* at the beginning of the negotia-tions by about 7, making them worth £5 at the end, were the contract to stand in its original form.

Belloc then allowed that there were other factors contributing to the rise, but said that it was the very large multiple of 7 that "struck us as abnormal."

I maintain, in common with those who have worked through this matter in many, many parts of the Press, and more so in all that section of public life that does not get printed, and which takes the form of important conversation, that a multiple of this sort is too large, and when a public contract increases the wealth of private citizens in that fashion, it is a very dangerous precedent to admit. That is the gravamen of the charges we have made. That is the root of the whole matter.

In common, Belloc continued, "I will not say with every man, because that would be an exaggeration, but with most educated men, and most men who meet other men and go about seeing people," he had heard rumours.

I did hear on authority which seemed to me sufficient, one definite statement that a man in a public position, whose name was not given to me, had, through his inside position, been able to multiply by three an investment made in Marconis. His name was not given to me and his name I do not know to this day. I used that as an illustration in an article . . . to illustrate what is undoubtedly true, and what this Marconi case has proved true, that men in an important position in the wealthier classes of society are in a position to increase their wealth perpetually, whereas the small investor is nowadays heavily handicapped. . . . Whom that statement referred to I do not know. If I had been given a name I should not have used it. . . . Proof there was that the shares had risen largely. Those shares, in my judgment, and I think in most sane judgments, rose mainly because of the contract. Undoubtedly the Postmaster-General was responsible for the contract, as undoubtedly the Chancellor of the Exchequer was responsible for allowing it to be put in that form—he is the guardian of the public purse—and as certainly the man principally benefited by the contract was the brother of the man who—without any quibbling as to when it exactly happened—was to become, or did become when the thing went through, a colleague of the Chancellor of the Exchequer and of the Postmaster-General.[5] That was the point I perpetually made. I made it in public speeches. I made it in articles. I make it now.

Belloc then passed to a different matter:

There appeared before you yesterday an unfortunate man who has

---

[5] This referred to the fact that Sir Rufus Isaacs was not a Member of the Cabinet until three months after the tender was signed, and witnesses were constantly interrupted to have the point emphasised.

published books for me, and who was, as I imagined, a man with capital sufficient to enable him, when there was talk of founding the *Eye–Witness*, to maintain that paper until it should be upon a paying basis . . . This unfortunate man—I do not desire to say one word against a man in a position so difficult and tragic—appeared before you and said that after I left the *Eye–Witness* it was handed over to him as editor, and further said that he was compelled to carry on the note that I had established, which I believe he described as antipathy to the Jews. Now I can give you this personal testimony which will be valuable to you when you call Mr Chesterton. When I gave up the *Eye–Witness* I said: "I cannot be any longer responsible for it, it interferes too much with my time: it is not a lucrative adventure, as you may imagine, and I am going from it. Mr Cecil Chesterton, I understand, is to be the editor and in full editorial control." I was told, yes, he was to be. I attached some importance, though there would be a great change, to the fact that that change would not be too abrupt, and that a paper with which my name had been connected should not too suddenly be printing things which might be odious to my religion or to my honour, lest confusion should arise. There was no question of Mr Granville being editor. He was the proprietor. Mr Chesterton has been responsible since I left, and is responsible to the present day for all that has therein appeared.

Belloc then turned to the charge that the attacks were inspired by his antipathy to the Jews, and he now made the famous remark that "anybody less Jewish than the Chancellor of the Exchequer I cannot conceive." He continued:

Now it will be obvious to the Committee that if it could be suggested that what, in my case at least, was honest indignation and an honest desire to criticise thoroughly—and I would go further and say, to expose—what I thought a dangerous piece of public policy; if it could be proved that this was but the result of a crazy piece of prejudice, such as some ill-balanced men entertain against Jews as Jews, then late in the day as it is for such a manoeuvre, that trick might score a point or two in favour of what I will call, by your leave, the other side. Now, for the protection of my dignity, and for the protection of my honour, as well as for the information of the Committee and all the public, I will at once proceed to deal with that falsehood.

Belloc then said that he had many friends who were Jews. "My life is open. I have written very many books and innumerable articles." His opinions, he said, were known to everyone.

I do feel in common with, I think, the great majority of educated men today, that cosmopolitan finance is a dangerous power, and a power particularly dangerous to the separate nationalities of Europe. . . . I recognise, as everyone must, that the racial Jewish element in cosmopolitan finance is a large element. Should it become, as it bids fair through the influence of America to become—I speak of cosmopolitan finance—a thing mainly Gentile and not mainly Jewish, I should hit it fair and combat it, precisely as I hit it fair and combat it today. I conclude by saying that in all I have written—and I have written freely and largely many books and many articles—there is not one word, I will not say of sneer or hatred, but even of jest, against a great mass of the Jewish race which is poor, and which is oppressed, and which is persecuted.

Now the Chairman returned to the question he had asked on Belloc's first appearance, and he quoted the sentence from the *Oxford and Cambridge Review*.

Q. Will you tell the Committee who that "one responsible for the conduct of public affairs" was?

A. I do not know. I was not given the name. I thought my informant a sufficiently good informant, and I should imagine, if you ask me, that it was a statement containing a kernel of truth, but not accurate in its details, and probably connected with what we know now has recently come out on the American Marconi deal, but I was not given the name and did not call for it.

Q. Are you willing to give the Committee the name of your informant?

168

A. No, I cannot do that. I cannot drag in anybody else. I repeat, had I even been given a name, I should not have used it. I do not think it is the way to fight this particular battle.

Mr Booth now took over the examination. It was a strange choice to confront the agile Belloc, but possibly Falconer felt by then there was neither information nor glory to be gained. Booth repeated the first of the two questions the Chairman had asked altogether six times. He elicited the information: "to my knowledge signifies—as it does nine times out of ten in human affairs—to my satisfaction as to the integrity and opportunity of knowledge of my informant." Apart from this remarkable definition he made no progress. The following dialogue ensued:

Q. That is to say a person whom you will not disclose——?
A. Certainly.
Q. Told you that some other person——?
A. Yes.
Q. Whom you never had identified——?
A. Certainly not.
Q. Had received confidential information?
A. That is it.
Q. Yet you used the words "one of those responsible for the conduct of public affairs has to my knowledge received information"?
A. I call that knowledge.
Q. You call that your own personal knowledge?
A. When the informant is good and sound, and is likely to know, I call that knowledge.
Q. Do you call it your personal knowledge?
A. Certainly.
Q. You say "to my knowledge" not "to his knowledge"?
A. I use that phrase in that sense. If it seems to you, as a critic of English, too strong a phrase, I shall take care, in my future writings, to use a little less force.
Mr Gordon Harvey. The demeanour of the witness is getting most insulting and he ought to be checked.

169

A. I shall be happy to apologise to the Committee for this remark. I put it this way: that if I see cause from the writings of others, or in my judgment, not to say things are of my knowledge when they depend on a good informant, I will do so, but I think the day is far distant.

Q. Did you have any personal knowledge?

A. Have I first-hand information? No.

Q. Do not you think you were mistaken, and those words were likely to mislead? I do not put it that you intended them to mislead, but looking at them now, do not you think that they did mislead people who read them?

A. If you had asked me that before certain revelations which have taken place, I might have had more difficulty in answering you, but I do not think anyone in the present state of the public mind reading that would be very much scandalised.

On this Booth abandoned the line of inquiry and asked whether Belloc had written any of the articles in the *Eye–Witness* and if so which. Altogether the members of the Committee asked over fifty questions directed to the same end, and to each Belloc replied that it was a principle of journalism that the editor is responsible for all unsigned articles and they must ask Mr Chesterton.

Q. But are you not putting all responsibility on Mr Chesterton?

A. Mr Chesterton and I discussed this together long before a decision was taken. It is a sound decision.

Q. May I take it that your evidence today is after consultation with another witness who is coming?

A. Undoubtedly.

Q. Is his own evidence arranged?

A. I know nothing of this whatever, but I have given him my assurance on this principle, and I mean to maintain it, and I should be a bad and disloyal friend and a bad journalist if I did not.

It was a long time before the Committee abandoned this line of inquiry, but in the end Mr Booth asked:

Q. You had some definite data for what you wrote?

A. Yes.

Q. Will you place it before the Committee.

A. I have already placed it before the Committee.

Q. Where?

A. As a member of the public criticising what I believe to be a contract detrimental to the public, I discovered, in common with thousands of other members of the public, that the Postmaster-General had advantaged in enormous degree the brother of the Attorney-General, and could only have done so in connivance with, or by permission of, if you prefer the word, the Chancellor of the Exchequer. That was the one on which I went. Beyond that I did not go. That is sufficiently great.

Q. I ask you again, had you any definite data?

A. That is the definite datum. There is not more than one.

Q. You only wrote one article?

A. No, there is one datum.

Finally Booth appealed to the Committee. He wished to know whether they "supported" him, by which he seemed to be threatening action of the kind earlier taken against Maxse. The witness interrupted to say "You will not get a different answer." Then the room was cleared and the Committee deliberated in private. Belloc was not recalled.

(13)

Ghastly Record: Isaacs v. Chesterton

1

The placards carried by sandwichmen which brought Cecil Chesterton to trial at the Old Bailey on a charge of criminal libel have never been completely explained. Chesterton said that he did not give the instructions which sent them out to patrol the streets in front of the House of Commons and the Marconi offices, but he took responsibility for the action of an underling. The *New Witness* at this date was an almost bankrupt concern and there is evidence of only one underling, the future Mrs Chesterton, and we have her own authority for accepting her responsibility.

> On publishing day we [she refers to herself and Chesterton] bombarded the House of Commons with a squad of sandwichmen who, selling quires of the *New Witness,* solemnly promenaded up and down outside the House displaying posters in huge type, "Godfrey Isaacs' Ghastly Record." This was the spectacle that met Sir Rufus, and all the M.P.'s on their arrival at the House.[1]

---

[1] *The Chestertons,* 94.

After preliminary proceedings before a magistrate at Bow Street Cecil Chesterton appeared in the dock at the Old Bailey on May 27.

For several months before this appearance he had from time to time appealed to the Select Committee to take his evidence and he had on several occasions publicly suggested that the members were unwilling to call him. When on April 28 he was finally called, he excused himself on two pleas—one, that he was ill, and two, that, as he was being prosecuted on a charge of criminal libel, his evidence should, in the first instance, be given in his own defence. In reply the Committee repeated their request that he should attend, and said that, if he feared any question might prejudice his trial, they were willing Counsel should appear to protect him, Chesterton replied:

> In reply to your letter of yesterday's date, I am afraid I must respect-fully ask the Committee to allow me to abide by the advice, medical and legal, which has been given me, and the effect of which was conveyed to you yesterday by my solicitors.

Lord Robert Cecil then proposed to his colleagues that Chesterton should be informed that "in default of sufficient excuse the Select Committee require your attendance." This was debated in private, according to *The Times* with some heat, and was the occasion of the only vote of any importance on which the Committee divided other than on party lines. Messrs Mooney and Harvey voted with the ayes, Amery and Sir Frederick Banbury with the noes. The latter being in the majority, Cecil Chesterton never appeared before the Committee of Inquiry.

The application to commit Chesterton for trial on a charge of criminal libel was heard at Bow Street on February 26 before Sir Albert de Rutzen. At this hearing Chesterton, appearing on his own behalf, objected that the summons would interfere with his evidence before the Marconi Committee and asked for an adjournment. It was his intention, he said, to justify in that court what he had published and to demonstrate to the magistrate that the alleged libels were for the public benefit. It would be obvious that if he was engaged in criminal proceedings it would be virtually impossible for him to give evidence before the Committee. Indeed he would suggest that this was just what the applicant desired.

Sir Albert de Rutzen said that in his opinion there was nothing to stop the case from going on.

Mr R. D. Muir, appearing for Godfrey Isaacs, stated that, the defendant having said he proposed to justify the libels, until that plea had been filed the prosecution would make no attempt to go into the merits of the case. He then described the libels, which included all those of the previous summer and the January articles on Godfrey Isaacs's record, saying again:

> When the proper time comes Mr Godfrey Isaacs, Sir Rufus Isaacs and Mr Herbert Samuel will appear in the witness-box and refute the charges made against them by the defendant. But it must be plain, in my submission, that they cannot be called in this court.

When Cecil Chesterton rose in his own defence he asked if the complainant was not going to give evidence, and on Mr Muir replying, "No, not yet," he turned to the magistrate and asked him to dismiss the case on the ground that no evidence had been produced on which a jury was likely to convict. The magistrate, after suggesting that Chesterton might like to have time to consider his statement, adjourned the Court until the following day.

Throughout the whole course of the proceedings at law Chesterton was to show the most astonishing inability to appreciate the simplest legal points. In his opening remarks he had made it plain that the defence was to be a plea of justification. This meant, as the learned Judge was to explain to him at the Central Criminal Court, that "the tables were turned." Chesterton became the accuser, Isaacs the accused, and, after filing the pleas of justification, the burden of proving the charges would fall on Chesterton. When the Court met on the following day he seemed no clearer on this point, and he immediately made a speech taunting Godfrey Isaacs for not appearing in Court:

> It is amazing that Mr Isaacs should not take the opportunity of denying on oath that the statements are true. Mr Muir has suggested that every tribunal seems to be the wrong one for me. I would also

suggest that every stage of these proceedings seems to be the wrong stage for Mr Isaacs to go into the witness-box to clear himself.

Chesterton was not a stupid man and he numbered among his friends some of the best intellects in the land; but he was conceited and arrogant, and all his life he had shone in debate. It seems probable that at this stage he was so convinced of his ability to outwit the lawyers on their own ground that he did not take the trouble to understand the legal points on which the argument turned.

Continuing his defence he said that the case Godfrey Isaacs would be called to answer related only to his own companies.

> If I am accused of libelling the Government, I will defend myself on that charge; if not, let the issue be confined to the ground of libelling Mr Godfrey Isaacs.

He said that his motive in bringing these charges had been solely one of public spirit. He believed that out of the secrecy which surrounded so much of politics many evil things were growing up which might be a danger to the public. He found that the Marconi contract was being hurried through with the idea that it should never be examined. He examined it and found it very bad. He went into the negotiations and found them most suspicious. He went into the record of the managing director of the Company and found ample ground for further suspicion and said so in his paper.

> By bringing this matter before the public some light has been thrown on the case. I hope that it is small as compared with the light which will be thrown when we get Mr Isaacs to present himself in the witness-box.[2]

---

[2] It can be seen that Chesterton, like Belloc, was concerned only with the charges of corruption, not that of gambling which, unfortunately for him, he had omitted to make.

175

The magistrate said that it was a case for a jury. When the time came Mr Chesterton would have every opportunity of raising any plea he wished. He committed him for trial on bail of £500 on his own recognisance.

2

When the trial opened at the Old Bailey on April 29, before Mr Justice Phillimore, Sir Edward Carson, K.G. and Mr F. E. Smith, K.C. led Mr J R. D. Muir for Godfrey Isaacs, Mr Ernest Wild, K.G. and Mr Rigby Swift, K.G. led Mr Gordon Smith and Mr Purcell for Cecil Chesterton.

Mr Wild asked for an adjournment. He said that with the consent of Mr Chesterton the trial had been fixed for that day. Mr Chesterton had every desire to defend himself and as regards preparations he was ready and willing to do so. Unfortunately on the previous Thursday he had developed a bad throat and was now suffering from laryngitis. He—Mr Wild—had therefore been asked to undertake the defence. It was a physical and mental impossibility for him to prepare the defence in the way it should be prepared without a considerable adjournment.

Mr Wilding Harmer F.R.C.S. then went into the box and stated that he had seen Mr Chesterton that morning. His throat was better but he did not think he was in a fit state to start the case that day. His voice would only last for an hour or so. When Sir Edward Carson asked him what the defendant was suffering from, he replied an inflamed throat affecting the larynx.

"It is in the nature of a cold."

It was not until May 27 therefore that the case was finally heard.

Sir Edward opening for Godfrey Isaacs, said that there were two series of libels. The first charged that Mr Herbert Samuel, the Postmaster-General, and Sir Rufus Isaacs, the Attorney-General, were both so corrupt, that Mr Godfrey Isaacs being also corrupt, a corrupt contract had been entered into. The second, referring to the companies of which Isaacs had been director, averred practically in so many words that Mr Godfrey Isaacs had been guilty of criminal offences for which he would be imprisoned if his brother did his duty.

Sir Edward said that the plea of justification of the libels was the most extraordinary he had ever seen.

It gives the go-by to many of the main charges that have been made, and seeks to justify a sentence here and there.

Speaking of the libels of 1912, he said:

The only plea of justification of this series of outrageous charges is that there was a secret arrangement because the contract was not placed on the table of the House of Commons until July 19, and that money would pass to the Marconi Company under the contract. Such a plea is really only joking upon a serious matter.

In the issue of August 15 there had occurred the words: "When Samuel was caught with his hand in the till (or Isaacs, if you prefer it that way) the shares naturally slumped." That was a charge of common theft.

Mr Samuel had also been charged with having promised "Isaacs's brother" a vast sum out of public funds and with having taken measures to see that the contract would go through without comment. The only justification for that outrageous charge was that the contract had not been tabled until July 19.

Passing to the more dangerous subject of the American deals, Sir Edward said that unless the other side was prepared to say that the fact that Sir Rufus took these shares long after the tender had been accepted was a ground for imputing fraud and corruption, there could be no object in putting this matter into the pleas. "It is put there no doubt for the purpose of trying to effect prejudice."

Upon the third count there was no justification pleaded as to any single line of the charges, although in the issue of December 5 there appeared the following passage:

We do not imagine that we shall succeed in driving these men from public life, though they would have been driven thence in any country but this, and in almost any epoch but ours. We think, however, that we shall do something. We think, for instance, that we shall prevent the fulfilment of the project for making Isaacs a judge, which has long been canvassed in political circles. The British ermine will be spared that last disgrace, and we shall not see this man bullying and torturing the poor and unfortunate from the Bench, as he has so often bullied and tortured them from the Bar.

In a number of points set out to justify another statement it was contended that the contract might have been better.

That is not what we are trying in this case—it is the charge of corruption, of jobbery, of criminal action on the part of Mr Godfrey Isaacs with members of the Government; and the defence always shirks the 'real reason for bringing them into Court

Turning to the last count in the indictment, which dealt with the articles concerned with Godfrey Isaacs's record, Sir Edward said:

There is nothing connected with these companies from beginning to end of which Mr Godfrey Isaacs has the least fear of investigation or the least fear of anything being brought to his discredit. From 1897, the earliest period they go back to, down to the present moment, no allegation has ever been made against him or his honour.

There were, he continued, some nineteen or twenty companies referred to. To show the malice or carelessness with which Chesterton had written of these companies, he would mention that out of thirteen cases there was no public issue except in two. In one of these the public subscribed some £4000 and the directors and their friends privately subscribed £24,000, Mr Godfrey Isaacs putting in £1000 which he still held. In another case, that of the Transvaal Co. Ltd, there was a prospectus issued to the public who subscribed £100,000, but Mr Godfrey Isaacs found a defect in the engineer's report which was incorporated in the prospectus, and thereupon insisted that the whole of the £100,000 should be returned to the subscribers and he himself left the board.

With a dramatic gesture and exclaiming: "Here is the thing which was paraded up and down outside his office for everyone connected with the Marconi Company to see!" Sir Edward Carson then held up a poster on which appeared the words: "Godfrey Isaacs' Ghastly Record."

"Some people might ask," he said, "why does he notice the *Eye–Witness* or the *New Witness?* It is impossible with a challenge like that outside his office that a man should not take notice."

3

The Ministers of the Crown were called early in the trial and gave the evidence which by now the public knew by heart.

When Godfrey Isaacs took the stand he was questioned for a long time on the companies of which he had been director. Nothing to his discredit emerged except that he had lost a great deal of money.

> *The Judge.* It is not an imputation against a man that he has been a failure. There is nothing in your libel to say that because Mr Godfrey Isaacs is a bad man of business the Government ought not to deal with the Marconi Company. The allegations were that the prosecutor is a fraud and a cheat.
>
> *Mr Wild.* There are two parts. First we say he is not the sort of man they ought to deal with because of the business failures. Secondly because . . .
>
> *Sir Edward Carson.* That he is a man that ought to be sent to gaol.
>
> *Mr Wild.* That is what I am coming to.
>
> *The Judge.* I have not seen the first part.
>
> *Mr Wild* (to witness). I suggest that you were not exploiting the public but exploiting these rich gentlemen?
>
> *Witness.* I was exploiting nobody, sir.
>
> *The Judge.* How can you exploit rich people if you are not a promoter?
>
> *Mr Wild.* The witness was in most of these companies from the start.
>
> *Judge.* That is not being a promoter.
>
> *Witness.* I do not think I ever invited people to put money into any one of these companies. I joined them myself as one of those who put money into somebody else's company.
>
> *Mr Wild.* Here are cases after cases of failure.
>
> *Witness.* That is my misfortune.

Judge. You might as well cross-examine any speculative widow, Mr Wild.

Mr Wild. A speculative widow would not be concerned in the management.

Later Counsel asked the witness whether he could point to one success except the Marconi Company in the whole course of his career.

Witness. In companies?

Mr Wild. Yes.

Witness. A complete success, no. I should not call any one of them a complete success, but I may say that each of them was an endeavour to develop something new. It is not one new thing in twenty which is a success.

Mr Wild. For the moment I am dealing with business failure apart from moral questions; do you think your business career up to 1910 qualified you to be managing director of a company like the Marconi?

Witness. That is not for me to say; but I can say that my business career qua business has always been a success. As a merchant I have been very successful.

The Judge, who constantly intervened, presently remarked :

It seems to me that a great deal of this writing is pure bungling wrong-headedness on the part of the person who wrote it—not venomous in intention, but simply in plain language stupidity.

When Signor Marconi took the witness-stand he was asked if he would explain how Mr Isaacs got 500,000 shares, for which there was an eager demand, without the English Company getting an opportunity of taking them. Marconi replied: "He got them by having the pluck to take them when no one else was likely to take them."

After several witnesses had given evidence as to the integrity and business capacity of Mr Isaacs the prosecution closed its case.

4

In his opening speech for the defence Wild said there were two sets of alleged libels. The first related to the contract between the Government and the Marconi Company. The people responsible for making the contract were attacked, and the defendant in making these attacks did undoubtedly use very strong language and imputed to the politicians concerned motives which he ought not to have imputed to them. But those politicians were not the prosecutors. It was open to Sir Rufus Isaacs and Mr Samuel and to Mr Lloyd George—whom they did not have the pleasure of seeing—if they were attacked by Mr Chesterton to bring an action against him.[3]

Dealing with the first series of libels Counsel made all he could of the American deals and accused Sir Rufus of having made a statement "subversive of public candour" in the House of Commons. When he turned to the attacks on Godfrey Isaacs, he took the line, not that Isaacs was a stupid man and a failure, but that he was a clever man with the intention to defraud. He had already remarked in the earlier part of his speech that Harry Isaacs had paid for the whole of his American shares and got some thousands in his pocket, and that Heybourn was put in the position of making from half to three-quarters of a million.

If the shareholders had been thought of instead of relatives and friends, this money should have gone into the pockets of the Company.

He now asked the jury a series of questions. As businessmen did they

---

[3]   F. J. Sheed comments *(Gilbert Keith Chesterton,* 300.):

All the discussion of the contract was given an air of unreality by the extraordinary line the Chesterton defence took. It distinguished between the two sets of charges, offering to justify the second (concerning Godfrey Isaacs's business record) but claiming that the first set brought accusation of corruption not against Godfrey but against Rufus and Herbert Samuel. . . . It was an impossible position to say that Ministers were fraudulently giving a fraudulent contract to Godfrey Isaacs, but that this did not mean that he was in the fraud.

really believe that Mr Isaacs had been making loss after loss? How did they think he lived? It had been said that there was no public issue. This was true in a sense, but instead it was when the shares had been worked up to a high price that the public came in. He suggested that the members of the boards were all Isaacs's creatures, and he said he would call a witness, a Mr Lockwood, to give evidence that Isaacs had asked him to report that the average yield of the St David's mine, a "pocketty" mine, was the yield of the pockets. Here both Sir Edward Carson and the Judge made one of many interventions to say that Mr Lockwood was not mentioned in the pleas of justification, and a further argument between Counsel and the Judge took place.

When the examination of Cecil Chesterton began, Sir Edward Carson constantly objected that the evidence was inadmissible and was upheld by the Judge. Finally the Judge addressed Counsel for the Defence.

> You must not lose your temper because the point is ruled against you. The witness is not being tried on an indictment for publishing a libel false to his knowledge. . . . We are not trying his *bona fides*. He might have honestly believed all those things.

And Sir Edward Carson interjected:

> The only reason I made the objection at all is that I do not want the jury to be misled into the idea that because a man has certain facts or theories in his mind he can therefore sit down and make charges against other people.

Later Mr Wild addressed the Judge.

> Will your Lordship allow me to take the witness through the articles?
> *Judge.* What do you mean by taking him through the articles?
> *Wild.* As to what he wrote and what he means?
> *Judge.* Surely you do not mean that? What meaning he intended to convey is immaterial.

182

After some further exchange the Judge asked Mr Wild if he would like to adjourn.

Wild. On your Lordship's ruling I think I have little more to ask.

The Judge then adjourned the Court so that Mr Wild might consider what to ask. On the following morning he upheld his ruling, and Sir Edward Carson began the cross-examination of Cecil Chesterton. Here is the whole of the evidence which is interesting today.

Carson. In relation to the Marconi contract do you now say he [Godfrey Isaacs] was guilty of any dishonourable conduct?

Witness. Which do you call the contract?

Carson. Take the tender first.

Witness. The only thing I should call dishonourable in his conduct was his request to Mr Samuel to have a clause kept secret and the issue of a misleading circular to the shareholders.

Carson. And you do not accuse him of any abominable business—I mean in relation to obtaining the contract?

Witness. Yes, certainly. I now accuse Mr Isaacs of very abominable conduct between March 7 and July 19.

Carson. Do you accuse him of fraud in relation to the contract?

Witness. Fraud? Well, I think one goes very near fraud.

Carson. I only want to get it from you because I could not follow your Counsel yesterday. Do you accuse him of fraud in connexion with the contract?

Witness. Am I obliged to say?

Carson. Yes.

Witness. I think some of his conduct went near it, but I will not accuse him of it.

Carson. Do you accuse him of having obtained the contract by any improper influence?

Witness. I would like to understand the question more clearly.

Carson. Do you accuse him now of having obtained the contract through the influence of the Attorney-General?

183

Witness. I do not accuse the Attorney-General of having influenced Mr Samuel in giving the contract.

Carson. Do you accuse him now of any corruption in his relations with the Postmaster-General?

Witness. No; I do not think I ever did.

Carson. Do you accuse the Postmaster-General of dishonesty or corruption?

Witness. What I accused the Postmaster-General of is having given a contract which was a byword for laxity and thereby laying himself open reasonably to the suspicion that he was conferring a favour on Mr Godfrey Isaacs because he was the Attorney-General's brother.

Carson. I must repeat my question. Do you accuse the Postmaster-General of anything dishonest or dishonourable?

Witness. After the Postmaster-General's denials on oath I must leave the question. I will not accuse him of perjury.

Judge. I think you must answer the question a little more precisely.

Witness. I think the natural interpretation of the Postmaster-General's conduct would be that he was unduly influenced in his public capacity by private considerations, but as he has denied it upon oath, it is a question of accusing him of perjury, and I do not know that I can take the responsibility of doing so.

Judge. That is a very argumentative answer.

Carson. Could you not answer Yes, or No?

Judge. Do you or do you not accuse the Postmaster-General of corruption?

Witness. That is the only answer I can give.

Judge. We do not want to know your motives. We want to know what you say now?

Witness. I say I do not accuse him on the ground I have given.

Judge. That is evasion. Do you or do you not accuse him?

Witness. I have said "No."

Later in the cross-examination.

Witness. My idea at that time was that Sir Rufus Isaacs had influenced Mr Samuel to benefit Mr Godfrey.

Carson. You have not that opinion now?

Witness. Sir Rufus has denied it on oath, and I accept his denial.

Carson. And you had no evidence of such a serious charge at the time?

Witness. I think it was a very natural inference to draw that in a great legal contract of this kind the chief legal adviser to the Crown would be a party to it, and, if he was, the extreme badness of the contract justified me in believing that he had behaved in an improper fashion in helping to draw up a lax contract for the benefit of his brother Mr Godfrey Isaacs.

Carson. You thought fit, as a respectable journalist, to charge Ministers of the Crown and Mr Godfrey Isaacs with corruption on an inference from the contract?

Witness, And the other facts, particularly the enormous Marconi gamble.

Throughout the cross-examination Chesterton made what play he could with the Marconi gamble, and in particular with the American shares. If his charges had been connected with the gamble, he might have made a better showing in Court. As it was the exchanges quoted here took place during the course of a long examination during which he sometimes scored debating points. This has some importance in view of the attitude he and his friends were later to adopt.

In an attempt to prove the charge of dishonesty against Godfrey Isaacs, the defence was neither more successful nor less undignified. They relied on the witness Lockwood, who was called in spite of an objection by Sir Edward Carson, with which the Judge was in sympathy, that he was not mentioned in the pleas of justification. Lockwood said that Isaacs had requested him to report the yield of the pockets of the St David's mine as the yield of the average. He provided F. E. Smith with an opportunity of which he took such advantage that the second Lord Birkenhead quotes the cross-examination in an account of his father's great achievements in Court. Only the wit of the advocate makes it worthy of record, however, because Lockwood was an unfortunate wretch of doubtful sanity, and an intelligent boy of fourteen could have disposed of his

185

evidence with the precision if not the brilliance of F. E. Smith.

Nothing was then left for the defence but to call witnesses to the character of Cecil Chesterton, and Maurice Baring and the Reverend Conrad Noel took the stand. They were followed by the defendant's brother, Gilbert Keith Chesterton, who, having said that he had been in close touch with his brother since birth, provoked laughter in Court by adding: "I envy him the dignity of his present position."

During the course of his summing-up, in which he inevitably directed the jury to find against Chesterton, the Judge made the following remark:

> With regard to the American shares, I think I may say in passing that there might be a claim by the English Marconi Company as a corporate body against Mr Godfrey Isaacs . . . because, although it was not anticipated that they would avail themselves of it, the shareholders had the right, if they chose, to take up the new shares.[4]

The jury, after an absence of five minitus, found that the defendant was guilty of publishing a defamatory libel of and concerning Mr Godfrey Isaacs on five of the six counts of the indictment, and that in each case the plea of justification had not been made out.

The Judge then addressed the defendant:

> Cecil Chesterton, it is right for me to say that though the verdict is the verdict of the jury, I entirely agree with it. It gives me pain to see a man of your position bearing an honoured name, with literary gifts and good friends, in such a position as you are in before this Court. I shall

---

[4] These words must have been encouraging to certain shareholders, but they did not suggest litigation because this was already under way. When Godfrey Isaacs arrived at the Old Bailey on the first morning of the Chesterton trial he was confronted by placards of the *Globe* and the *Pall Mall Gazette announcing* a million-pound claim. He was granted an injunction to stop this publicity, which was obviously prejudicial to the present case, and, owing to interminable legal quibbling, the action of the shareholders did not reach a court of law for four years. It is discussed in the last chapter of this book.

bear in mind that you have sworn upon oath that you honestly believed the matters which you have written and published. I return to a remark I made somewhat earlier in the case, which I hoped at one time might possibly have been taken to heart by you and your advisers. It seemed to me that really a good deal of this matter was due to what the theologians would call invincible ignorance—to ignorance of business and prejudice . . . I still think that you, and possibly those who were behind you, have been partly instigated by racial prejudice and partly blind to business matters, which has led to the extraordinary series of libels that you have published upon Godfrey Isaacs . . . Upon each one of the five counts upon which you have been convicted you might have been sent to prison for a year, and you might in addition be fined as well as having to pay the costs of the prosecution. That is the maximum, and it is not the punishment I propose to award. When I consider the cruelty of some of these charges and the fact—I daresay not considered—but obvious to anyone who did consider them—that they might have rendered Godfrey Charles Isaacs a beggar and driven him from his employment, as well as from the fame and respect of good men; when I remember the sending of those placards along the front of his place of business in the Strand, it is extremely difficult to refrain from sending you to prison. But on the whole I hope that what I have said, and the opinion of your countrymen, as expressed by the verdict of the jury, will be sufficient with the punishment I propose to inflict. You will be fined *£100* and according to the ordinary course of the Court, you will be imprisoned until the fine is paid. You will further have to pay all the costs of the prosecution. I say all, because the statute enables the Court to award either the whole or the part. I know that will come very heavily upon you, but I cannot help that. It is your plea of justification—and the statute expressly directs that the Court should take into consideration the plea of justification in awarding punishment—it is your plea or pleas of justification and the way they have been supported in the case which has increased the costs to the enormous amount to which they will extend. That is the sentence of the Court upon you.

Then a very curious thing happened. Although Chesterton under pressure had withdrawn the charges against the Ministers and had been shown to have no evidence to support the charge of dishonesty against Godfrey Isaacs; although his defence had been a series of *non sequiturs* based on a set of assumptions for which there were no serious grounds; although the Judge had summed up against him and delivered a severe rebuke, there is some evidence to think that Chesterton and his friends had not understood any of this. They had not, it has already been suggested, taken the trouble to understand the legal points, and, although they had realised the case was going against him, their views on public corruption made it easy for them to believe that this was a result of the natural hostility of the Judge towards someone who had made an attack on public men.[5] In criminal libel the question of damages does not arise as it does in a civil action. The sentence can only be imprisonment or a fine. Cases of criminal libel are very rare, the sentence of imprisonment almost unknown, and there is no doubt that, when he imposed all the costs as well as the fine, the Judge considered he was punishing Chesterton harshly.[6] All the evidence suggests that this again was not understood. Chesterton was prepared for imprisonment and the martyr's crown. The £100 fine seemed to him and his friends the equivalent of a farthing damages in a civil suit. They hailed it as a victory and have ever since believed that it was. The idea was probably conceived as the result of the demonstration that took place in Court from the relief of Chesterton's friends and the surprise of the crowd, many of whom were hostile to the Ministers, the moment the Judge ceased to speak.

Mrs Chesterton gives the following account of the scene:

> There was a moment's silence after the judge had stopped speaking, and then the pent-up feelings of the crowd were released in a roar of cheers. The Court seethed with excited jubilation and a huge wave of

---

[5] Reginald Turner, writing on 3 June 1913 to Max and Florence Beerbohm in Rapallo, said: "Are you interested in the Chesterton case? Had he written more soberly he would have had a better case, but then if he had I suppose Isaacs would not have taken action. Wells (who has been here) told me that Belloc has *assured* him the Government had arranged that the jury should disagree. Funny, how French blood will out."

[6] In addition to his own costs, Chesterton had to pay £1504. 6*s*. 1*d*. and, as he was unable to find any of the money, a collection took place among his friends.

humanity swept towards the hero of the day. It was a moment that quickened the imagination. Against the Marconi Goliath of wealth and power David had more than held his own; he had breached the citadel of Cabinet security, and forced Ministers of the Crown to face public opinion. No wonder Cecil's sentence of a fine was regarded as a victory for clean government.[7]

This is largely the work of a quickened imagination and should not be taken as an objective account of what happened, but there is no doubt that Chesterton and his friends were encouraged in Court to believe a victory had been won. A close reading of the press on the following day might have dispelled this notion, but in the Marconi case everyone always believed unwelcome views to be equated with strong and discreditable party feeling.

The Chesterton view of the case is romantic and, while ignoring that Cecil withdrew, also makes ridiculous claims. If the doubtful honour of having brought the charge of corruption is to be competed for, acknowledgement must be made to Lawson as the first in the field; and, if any journalist was responsible for "forcing the Ministers to face public opinion," this could only have been Maxse. Mrs Chesterton speaks of the sensation in Court when Sir Rufus had to admit to the American deals. But this was three-months-old news and the public were heartily sick of hearing about it.

Belloc said of Chesterton: "His courage was heroic, native, positive, and equal: always at the highest potential of courage."

In the perspective of today his courage seems excitable, reckless, unequal, the courage of a delinquent child. Discretion is at least some part of valour, justice of honour. Chesterton withdrew under pressure in Court, but he never withdrew anywhere else. Yet courage, discretion, honour all demanded that charges of the vilest and most scurrilous kind, framed in the most insolent language, which when tested could not be substantiated, should be completely and whole-heartedly withdrawn and some apology made. Chesterton and all his circle remained convinced that a blow had been struck for public morals and they have boasted ever since of the part he played.

Probably the strangest thing in the Marconi case is that they do not seem

---

[7] *The Chestertons*, 110.

Mr. CHESTERTON FINED £100.

ORDERED TO PAY ALL THE COSTS OF THE PROSECUTION.

JUDGE AND MARCONI SHAREHOLDERS.

Mr. Cecil Chesterton was found guilty at the Old Bailey on Saturday of publishing defamatory libels about Mr. Godfrey Isaacs, managing director of the Marconi Company. He was sentenced by Mr. Justice Phillimore to pay a fine of £100, and to stay in prison until the fine is paid.

Mr. CECIL CHESTERTON.

He was also ordered to pay Mr. Godfrey Isaacs' costs, which will amount to thousands of pounds. Mr. Isaacs was represented by Sir Edward Carson, K.C., M.P., Mr. F. E. Smith, K.C., M.P., and Mr. R. D. Muir, senior counsel to the Treasury, and Mr. Chesterton by Mr. Ernest Wild, K.C., Mr. Rigby Swift, K.C., and Mr. Purcell.

From the *Daily Express*, 9 June 1913

even to have understood that he withdrew. In their self-engendered excitement they noted only that he scored a few points on the Stock Exchange gamble and the American deals. When, for her biography of G. K. Chesterton, Maisie Ward was preparing a chapter on the Marconi case, she wrote to Mrs Chesterton to ask her why Cecil withdrew. Mrs Chesterton replied with a long and detailed explanation that violent pressure had been exerted both by Gilbert and his father, who were in a panic over the trial. Miss Ward says:

> Unlikely as this seemed, especially in Gilbert's case, the account was so circumstantial, and from so near a connection, that I felt almost obliged to accept it. What was my amazement a few months later at receiving a letter in which she stated that "after a great deal of close research, re-reading of papers, etc." (in connection with her own book *The Chestertons)* and after a talk with Cecil's solicitors, she had become convinced that Cecil had acted as he had because "the closest sleuthing had been unable to discover any trace" of investments by Rufus Isaacs in English Marconis. "For this reason Cecil took the course he did—not through family pressure. That pressure, I still feel, was exerted, though possibly not until the trial was over."

Since Chesterton's charge had been one of corruption in the placing of the contract and not of gambling on information, the second reply explains even less than the first. It seems likely that Mrs Chesterton's hesitations were due to the fact that this was the first time she had properly understood that Cecil withdrew.

The degree of unbalance in the participants on both sides of this controversy is extraordinary. Men whose lives and careers were at all other times distinguished by courtesy, goodwill and intellectual integrity seem to have taken leave of their senses. No example is more striking than that of G. K. Chesterton, who was and remained all his life obsessed by the case.[8]

---

[8] Mr Leonard Woolf, writing of the Chesterton brothers as young men, says: "I never liked Cecil Chesterton, partly because his physical appearance was so unprepossessing, and partly because even then he had a streak of that kind of

He was not personally concerned with the investigation of political scandals; he took his views from his brother. He remained to the end of his life convinced that Cecil had been the champion of public morals against corrupt and evil men, and this belief led him to the most astonishing excesses.

The death of his brother coincided with a civil libel case in which the plaintiff, Godfrey Isaacs, was defeated. Chesterton used the occasion to address an open letter to Lord Reading in the *New Witness*. It is written in a spirit of self-righteousness and with an ironic assumption of charity masking a hatred and contempt for which it would not be necessary to be a Christian to be ashamed. It repeats the infamous charge for which his brother was quite properly fined, and Chesterton seems, in addition, to be under the impression that Cecil had charged speculation. It is given as an appendix on p. 256.

---

fanatical intolerance which seems to be fertilized, not by profound convictions, but by personal animosities. Gilbert was a very different kind of person. . . . Whereas Cecil seemed to have a grudge against the universe, the world, and you in particular, G. K. gave one the immediate impression of goodwill, particular and general." *(Sowing,* 92.)

(14)

The Select Committee:
7. An Absconding Stockbroker

When the Master of Elibank resigned his position as Government Chief Whip in August 1912, his action seems to have been in no way connected with his participation in the American dealings, because he had told Asquith of his desire to resign in the February before and had made arrangements to join the Pearson company. He remained in England for rather more than two months after the Select Committee had begun its sittings, but at the time the American dealings were made public at the *Matin* trial he had already left England for South America on a tour of Lord Cowdray's interests there.

On 7 April 1913 the Chairman of the Select Committee sent him a telegram asking him when he could attend to give evidence. Lord Murray replied from Bogota:

> In reply to your cable of April 7 received today: shall be glad to testify on my return. May I explain that I am over one month's journey from London and in the midst highly important negotiations with Colombia Government for my firm. That when I have finished my

work here I have urgent engagements in Mexico, where we have important interests, as well as subsequently with my officials in the West Indies. In ordinary circumstances I calculate to return July. I trust delay will not be gravely inconvenient. Please inform Committee that I have never held any interest whatever in English Marconi Company. In any case I shall desire make personal statement in Parliament on my return.

On April 28 Sir Alfred Spicer sent a further telegram:

July too late. If you desire give evidence give earliest date arrival in England.

And to this Lord Murray replied:

In reply to your further cable recently despatched to Bogota, I much regret that for reasons carefully ex-plained . . . in reply to your cable of 7 April unfortunately I will not be able to return home before July.

When the Select Committee had heard all the evidence related in previous chapters they fell out among themselves over the question whether Godfrey Isaacs should be recalled and further examined. They had by now had an opportunity to peruse the books of the Marconi Company and the various other documents he had supplied at their request, and since there were some discrepancies between the information these revealed and his verbal statements, the Tory members wished to re-examine him. They were again over-ruled by the Liberal majority, and in the atmosphere of hostility thus achieved they began an attempt to agree a report of their findings.

The unpeaceful quiet which now reigned was once more broken from outside—this time by a coup on the part of the *Daily Express*.

On May 31 under the headlines "MYSTERY OF MISSING STOCKBROKER," "WHERE IS MR CHARLES EDWIN FENNER?" the *Express* asked:

Will the Marconi Committee, in view of the fact that in usually well-informed financial circles Mr Fenner's books and documents are believed to contain interesting records of the dealings of certain prominent persons in Marconis . . . subpoena Mr F. S. Salaman, trustee of the estate of Mr Charles Edwin Fenner?

Three days later the *Globe*, a Conservative evening paper, took this up. The headline this time was "LORD MURRAY'S ABSENCE," and the paragraph read as follows:

> A firm of stockbrokers has recently become bankrupt, a leading member of the firm has been declared in court an absconding bankrupt, and the affairs of that firm are now the subject of investigation by an officer of the court. It is in connection with that firm that fresh rumours have been set on foot, and Lord Murray's name is mixed up with them.

As a result, Mr Frederick Seymour Salaman was called before the Committee. Mr Salaman was the Trustee in Bankruptcy elected by the creditors of Mr Charles Edward Fenner, who had practised as a stockbroker under the name of Montmorency & Co. Mr Fenner had been made bankrupt some months before, after absconding: and it may here be remarked that the "Marconi Ministers" were dogged by unusual bad luck, because Mr Fenner had been conducting an apparently high-class business and had shown no sign that he was a man on whom it might be unwise to rely.

Mr Salaman was accompanied by Counsel, and, after some discussion as to whether the confidence normally reposed in the discretion of a stockbroker could be extended to apply to him, he was ordered to reply to the following question put to him by the Chairman:

> Q. As far as your information goes, is there any entry or entries in any of the books in your possession as trustees of the estate of Mr Charles Edward Fenner, Stockbroker, which relates to the dealings of Ministers, or ex-Ministers, or Public Officials in the shares of the Marconi Company?
> A. Yes, sir, there are. I have the books here.

The Master of Elibank had purchased 2500 shares in the American

Marconi Company on April 18 for coming out settlement at £3–5s. 0d., and on May 14 he had purchased a further 500 shares at £2. 8s. 9d.

The sensation this caused and the chagrin of the Liberals was immediately increased by the revelation of a further circumstance. It seemed likely that the shares had been bought not for the Master of Elibank's personal account but for a trust for which he acted. There was some doubt about this. In the books of the absconding stockbroker there was a page headed The Master of Elibank Trust Account. On this page there was no record of any dealings in Marconi shares, but the ledger had been balanced and appeared to be carried forward to another page. The uncertainty was because this second page, on which the Marconi deals were recorded, was headed merely The Master of Elibank, the words Trust Account having been left out. Mr Salaman gave it as his opinion that the two pages referred to the same account and not to two separate accounts. In giving this opinion he laid himself open to hours of bullying from the Liberal members of the Committee.

At this stage of the Committee's proceedings witnesses were often subjected to an ordeal which must have prevented any normally sensitive person from contributing relevant evidence unless forced to do so by law. When a witness gave some evidence in his original examination which pleased one of the two completely divided groups, it inevitably displeased the other. He was then hectored individually by each member of the dissatisfied group in an attempt to break his opinion, and then re-examined by the opposing group, this time the questions tending to restore his original statement. If some small new fact emerged, he was immediately taken through the whole procedure again. Mr Salaman endured this for several days.

Falconer and Booth now behaved like buffoons. In face of the evidence which made it practically certain that both pages of the ledger referred to a Trust Account, they were determined to establish that there were two accounts and that the Marconi shares had been purchased by Lord Murray for himself. Lord Murray was a man who might easily have been managing a trust for relations or friends, but the tremendous anxiety of the two Liberals made it plain they had seen at a glance the direction from which some new blow might hit them, and the pain it would cause if it fell. Lord Robert Cecil scored by pointing out that cheques to the value of £9000 had been given immediately in payment. Sir Rufus Isaacs, he reminded the Committee, had claimed acquaintance with Lord Murray's financial position and had seemed in doubt as to how easily he could produce a cheque for £2000.

But if the fears of the Liberals were quite obvious, their power to rule out questions they did not care for was well known, and it is not surprising that the rising temper of the Tories, so long under control, now burst out. When Lord Robert Cecil asked Mr Salaman whether he had been able to form a judgment as to the persons for whom the Master of Elibank had acted, the witness replied that he had been told it by Mr Fenner's clerk. Immediately several voices spoke to rule out hearsay evidence, and this proved too much for Amery.

> *Mr Amery.* You want to prevent the truth coming out, and you might be decent in doing it.
>
> *Mr Mooney.* That is not a remark any Member of the House should address to another Member.
>
> *Mr Booth.* It is a Party remark.
>
> *Mr Amery.* I apologise for having made a remark which may be out of but which I believe to be true.
>
> *Mr William Redmond.* It is out of order.
>
> *Chairman.* Please withdraw the remark.
>
> *Lord Robert Cecil* (to the Witness). Do not answer the question until objection is taken, if one is taken, and the Chairman has ruled upon it. Does your information on the point come from Mr Fenner's clerk?
>
> A. Yes.
>
> Q. Is Mr Fenner's clerk available as a witness?
>
> A. He is here now.

Mr Fenner's clerk was a disappointment. He was not the head clerk, who by now had employment elsewhere, and several more witnesses were called before progress was made. Before this time Mr Mooney, still speaking publicly, had again addressed the Chairman on the subject of Mr Amery's remarks:

> *Mr Mooney.* I would like to ask you, sir, whether it is in order for an honourable Member under the guise of withdrawing a charge which

has absolutely no foundation in fact, to make accusations of this kind against other Members of the House?

Mr Amery. Before you express an opinion, sir, I should like to say that there seems to be some misapprehension in Mr Mooney's mind. I was not intending in any way to withdraw what I said, but I did express regret to the Committee for feeling impelled to say what I said. When the Witness was about to answer a question I heard interruption, not only from Mr Mooney, but I think I heard it more specifically from Mr Booth—that was my impression. Though I regret very much that in the proceedings of this Committee anything that is in any way unseemly should be introduced, I must express the conviction which has come upon me after many months, that, whenever there seemed at any moment an answer likely to lead to the discovery of anything which seemed unpleasant to one or two Members on the other side, particularly Mr Booth, that answer was invariably interrupted: and there is that other fact, which is notorious to the whole public, that certain information most vital to this Committee and affecting all the proceedings . . . was held back for a space of something like two months. Under the circumstances, I do feel that my observations, however technically unseemly—and I regret that they should have been unseemly—were in substance justified, and I have no intention of apologising for them or withdrawing them.

The row broke out in all directions at once. Falconer felt impelled to make again his long and incomprehensible explanation as to why he had felt it necessary to withhold from the Committee his knowledge that Ministers had bought American shares, while other Members wished to discuss the point more immediately at issue. The Tories made good use of the occasion to complain of the treatment they had received from the Liberal majority.

When Amery made his interjection he had most probably lost his temper. If so, he had the sympathy of much of the public. *The Times* now devoted a leader to the Marconi case in which the whole of the events were reviewed. Having referred to the October debate and the unexpected disclosure at the *Matin* trial, this continued:

198

Only persons of the most scrupulous honour who desired that nothing whatsoever should remain hid would, it was suggested, have thought necessary to mention it at all. But even while public opinion was still occupied in adjusting itself—somewhat painfully it must be admitted—to this unexpected admission, it was startled still further to find that the chivalrous candour displayed at the *Matin* trial had allowed something not wholly unimportant to remain undisclosed.

After describing the circumstances in which it had been revealed that Mr Lloyd George and the Master of Elibank had made further purchases, it then continued:

> Once again, therefore, public opinion was asked to adjust itself to a new set of facts without abandoning the theory that all the Ministers concerned had acted throughout, not merely innocently, but with a perfect propriety and discretion. Any person who ventured to suggest the contrary was immediately trounced as a calumniator by the most respectable organs of the Liberal Press. . . . It was absurd and unnecessary to put Lord Murray to the inconvenience and expense of a journey from somewhere in the middle of the South American continent merely in order to confirm—for of course he could not amplify–the quixotic admissions of his colleagues and friends.

After relating the story of the absconding stockbroker and speaking in severe terms of the reticence of Mr Falconer and Mr Booth, it concluded:

> Mr Amery may have expressed himself the other day with more heat than propriety upon this aspect of the matter; but there is not much doubt that public opinion endorses his complaint that certain members of the Committee have for months past been desirous of preventing unpleasant facts from coming to light.

It is possible, however, It is possible, however, that Amery did not lose his temper, but made this public and unseemly protest deliberately, as the only way of making it too hot for the Liberals, of preventing them from ruling out

199

questions which might expose the truth. If so, he succeeded.

It took some time and the exhaustion of several witnesses, but it was eventually established that the two pages of the ledger referred to the same account, the Master of Elibank Trust Account, and that this was held jointly in two names. The second was that of Mr Percy Illingworth, Government Chief Whip and Patronage Secretary to the Treasury in succession to Lord Murray.

This was a sad day for Mr Falconer and Mr Booth and indeed for the whole of their Party. The explanations were still to come, but no one now had any doubt that the Master of Elibank had bought 3000 shares in the American Marconi Company for the Liberal Party Fund.

Mr Illingworth and Captain Arthur Murray, brother of the absent Elibank, were called to explain what they knew of the transactions.[1]

Captain Murray said that, when his brother was about to leave England, he had given him 3000 American Marconi shares which he said he had purchased on behalf of the Liberal Party. Lord Murray had said that he had told none of his colleagues about these shares, although he had consulted his legal adviser, because he proposed to keep them until the Marconi business was "cleaned up."[2] It was thus made plain that no one, and certainly not Mr Illingworth, had had any knowledge of the purchase until the breach of confidence of a clerk to an absconding stockbroker had informed the press.

These events concluded the hearings of the Select Committee. For almost nine months their questions had ranged so widely, their procedure become so undisciplined, their disagreements so obvious, that it is doubtful whether anyone could have followed the reports of the proceedings as they appeared daily in the press. It was essential therefore, if they were to conclude their task, that a distillation of the facts that had emerged from their endless discussions should now be presented in an agreed statement.

---

[1] Captain Murray was to write a life of his brother, entitled *Master and Brother*, in which the word Marconi is not even mentioned.

[2] This phrase gave great joy to Leo Maxse.

(15)

The Reports

It had for some time seemed unlikely that the Select Committee would be able to agree on a report, since it was incredible that the Tory members would be able to sign any document that satisfied the views of Mr Falconer, Mr Mooney and Mr Booth. It was a surprise when they issued not merely two reports, a majority and a minority, but three; and concluded their labours as incompetently as they had conducted them, the findings on most of the matters they had discussed remaining as much the subject of conjecture and opinion as before.

What happened was this: the Chairman drafted a report on behalf of the Liberal members, while Lord Robert Cecil and Mr Amery collaborated on an alternative draft. The Chairman's draft was proposed, and Lord Robert's proposed as an amendment. The amendment was voted on first and rejected. At this moment there was a distinct if small possibility of agreement. The two drafts were not as dissimilar as might have been expected, and the difficulty of reconciling them not insuperable. Both documents unequivocally repudiated the charges that Ministers had been influenced in their public duties by private or personal considerations, and that they had used privileged knowledge to gamble in Marconi shares. Both recorded the opinion that the purchase of American shares had been indiscreet, and both regretted the lack of frankness with the House of Commons in the debate of 11 October 1912. The serious difference was that, where the Chairman used kindly, rather timid terms in these paragraphs, the Tories were far more severe. It was said at the time that the Tories accepted the fact that they had no chance of getting their own draft through, and were prepared to vote for the Chairman's.

Then Mr Falconer went to work. Nominally accepting the Chairman's draft, he proposed amendment after amendment, which the majority carried, until it was altered beyond recognition. Of nine pages of findings, seven and a half were struck out altogether, while, in place of the Chairman's mildly condemnatory conclusions, lyrical and complete acquittals of the Ministers were inserted.

A Select Committee of Inquiry, unlike a Royal Commission, which may publish a majority and a minority report, is confined to one. The majority report, Mr Falconer's, thus became the Report of the Select Committee of Inquiry. Lord Robert Cecil defiantly published the Tory report as a draft, and the Chairman unexpectedly struck a blow for the honour of the Liberal Party by also publishing his own.

The Majority Report and Lord Robert Cecil's draft are given as an appendix. The Chairman's draft is only of importance because he felt strongly enough to publish it and because he stated that the Ministers' "purchase of American shares was liable to give rise to misconception," and secondly that "if it had occurred to them" to make a full statement in the debate of October 11, it would have "tended to avert much misunderstanding, and to lessen, in considerable measure, the labours of your Committee."

The Majority Report clears the Ministers of all blame in terms that must be read to be properly appreciated, since no account can do justice to the levity and hypocrisy with which the Liberal politicians reported to the House of Commons on matters at least sufficiently serious to have occupied their attention for nearly nine months. It is enough to say here that they were agreed that the American Company had no interest, direct or indirect, in the contract with the British Government, and that the Ministers had assured themselves of this before they purchased the shares; that the Ministers had received no favour from Mr Godfrey Isaacs but had bought the shares from Mr Harry Isaacs at "market price"; that on October 11 Sir Rufus Isaacs had taken the opportunity to inform the House on behalf of himself and his colleagues that all "such statements or suggestions" as had been rumoured against them were baseless fabrications. They concluded that the Ministers had acted throughout in the sincere belief that there was nothing in their action which could in any way conflict with their duty.

The only one of the three reports that need be discussed in detail here is the minority report, usually referred to as Lord Robert Cecil's. This was often subjected to that most scornful of epithets, beloved of Mr Booth, "a Party document," and indeed there were many circumstances that might have made it so. Apart from the long-sustained warfare between the opposing parties, Mr Falconer had stepped down to make way for Lord Robert Cecil in the main examination of the journalists who had contributed to the rumours. Lord Robert had then conducted this part of the inquiry with an air of revolted surprise and a determination that would have been impossible to anyone aware that, although the charges made against the Ministers were untrue, a major indiscretion had, nevertheless, taken place. He must have felt fooled when he realised the use that had been made of him, and, in any case, he had personally to receive the complaints of the journalists who felt they had been unfairly treated. But he and Amery were aware that, if a minority report was to be influential, it had to be just. One of them said later that every paragraph was scrupulously tested against the evidence and all struck out that could not be justified.

The result is a document of which in the main the worst that can be said is that it is harsh. The conclusions drawn from the evidence would hardly be disputed today. In two places, however, an opinion is formed or a suggestion made that is, at the least, ungenerous, and this was to mar its reception. It remains the only one of the three reports that gives a full account of the findings, and it was this account that the House of Commons was later to debate.

Reasons are early adduced for believing that the contract with the British Government would be of great if indirect benefit to all Marconi Companies. Chief of these was that "the erection of a chain of stations half-way round the globe would not only provide an additional traffic to existing longdistance stations on the Marconi system, but would . . . constitute an inducement for the erection of further stations, public or private, on the Marconi system rather than any other." Further, the five years' monopoly to build stations in the British Empire would put the Marconi Companies in a position of great advantage over all possible future competitors and act as a powerful lever to induce inventors to sell their patents to them.

In support of this reasoning, details are given of the effect of the signing of the tender, not merely on the English shares, but on the shares of all other Marconi Companies. During 1910 and early 1911 the shares of the English Company had stood between 12s. 6d. and 17s. 6d. From the start of the negotiations until April 1912 they rose steadily until they reached the figure of £9. 17s. 6d., and in the later stages this upward movement was closely reflected in the shares of other Companies such as the Canadian and the Spanish.[1]

After giving an account of the transactions by which Ministers acquired the shares and explaining that the only shares not under the control of Mr Godfrey Isaacs were those for which the American shareholders could apply, the report states that, although a few shares were sold to New York dealers, in general the shareholders could not be informed of their rights before the morning of the 19th. Paragraph 17 reads:

> A leading arbitrage dealer stated before the Committee that if he had been given an order for 10,000 shares on the evening of the 17th he would have had to pay 14 dollars (58s. 4d.). Even, therefore, if the transaction had been carried out in New York through arbitrage dealers, a purchase of 10,000 shares could not have been made at £2 on the evening of the 17th.

And paragraph 18 explains that the British public were not, in fact, given an opportunity of buying in New York, because the leading brokers and dealers agreed not to deal in the shares until the 19th. The brokers were all referred to Messrs Heybourn & Croft, and no order would have been carried out until opening day when the purchaser would have had to pay £3. 5s. 0d.

---

[1] The whole of this argument was controversial because the Liberals had made the most of the fact that there was only a small rise immediately after the signing of the tender. The Tories believed that acceptance had been anticipated and the rise had taken place beforehand. In any case, shortly afterwards the shares of all Companies rose again.

Nor would any ordinary member of the public have had information about the agreement with the Western Union Cable Company.

Having described the "atmosphere of reckless speculation and excitement" in London, the report states that, assuming a demand for the shares, as it was tolerably certain there would be, Messrs Isaacs and Heybourn were enabled to regulate the price within fairly wide limits.

> The offer, therefore, of April 9 to the Attorney-General was almost equivalent to an offer of a considerable though uncertain amount of money.

Finally it should not be forgotten that the rights to the shares offered to Sir Rufus actually belonged to the Marconi Company. "It is true that Mr Godfrey Isaacs told us that they had been sold to him. This account of the arrangement is not borne out by the minutes of the Company, very reluctantly produced by Mr Godfrey Isaacs, nor did Mr Marconi's recollection on the subject appear to be very clear." In any case, Godfrey Isaacs's rights to the shares were subject to his undertaking to place them, and they never actually came into his possession. When issued they belonged to the English Company, and were at the disposal of Mr Isaacs as agent of that Company.

Elsewhere the authors of the report say that, even if there had been no association between the British and American Companies, "the impropriety of which the Ministers . . . were primarily guilty, was that of making an advantageous purchase of shares upon information received from a government contractor, and that impropriety would remain the same whatever the character of the shares purchased." They say, however, that they do not accept that there was no association, because "the acquisition of the assets of the United Wireless Company . . . the arrangement with the cable companies, and the subsequent financial expansion of the American Company were all initiated and in the main carried through . . . by the English Company, whose prestige and financial position were essential to the success of all these operations. Moreover, the patents belonging to the American Company were the same as those of the English Company."

The authors speak throughout in severe terms of Godfrey Isaacs. Referring to the omission of Clause 16 from the circular announcing the terms of the tender, they say they were unable to accept "this curious explanation . . . and Mr Isaacs, in fact, regarded the condition as of so much importance that at first he asked that it should be kept secret."

They then say that Isaacs's account of the transactions was "not satisfactory," and that "owing to a decision of the majority of the Committee we were precluded from recalling Mr Isaacs in order to explain the discrepancy between his statements and the records produced."

In a further paragraph they seem to be grossly unfair to Isaacs. They suggest that, while the Attorney-General attributed the offer of shares to fraternal affection, it may have been due to other and less creditable motives—a suggestion of complete dishonesty in everyday dealings with family and friends. Yet if Isaacs had a fault, it is more likely that he interested himself too much in the advancement of his immediate circle. The Liberal press were not slow to point out that the Attorney-General was a very rich man in a distinguished position. If family affection was insufficient to secure his influence, why should Godfrey suppose that the offer of shares might be more successful?

Paragraph 45 of the Report contains the conclusions. Having acquitted the Ministers of the main charges of corruption and use of privileged information, the authors state that in their opinion the Attorney-General acted "with grave impropriety" in purchasing the shares "upon advice and information not then available to the public, given to him by the Managing Director of the English Marconi Company, which was in course of obtaining a contract of very great importance—a contract which even when concluded with the Government had to be ratified by the House of Commons," and that the Chancellor and the Chief Ministerial Whip were open to the same censure. The impropriety was increased, they continue, because the shares were taken from Mr Harry Isaacs, who had taken them on even more advantageous terms from Mr Godfrey Isaacs, at a time when the shares could not have been bought on the Stock Exchange and at a price at which they could not have been bought by any ordinary member of the public. They state that in their opinion the Marconi Company of America was materially interested, although indirectly, in the contract and that it was therefore, "apart from any question of purchase on special information, or on special terms, highly inadvisable for Ministers to take shares in the American Marconi

Company, while the agreement was pending."

Then, having said that they held that the transaction of the Chancellor of the Exchequer, and to a lesser degree that of the Attorney-General, were in the nature of speculation rather than investment, and having censured the Postmaster-General for trying to obtain ratification of the contract after he knew of the share transactions, they state:

> We find that the rumours current in the City of London as to the connection between Ministers and Marconi shares, however recklessly and inaccurately expressed, arose chiefly from distorted accounts of Ministerial dealings in the shares of the American Marconi Company, and that they were not the mere invention of journalists. . . .
>
> We are of opinion that the persistence of rumours and suspicions has been largely due to the reticence of Ministers, particularly in the debate of October 1912. We regard that reticence as a grave error of judgment and as wanting in frankness and in respect for the House of Commons.

(16)

The Final Debate

1

After the sensation of the absconding Mr Fenner and with the publication of the Reports the Marconi case overshadowed all other topics of public affairs in the news In the month of June 1913 *The Times* published altogether six leaders on the subject, five of them first leaders.

The Majority Report outraged Conservative opinion without pleasing Liberal. It was immediately labelled a "whitewashing report" and those Liberal papers which could not join with the Conservative press in condemning it gave it little space and concentrated on criticism of Lord Robert Cecil's. Government opinion did not underestimate the seriousness of the situation. In the *Nation* of June 14 a writer under the title "A Wayfarer" said:

> Liberal members of the Committee are perhaps surprised to find how gravely the current of feeling runs. The *mot* of a Liberal Member best crystallises the view of one section:—"Murray should be repudi- ated, Isaacs should resign, George should express regrets."
>
> I think most are definitely against the Chancellor's resignation, and deem it quite sufficient that he should express regrets. . . . No such

feeling exists in the case of Sir Rufus Isaacs, who may be a great lawyer, but is not a great politician, and to whom belongs the initiatory blame. Much depends on how he shoulders it, and a good deal on the tone of Mr George's speech.

While H. G. Wells, writing as a Liberal, said:[1]

> What has gripped our imagination is not Mr Lloyd George trying, as most of us would be quite ready to try, to improve a modest and justifiable little income in investment by a favourable purchase, but Mr Booth and Mr Falconer interrupting questions: that is the real scandal. What was at the back of the minds of these portentous gentlemen? No doubt there was nothing to hide; but what did they think they were hiding?[2]

And a *Times* leader probably summed up general opinion when it remarked that the pailful of whitewash instead of whitening Ministers had blackened the Committee.

More serious for the Government than any press comment were the results of two by-elections, at Newmarket and at Altrincham. Previously it had been difficult to assess the true state of public opinion on the Marconi case because of the rigidity of the party split. The Liberal press had on the occasion of each new revelation been ready to accept the most implausible interpretation of the facts and to adopt the view that criticism of the Ministers was part of an unworthy political campaign. Now at these two by-elections, during both of which the Marconi case was treated as a major issue, the electorate

---

[1] Quoted by Bonar Law in the House of Commons.

[2] Mr Booth was in 1917 the defendant in the celebrated case of *Gruban v. Booth*. Sir Patrick Hastings in cross-examination exposed a peculiarly cruel fraud against a business partner who, being of German origin, was very vulnerable at the time. During the course of perpetrating this fraud Booth had boasted of his power over Lloyd George, who, he claimed, was indebted to him for services in the Marconi scandal. Damages of £4750 were awarded and Mr Booth's public career was at an end.

registered their opinion in two decisive Government reverses.

The Select Committee having achieved nothing but an increasing contempt for the Liberal Party, it became perfectly clear that the issue must be decided in the House of Commons itself, and that more than the careers of the Ministers might rest on the result of the debate.

Sir Rufus Isaacs and Lloyd George had steadily refused to admit any of the implications of their transactions, but there is no doubt they both understood that their future depended on the imminent verdict of the House of Commons, and that they suffered terribly under the strain. Lord Reading says that, although outwardly calm, in his own family circle Sir Rufus was sadly changed.

> One day at the height of the controversy I came unexpectedly into his room . . . and found him sitting at his desk, his head resting on his hands, gazing silently before him. For some minutes he neither moved nor spoke and then, turning towards me, he said:
>
> "I had hoped to hand on to you so much, and now it looks as if I shall have nothing to hand on to you that you will want."[3]

And Mr Frank Owen speaks of Lloyd George in highly dramatic terms:

> He lost weight, lost vitality, fell ill again, and his black hair grew grey, the lines began to mark his face, and for the first time in public he was seen to use spectacles. A great life poised on the edge.[4]

At this time the Prime Minister made his only recorded intervention. He called Haldane into consultation and together they saw the Chancellor and the Attorney-General. Of this interview Haldane wrote to his mother:

> An unpleasant and to me very distasteful business. I hate saying "Thank God I am not as other men are," but I am heartily thankful

---

[3] *Rufus Isaacs*, 273.
[4] *Tempestuous Journey*, 236.

that I have never had any temptation to try and make money by investments. It is apt to be a slippery business. I don't think that in this case there has been more than indiscretion, but the public incited by an opposition out for party gains always believes the worst, and even a small indiscretion may do much harm. Asquith as usual is very calm and judicial but it adds to the difficulties of which he has enough on his hands.[5]

2

The Times suggested that the Government had difficulty in finding a form of words for the Motion, and that, while this difficulty was still unsolved, the Opposition, taking them by surprise, placed a Motion on the Order paper. In any case on June 18 Mr Cave moved a resolution for the Opposition in the following terms:

> That this House regrets the transactions of certain of His Majesty's Ministers in the shares of the Marconi Company of America, and the want of frankness displayed by Ministers in their communications on the subject to the House.

The debate lasted two days and during the whole of this time the House of Commons was overcrowded with Members from both Houses and with distinguished visitors. Among those who sat right through the two days in the Strangers' Gallery was Godfrey Isaacs.

Cave moved the Resolution in terms which won much praise for his moderation and fairness from both sides of the House and from the Attorney-General himself. He suggested that there were three rules which a Minister of the Crown must observe. (1) In choosing his investments he should not make use of confidential information which comes to him as a Minister of the Crown. (2) He should not invest in companies whose profits or dividends depend directly or indirectly upon contracts entered into with

---

[5]   Maurice, *The Life of Viscount Haldane of Cloan*, 1, 329.

the Government. (3) He should not receive, in relation to his investments, or for any other purpose, any favour or advantage direct or indirect from a person contracting or proposing to contract with the Crown.

He completely absolved the Ministers of any infringement of the first rule, but he thought the second and third had not been fully observed.

When he sought to show that the Ministers had taken an interest in a company which had an interest in a government contract, he remarked it had been said that the Ministers had not realised it was so.

Well, sir, I am anxious to believe that. But I am afraid if that defence is accepted as excusing the breaches of the rule, it must be at the expense of the reputation of those gentlemen for intelligence. The facts . . . were open to them. . . . I notice that one hon. gentleman opposite who volunteered an apology or defence of the Chancellor of the Exchequer put his defence in this way . . . He said: 'The Chancellor of the Exchequer is a child in these things, artless, ingenuous, impulsive and confiding."

Is that the defence which we are to hear, and is the description accepted by the Attorney-General also?

Of the investment of Liberal Party funds he said:

Lord Murray has the advantage, or disadvantage, of being absent, and we have yet to hear his explanation . . . But there is this consideration which lies on the surface. If this was a purchase simply for re-sale, it is a matter which does not concern us so closely as hon. gentlemen opposite. It is for them to say how far they are satisfied that party funds should be used in a Stock Exchange speculation, and that funds to be utilised for the promoting of the political objects they have in view, such for instance as the Disendowment of the Church, should be obtained by a gamble on the Stock Exchange. If, on the other hand, it was a purchase for investment . . . the effect was this, that the financial interests of the party opposite and the whole influence of their Chief Whip were involved in the success of the American Marconi Company, which itself depended to some extent upon the Parliamentary confirmation of

212

the contract . . . If hon. gentlemen are satisfied with that transaction they will tell us so presently.

The second charge was of want of frankness with the House, and Mr Cave told the whole story of the October 11 debate, the *Matin* trail, the failure to inform the and remarked that Lord Murray at least had made it quite clear that he had not intended to disclose his transactions, while only the absconding Mr Fenner had revealed the purchase for the Liberal Party Fund. Then he passed to the Reports of the Committee. Speaking of Lord Robert Cecil, he said:

> He proposed to state the facts as he viewed them, and I am not sure that his view of the facts differed very much from the view of the Chairman of the Committee. He proposed to censure, in somewhat more severe terms, I agree, the action of the Ministers impugned, also upon the grounds which I have put before the House. What did the Committee do? The majority rejected both those reports. They threw over entirely the draft of my noble friend. They nominally took the draft Report of the Chairman of the Committee. They struck out of it the bulk of the facts—twenty-six paragraphs went at one blow in one amendment. The other paragraphs were mutilated beyond recognition, and in the result, without finding the facts, they put before the House their conclusions. They brought in an acquittal—an acquittal in, I think, somewhat fulsome terms—of the Ministers concerned on the charges of corruption which had been made by some persons against them—an acquittal which was perfectly just, and which appeared in both of the draft Reports. But as regards the other matters to which evidence given before the Committee had been directed . . . they not only omitted to find the facts, but they thrust the charges aside with the flimsiest possible excuses—excuses which will not bear a moment's investigation. . . . I say that in taking that course the majority of the Committee did not perform their duty to the House. They rendered the worst possible service to their colleagues in the Cabinet, and they are directly responsible for the Motion which I am bringing forward.

He concluded his address to the House by asking:

Are you going to say that the Ministers are without blame? Are you going to say that in their place you would have taken the same course, and that, if the opportunity arises, you will take the same course in the future? If so, I think you will strike a blow not only at the position and influence of this House, but at all the rules which ought to regulate public life. Our course is perfectly clear. . . . What we want to do is to place upon the Journals of this House a Resolution which shall show clearly that, in the opinion of the House as a whole, the course taken by Ministers concerned is a breach of the best of our traditions, that our Rules have been infringed, and that they shall never with impunity be violated again.

Viscount Helmsley, seconding the Motion, complained that no Minister had made the slightest suggestion that he regretted his action. "Ministers have up to the present said that their action is entirely without blame." If they had a regret, he thought it was only in the light of subsequent events. He accused Mr Samuel of having tried to push through the contract because it would be to the advantage of his colleagues, and he said that there had been an effort, "and it looks to me like a resolute effort," not to disclose anything to the House or the Committee which they did not already know or to admit to any indiscretions of any kind.

When he sat down, Sir Rufus Isaacs, amid the cheers of his own party, rose in his place. He said first that, in accordance with precedent, when he and the Chancellor of the Exchequer had made a statement they would leave the House. They were therefore entitled to assume that all that would be said against them had been said by the hon. and learned Member who moved it and by the Noble Lord who seconded it. Then he turned to address the House.

Sir Rufus had not the command of language which was to distinguish much of the rest of the debate. But he was fighting, one might say, for his life, and he made an able speech, while his appearance and delivery awoke sympathy. He began by saying that he rose first because in historical order he was the first in the transaction. Whatever blame was attached should fall on him.

214

Dealing then with the charge of concealment, he said that Mr Cave had made no charge of intentional concealment. "What I understood him to say and the complaint which he made was that we had not stated all these facts on the occasion of October 11. I agree with him . . . and I say to the House as a whole . . . that the course we pursued, and which I will explain in a moment in a little more detail, I think now and by the light of all that has happened was a mistaken one." But he thought this was not really the matter that was before the House, since the words of the Resolution, if placed on the Journals of the House, were wide enough to suggest intentional concealment.

In case there should be any doubt in the minds of any as to the meaning . . . the Noble Lord has made it perfectly plain so that no one can have any doubt. As I followed what he said—and again I say he will correct me if I am wrong—he did say, as I thought, very deliberately that there was intentional concealment.

Viscount Helmsley. I do not know what the learned Attorney-General means by the word "intentional." I presume that it must have been discussed whether it should be mentioned or not, and it was decided not to mention it.

Sir Rufus Isaacs. The Noble Lord, I am sure, does not wish to shelter himself behind any quibble. . . . There can be no difficulty in understanding what I am saying. . . . To come to a conclusion that a thing need not be stated, may be, of course, a perfectly honest and a perfectly moral transaction, and at the same time may be one which you may regret hereafter. But to come to a conclusion that you will make a statement for the purpose of covering up a transaction so as to deceive those who are listening is a very immoral transaction. . . . If he means the first, I quite follow him. Does he mean that in the statement that was made, and in the course that we took, we intended to deceive?

Viscount Helmsley. What I mean by "intentional" is this: presumably the alternative courses were discussed by the Attorney-General with other people whether or not to mention it, and he decided not to mention it. In that case his decision was intentional. I also think he thought it was wiser that the House should not have that information on that date.

Sir Rufus Isaacs. I will not pursue the matter, but I am still rather at a loss to understand the Noble Lord.

Sir Rufus now returned to the circumstances of the debate. He said little that was new, stating as so often before that he had thought the Select Committee the proper place to make a full statement. Ministers had expressed their willingness to appear.

> The moment you have got that fact, I submit to the House that any intentional concealment, in the sense of deceiving the House, absolutely disappears. There is no charge which to my mind is so odious as that which imputes to men who stand in the relationship which we do to each other as Members of this House, that one Member has attempted in a statement or explanation given at the Table to deceive. I am sure there is no Member of this House who would not resent, and resent most bitterly, even the faintest suggestion of any such intention. I assure the House that no such intention was ever present in our minds—that all we meant was that this was not the opportunity; that the proper opportunity was at the Select Committee.

Sir Rufus said that he should not be judged on the facts as they had afterwards emerged, but on the facts as they were known to him at the time. He had regarded the tender as a "business agreement" and he had known of no wireless Company other than the Marconi "except the Lodge Muirhead, because I knew of a patent action which took place a year or eighteen months before." He insisted again on the distinction between Godfrey and Harry, and then he said:

> Let me add one word further, that the offer was never made to me by him as a Government contractor. It was made by him as a brother to me and to my other brother. Let me ask, would the rule . . . apply to my brother, who chose, for example, on my silver wedding day to send me a present on which he may have spent a couple of hundred pounds? It would apply to a Government contractor in the ordinary way.

216

Sir Rufus said that he did not want the House to judge his transaction on any standard lower than had been applied by the House at any time.

> Aye, I go further, and say that I do not ask the House to judge my conduct by any lower standard than has been imposed by the Liberal Party as applicable to Ministers and that is the higher test. (A Right Hon. Member: I do not think so.) I think I am justified in saying it is the higher test. . . . I put forward this rule which I think is the closest to the case. A Minister should not place himself in a position which might reasonably expose him, in the opinion of fair-minded men, to the suspicion of corruption even though his own conscience is clear. . . . In my view no one can protect himself against the suspicions of prejudiced persons. No one can guard against the suspicions of the evilly-disposed. . . . It never occurred to me that any human being could suspect me of corruption because I purchased American Marconi shares some six weeks after the announcement was made of the acceptance of the tender of the British Marconi Company by the British Government.

He then made the statement from which the phrase italicised has been quoted by various writers with equal conviction to show his innocence and to show the ludicrous vanity of the claims he made.

> I say now that if I had had all the facts present to my mind at the time I entered into the transaction, if I had known then all that I know now, if all had been disclosed to me which subsequent events have revealed, *if I had realised that men could be so suspicious of any act of mine*, if I had thought that such misrepresentation could possibly exist, I state plainly that I would not have entered into the transaction.

And he added:

> I have the gravest doubt at this moment whether the rule that I formulated can be said to apply to this case—I have the gravest doubt whether it could be said that any fair-minded man could have come to

the conclusion or could have suspected that I had been guilty of corruption if he knew that I had bought American Marconi shares—but I will not balance it on too fine a point; I will state that I should not have gone into the transaction.

Then he concluded:

> This House may lay down rules, but in the end it is not rules but the high principle and the public honour of our public men, to whatever party they belong, which are the best safeguards for the purity of our public life.

When the Chancellor of the Exchequer arose he was in a more belligerent mood. He began by saying that he would have liked to examine the rule that Ministers ought not to have shares in companies which contract with the Government in the light of precedents, but he refrained because he did not wish to appear to escape from his responsibility by recriminating on political opponents.

He assured the House there had been no intention of concealment on October 11 and then he spoke at length and with great and justifiable bitterness about the rumours and the newspaper slanders. He fell into a wrangle with Walter Guinness, the owner of the *Outlook*, which was later to cause an interruption while Guinness made a statement, a fairly unsatisfactory statement most people would think. Lloyd George said it was impossible to consider the charges of indiscretion in the atmosphere created by the grosser charges. There was an inaudible interruption when he said that the Committee had found nothing to justify any man in suspecting corruption, and Lloyd George turned and asked:

> Does any hon. gentleman say that there was ground for suspecting corruption? Is not that exactly what I said? Although it is indiscretion on paper . . . in the background it is corruption, which you will hear for months when it cannot be refuted. The charge has been exploded, but the deadly after-damp remains and the noxious fumes of these slanders are at this very moment poisoning the blood of people who are

considering even minor charges which are brought against us.

He then appealed to the House to consider the charges fairly and as remotely as possible from the atmosphere created, and he said:

> I am not going to qualify any statement I will make as to whether it was judicious. I do not mind whether you use the word "judicious" or "wise" or "discreet." I say that looking at all the circumstances it was neither. I do not want to palter about words. I do not care which of the three words is used. I accept any of them. It was not. I would certainly not have gone through it again.

He said that there was, nevertheless, a vast difference between an indiscretion that may be rebuked and an indiscretion that warranted a solemn vote of censure from the House. He described how he had come to make the purchase and said he had had nothing to do with the negotiations and had thought the contract was definite.

> I did not know all the details. I did not examine the charters of incorporation. . . . The utmost that the hon. and learned gentleman can say is that I ought to have scrutinized all these documents before I entered upon this transaction. I realise frankly all the misconstruction that can be placed upon it—the same name, Marconi, an honoured name and still will be when all this is forgotten. Had I foreseen that the whole contract was going to be made a matter of fierce controversy between the parties; had I foreseen that the very name Marconi would rouse the most fierce political passions; had I foreseen that charges of corruption would be brought against Ministers, it would have been crass folly to have entered into that transaction at all.

Finally he dealt with the question of speculation. The point he made was that he could have paid for the shares and was not forced to borrow from his brokers. "I was in a position then to pay, and I can only say it was carelessness on my part."

Then he concluded:

219

I am conscious of having done nothing which brings a stain upon the honour of a Minister of the Crown. If you will, I acted thoughtlessly, I acted carelessly, I acted mistakenly, but I acted innocently, I acted openly and I acted honestly. That is why I, with confidence, place myself in the hands, not merely of my political friends, but of Members in all parts of this great assembly.

The Attorney-General and the Chancellor of the Exchequer then withdrew.

3

Lord Robert Cecil followed the two Ministers and in a long speech dealt with all the questions discussed in his report and with the conduct of the Inquiry. He made one rather remarkable statement. He said:

I have been told that in the Report which appears in my name I have endeavoured to make the worst of the charges against Ministers. . . . But it is not true. I can assure hon. Members that if I had really wished to make a flaming Report against them I could have said a great many things which I did not say, because I thought it would not be fair to put in the Report what I considered was not supported by evidence. I am quite willing to tell any hon. Member frankly some of the things which I did not put in the Report, and in regard to which I do not think there is sufficient evidence on which to put them before this House and the country.

Mr Chiozza Money. You ought to state them.

Lord Robert Cecil. I shall be very glad to tell the hon. Member privately but I do not think it is fair to state in public what I do not think there is sufficient evidence to justify my putting into the Report.

Mr Chiozza Money. The Noble Lord has made them now by innuendo.

Mr Buckmaster (Liberal) now moved an Amendment:

220

That this House, after hearing the statements of Mr Attorney-General and Mr Chancellor of the Exchequer in reference to their purchase of shares in the Marconi Company of America, accepts those statements, and deems it right to put on record its reprobation of the false charges, of the gravest description, brought against Ministers, which have proved to be wholly devoid of foundation.

Later Mr MacMaster, Sir Walter Essex and Sir Frederick Banbury spoke and showed, as later Mr Falconer would also, that party feeling, ill-will and an irresponsible approach to matters of supreme importance to their fellow-men were not confined to either side of the House. MacMaster presented the facts in a really evil light, suggesting motives that had not before occurred to anyone. Falconer spoke for over two hours. It was a speech his colleagues on the Committee had constantly heard, and, although he considerably expanded it, he made it no more comprehensible. Its reception was ironic.

When Mr Samuel rose to make the explanation he had also often made before, he complained that, although his name had been connected with the charges and he had been completely cleared, no one had felt it necessary to exonerate him in the Motion before the House. To this Mr Alfred Lyttelton replied: "His complaint was that he was not included in the Motion . . . submitted to the House. I should have thought he would have been very glad not to have been included."

This speech concluded the first day of the debate. On the following morning *The Times* published a leader which has become famous in this case.

We have no wish to treat an apology ungenerously, and we are very glad that it has been made; but we are bound to point out that neither Minister seems to understand how their conduct strikes the public. It may be put by way of a metaphor. A man is not blamed for being splashed with mud. He is commiserated. But if he has stepped into a puddle which he might easily have avoided we say that it is his own fault. If he protests that he did not know it was a puddle, we say that he ought to know better, but if he says that it was after all quite a clean puddle, then we judge him deficient in the sense of cleanliness. And the British people like their public men to have a very nice sense of cleanliness. . . . If Ministers are so innocent and careless as not to know a puddle when they see one, then they ought not to occupy their extremely responsible positions.

4

When Asquith rose on the second day of the debate he began with an attack. He spoke in strong terms of the rumours and slanders in the press and said that no one who had followed the history of the case could be blind to the fact that "the most disgraceful appeals were made from the beginning to racial and religious animosity." He said that the charges had been rejected by unanimous and emphatic decision of the Committee, but he was bound to call attention to an observation made by Lord Robert Cecil which it was impossible to pass. He then quoted the first of the passages from Lord Robert's speech quoted here and said: "What an extraordinary dictum from a judicial mind. Not content with that the Noble Lord goes on to say very kindly"—and here he quoted the rest of the exchange with Mr Chiozza Money. "I make no comment upon that. It is a passage that speaks for itself, and which, I am afraid, throws some light on the spirit in which the Motion has been moved."

The Prime Minister went on to say that the charges against the Ministers having been declared without foundation by unanimous and emphatic decision, this surely ought to have been in the very forefront of the Motion. When he said that this was no doubt what had led Mr Buckmaster to supply what was wanted, there was laughter in the House and he continued:

> Is it not wanting, an omission of so grave a character, if the House is to record its judgment on the subject, and to declare that it is the unanimous opinion of this House that Ministers have been foully traduced? But there is another aspect of the hon. and learned gentleman's Motion . . . to which I can in no circumstances, and certainly not after what happened yesterday, advise the House to assent. It is, both in substance and in terms, a Vote of Censure upon the Ministers concerned.

Asquith now spoke of the two charges and of the Ministers' statements. At the time it was a very effective speech and it was acclaimed as a great one; but when the life has gone, when the prestige of the Leader of the House and the dignity of the great personality are no longer present, it takes more than a high intellectual manner, a lofty moral plane to impress—it needs a good brief. He had made the most of the opportunity to put the Opposition in the wrong, and now he made the most of the Ministers' statements. At times he gave the impression that he was incompletely informed on the facts of the case, and this in itself was curiously effective, since it implied that here was a molehill blown to a full-sized volcano by the breath expended on it.

The House has heard from my two right hon. friends what they have to say. . . . I do not think I have ever heard, or that anybody has ever heard, a franker or more manly explanation. They both admit fully and freely that it would have been better for them at the time of the debate in October to have given to the House a full statement of these transactions, and they regret that they did not do so. But at the same time they both give reasons for their reticence, if that is the proper term to be used, on that occasion which seems to me and I think must seem to all fair-minded men . . . to acquit them of the very serious charge of want of frankness.

He then spoke of his own part. He said that he had been told of the transaction by the Master of Elibank at the end of July or the beginning of August and later in a letter from the Attorney-General which he was sorry he had not kept. He did not know the date of the transaction, he did not know the amount of the purchase, he did not know the price given, and he did not know any of the circumstances of the transaction.

I am bound to tell the House that, not because it has any bearing on the question of the conduct of my right hon. friends, but because it is my duty, as it is the duty of everybody, to make a perfectly full disclosure. I was not present at the Debate which took place in October . . . through a slight indisposition . . . and I held no communication of any sort or kind with my right hon. friends with regard to statements they made. But I read them, and so little importance did I attach to what I had been told—and I have told the House the whole of it—that I really believe that at that moment it had almost passed out of my mind. It seemed to me to have no relevancy of any sort or kind to these calumnious rumours . . . I thought this was a matter of no concern.

Having said that the Ministers had meant to seize the earliest opportunity to go before the Committee, he continued :

> For some reason or other which I do not know, the Committee had been occupied, I daresay quite properly, in the intervening weeks, in the discussion of other aspects of the matter, and my right hon. friends assured me that it was their desire to go before the Committee and tell them everything.
>
> *Lord Robert Cecil.* Why did they not do so?
>
> *The Prime Minister.* That is exactly what they did. . . .
>
> *Mr Goulding.* They told two colleagues on the Committee.
>
> *Prime Minister.* I know nothing about that. They went before the Committee. They told the Committee every detail of the story without any kind of concealment, reservation, or equivocation whatsoever. The Committee was put by them in possession of the whole of the facts.

The Prime Minister now passed to a consideration of the code of rules of conduct for Ministers and other persons in official positions. He remarked that a most extravagant and hysterical standard was being set up which would make the carrying on of the government of the country by business men absolutely impossible, and he illustrated this thesis. He then defined the rules which, in his opinion, must be observed, and, although these did not differ materially from those laid down by Mr Cave, the Asquith rules have acquired some authority over the House of Commons and have since been referred to when the conduct required of Ministers is considered. He said:

> The first of course, and the most obvious is that Ministers ought not to enter into any transaction whereby their private pecuniary interests might, even conceivably, come into conflict with their public duty. There is no dispute about that. Again, no Minister is justified under any

circumstances in using official information, information that has come to him as a Minister, for his own private profit or for that of his friends. Further, no Minister ought to allow or to put himself in a position to be tempted to use his official influence in support of any scheme or in furtherance of any contract in regard to which he has an undisclosed private interest. That again is beyond dispute. Again, no Minister ought to accept from persons who are in negotiation with, or seeking to enter into contractual or proprietary relations with, the State any kind of favour. That, I think, is also beyond dispute. I will add a further proposition, which I am not sure has been completely formulated, though it has no doubt been adumbrated in the course of these debates, and that is that Ministers should scrupulously avoid speculative investments in securities as to which, from their position and their special means of early or confidential information, they have or may have an advantage over other people in anticipating market changes. . . .

Those, in my opinion, are rules of positive obligation. . . .

I go a step further, and I say that I think in addition to those rules, which I have described as rules of obligation—because it seems to me that they have an ethical value and sanction, as well as being based on grounds of expediency and policy—there are, or there certainly ought to be, rules of prudence specially applicable to Ministers and to persons in positions of official responsibility, rules which perhaps never have been formulated and which it would be very difficult to formulate in precise or universal terms. One of those rules is that in these matters such persons should carefully avoid all transactions which can give colour or countenance to the belief that they are doing anything which the rules of obligation forbid. It was that rule, which I call a rule of prudence, which, in my opinion and in the opinion of my right hon. friends and colleagues, was not fully observed, though with complete innocence of intention, in this case.

Speaking of Lord Murray, Asquith said:

I owe to him for his loyalty, assiduous and faithful service . . . a debt which it is impossible for me to measure, and during the whole

225

of that time I never saw anything in his language or his conduct which led me to entertain the faintest doubt, either of the soundness of his judgment or the integrity of his character. I say therefore in regard to this charge of want of frankness, it is impossible that it can be substantiated, and it ought not to be assented to by the House of Commons.

And finally, of Rufus Isaacs and Lloyd George:

Their honour, both their private and their public honour, is at this moment absolutely unstained. They have, as this Committee has shown by its unanimous verdict, abused no public trust. They retain, I can say this with full assurance, the complete confidence of their colleagues and of their political associates. We ask the House, in view of what they said yesterday, and of the considerations which I have endeavoured to summarise today, to say in the language of the Amendment . . . that it reprobates the infamous calumnies—that has been conclusively disproved—by which the characters of these Ministers have been assailed, and that, having heard their statements with regard to this particular transaction in which their honour is not involved, though their judgment may be impeached, the House accepts those statements, and desires to put that acceptance on its records.

When Asquith sat down it was felt on the Government benches that a great advance had been made. His attack on the generosity of the Motion and his lofty view of the issues involved had put the Opposition for the first time on the defensive. Then Balfour rose to make one of the finest speeches of his career. He spoke immediately of Asquith's complaint, and having pointed out that all three reports unequivocally rejected the charges of corruption, he said:

It is quite true that no such protest appears in the terms of the Resolution, but, speaking for myself, I can most truly say that it never even occurred to me that in this House any such protest was necessary. I have spoken, as everybody in this House has spoken, on countless occasions with Members of the House, and with persons of repute and

226

credit outside the House—indeed this wretched subject could not be avoided wherever one went, unless one buried oneself in the heart of the desert of Sahara—and in not one of those conversations from any man that I came across in personal intercourse in this House, or out of this House, did I ever yet hear the suggestion that either the Chancellor of the Exchequer or the Attorney-General had been guilty of personal corruption (Hon. Members: Oh, oh!). It may be that I have been more fortunate in the company I keep than hon. gentlemen opposite. I can most sincerely assure the House that is the absolute fact. . . . After all, neither the Committee nor this House approaches this sort of questions, or ought to approach them, as I suppose such questions might be approached in a Police Court or a Criminal Court. . . . We do not go about saying "So-and-so is innocent, I believe, because he is not proved guilty." . . . It never occurred to me to trouble my head about the truth of these accusations against the Attorney-General and the Chancellor of the Exchequer, not because I examined the evidence: I do not know even that I would take the trouble to examine the evidence on that particular aspect of the question, because I think the thing is absurd on the face of it. Remember, I have sat opposite these gentlemen through their whole Parliamentary career. I have been able to judge them as we all judge each other. There is not a Member of the House who has taken any active part in our Debates, and who is known, who has not got his character well established in essentials in the judgment of any of those, be they his friends or enemies, with whom he has ever come in contact, and I would no more believe, with or without evidence, that the Chancellor of the Exchequer and the Attorney-General had been guilty of putting their hands into the till, or that they had done a thing which no man of honour could do, or that they had done things for which men should be hounded from private and public life—I would no more believe that, with or without evidence, than I would believe a similar charge against my own nearest relation . . . If the Government think, after what has occurred, that really this particular certificate of character should be given to their colleagues, I for my part am perfectly ready to endorse it, and I do not believe there is a man on this side of the House, not the severest critic of the conduct of the two right hon.

gentlemen, who would not be delighted to say, if thought necessary, not only that they had not been proved to be guilty of corruption, but, much further than that, that the idea of corruption was utterly out of the question, and that it was not before us at all.

When Balfour turned to the charges that were before the House he scored heavily because, almost for the first time in the whole of this case, he broke through the construction of artificial verbiage that had been built round it and spoke in real terms of the events that had occurred. He said, speaking of October 11:

> I think I understand the sort of thing that occurred, though I admit that the explanations given yesterday to me do not seem to throw much light on it. What I believe happened was this, that the Attorney-General and his colleagues, conscious that they were perfectly innocent of any corrupt motive or any corrupt proceeding, began to be uneasy, in face of those rumours, about their connection with the American Marconi Company, and they did consider, and they must have considered, whether they ought or ought not to give all their information openly to the House on 11 October. They must have thought about that. I think they said so, but, whether they said so or not, the thing is obvious. I suppose they decided that in their view at the time there was no connection between the companies—an erroneous view—and they based upon that in their own minds and consciences the conclusion that the House had really no right to know about their private investments, and that unless those investments touched upon the public case they were not travelling beyond their duty when they maintained this most unfortunate and most unhappy reticence. We are all apt, in such cases, when our own conduct is in question, to take the wrong course; we are all apt to err, or there is a certain inclination to err, on the side of want of frankness. They did err on the side of want of frankness, and there has been no defence really put forward on this point. How, for example, is this simple question going to be answered? . . . The Attorney-General, as I understood, said it was not proper to tell all to the House of Commons, but it was proper to tell it to the Committee.

Mr Booth. To the Committee first.

Mr Balfour. To the Committee first . . . Honestly, I do not see the point of that, and he gave no reason or explanation that I remember for it. But let us grant that there was a reason . . . grant that, and would not the very first thing that would have occurred to anybody be that they would write to the Chairman of the Committee and say to him: "There are things that we did not think it appropriate or relevant to say on 11 October before the House, but which we think you, who are investigating this matter, ought to know. Will you call us, and we will tell you all about it?" . . . The whole matter would have been frankly put before the Committee and the public, instead of coming out this in one way and that in another, a Law Court here, a stockbroker there, and all the various accidents through which the Committee at last arrived at the full knowledge of the facts. That is the reason why I am quite unable to accept the statement of the Prime Minister that this House, or the Committee representing this House, has been treated with anything deserving to be called frankness.

Later he said:

I think I told the House I thought I understood what had really passed in the minds of Ministers when they refused to take the House into their confidence on 11 October. May I say now what I think passed in the minds of the Attorney-General and the Chancellor of the Exchequer and of Lord Murray when they bought the shares. The Majority of the Committee with that, I was going to say partisan ineptitude, at any rate with great ineptitude, said . . . that "the Attorney-General, after carefully considering"—is not that the phrase—came to the conclusion that the transaction was perfectly proper. If the Attorney-General had carefully considered it, . . . he never could have come to the conclusion that it was a proper transaction. The real fact is he never did consider it. That is the naked truth of the matter. . . . I say that if the Attorney-General really made special inquiry, as this unhappy Majority assert, his case would be absolutely indefensible, and not all the advocacy of that Front Bench could justify the course which he pursued. But, of course, he made no inquiry, no special inquiry, at all. He merely asked his brother, I suppose, such questions as whether if the British company made large dividends, the American company would share, or whether any direct profit would come to the American company from the success of the British company; and, of course, his brother, who is a financier and not a statesman, said quite truly that the mere addition of dividends to the British company would not affect the American company. He never pointed out—why should he?—why should it occur to him?—that he was in the middle of contractual arrangements with the Government, that he was offering to his brother special terms, that he was offering special terms to a member of the Government who might be brought into consultation on the matter either at that moment or years afterwards . . . and that the fortunes of the American company would be disastrously affected if the arrangement with the British company fell through . . . If the Attorney-General had made special inquiry he must have known that all these things were true. If he had known that all these things were true he could not as a man of honour have taken the shares. . . . He rushed, most unfortunately, into the matter, and, as he went in, I admit that I am not at all surprised, nor do I blame the Chancellor of the Exchequer and the Patronage Secretary for thinking that where the head of the English Bar, accustomed to commercial matters, thought he might safety tread, they might safely follow. I have no doubt that that is the real account of what occurred. But is that a justification, is that a reason for this House not expressing regret that such a course should have been pursued? I think not.

Balfour expressed his disapproval of the speculative nature of the Chancellor's transactions, and then he turned to the point which, in the end, was to divide the House.

The real truth is again that while the Prime Minister told us throughout his speech that the Ministers, with whose conduct we are concerned at the moment, had expressed regret, the word "regret" appeared very seldom, if at all, in the course of their speeches. If it appeared it was

230

regret that such difficulties had arisen subsequent to their operations, and in consequence of events for which I am bound to say they were not themselves responsible. I do not remember any regret being expressed. I may be wrong; I hope I am wrong; but I do not remember the Attorney-General saying that he greatly regretted that he had not looked carefully into the character of the stock which he purchased, and I do not remember the Chancellor of the Exchequer saying that he greatly regretted having, when he purchased that stock, used it for speculative purposes. They gave explanations which did not explain either of these things. Nor can they be explained. They are the blunders which honest men may fall into; which honest men in this case have fallen into; and whenever they are fallen into, the best that those concerned can do is, without any attempted explanation, simply to say that they made a profound mistake and are very sorry for it. . . .

May I put this question to the Leader of the House? When he got up he said he had hoped we might come to a unanimous conclusion in this debate. There are two proposals before us. . . . We entirely agree with the substance of the Amendment moved by the learned gentleman opposite. Do hon. gentlemen opposite agree with the substance of the Resolution? If that is so, by the mere process of running the Resolution and the Amendment together you may obtain complete unanimity.

Balfour then said that he feared the Prime Minister might not be prepared to accept his part.

Apparently his reason for not doing so is that it would be a Vote of Censure on the Ministers. I do not in the least care about censuring Ministers. I have no wish to do it one way or the other. What I do wish the House to do is to leave on record something which indicates regret at what has taken place.

He then said that he believed in its heart the House was absolutely agreed on both the Resolution and the Amendment and that if the Prime Minister would find a form of words to express what they all felt, he would find no enemies among them.

If you do not do that . . . in what position is this House going to be? The one document . . . which will remain on public record will be the Majority Report of the Committee upstairs, a Report which not only does not express regret, but rejoices in the whole performance.

If, he said, the party majority rejected the Opposition half of the joint Resolution, many a Liberal would leave the House knowing he had voted against his convictions, and they would have to confess that after all the talk of purity and honour they had been unable to find a form of words to indicate even the smallest regret that the Leader of the Bar and the Chancellor of the Exchequer—"men who, however we may differ from them . . . we all know to be men of honour"—should have so rashly embarked on an undertaking which they ought to have left severely alone.

That surely would be a most unhappy result of these two days' debate. Though I ask no immediate reply either from the Prime Minister or from any of his colleagues who may follow me, I do beg of him to think, before the Division comes, whether they cannot find some course more consistent with the credit of this assembly, and more likely to maintain the purity of the public service.

Balfour's speech took the whole House by surprise. There was a feeling among the more aggressive of his followers that he had given the day away, while the Government was unprepared for his offer. The Debate continued, but the occupants of both Front Benches disappeared, presumably to negotiate. When a little late Buckmaster withdrew his Amendment to make way for a new one moved by Sir Ryland Adkins, many people supposed that agreement had been reached.

The new Amendment stated "That this House after hearing the statements of the Attorney-General and the Chancellor of the Exchequer . . . accepts their expressions of regret that such purchases were made and that they were not mentioned in the Debate of October 11," and acquitted the Ministers of acting otherwise than in good faith and reprobated the charges of corruption.

Negotiations had been undertaken, but they had broken down on this essential difference between the two parties. The Tories were not prepared to agree to a form of words by which the House merely accepted the Ministers' regrets. They insisted that the House itself must register regret. On the Government side, Lloyd George, who had offered his resignation, was determined to go no further than he had in his statement, and he insisted that he would resign if the Tory view was adopted. Mr Churchill, on this as on previous occasions, acted as his emissary to the Prime Minister. Asquith decided to back his Ministers.

The Debate continued for some hours, during which Major Archer-Shee made an attacking speech, and it was not until Bonar Law rose that the House was informed of this irreconcilable difference. The Leader of the Opposition stated without preamble that the Amendment before the House had been sent to him, but that he had been unable to agree to it. He said he adhered to the letter and the spirit of everything Mr Balfour had said, and in order to show this a new form of words had been prepared.

> That this House, having heard the statements made by the Attorney-General and the Chancellor of the Exchequer, acquits them of acting otherwise than in good faith and reprobates the charges of corruption which have been proved to be wholly false, but regrets their transactions in shares of the Marconi Company of America and the want of frankness displayed by them in their communications with the House.

He went on to say that the Amendment before the House asked them to accept the Ministers' explanation as adequate.

> Well, sir, we cannot accept it as adequate. I know thoroughly the difficulty in which these Ministers were placed. They had maintained up to the last moment that they had done nothing which they would not be entitled to do again tomorrow. It was therefore very difficult for them to come down and say something entirely the reverse, but I listened to every word which they said with the intention, after consultation with my colleagues, of changing what we had intended to be the order of the Debate, and getting up and speaking then . . . if these Ministers had said

what we thought they ought to have said, that they had done things which they ought not to have done, that they were sorry apart from what happened afterwards, apart from all controversy, that they had done it. That is our reason for not accepting the form of words which was submitted.

He then said that they had been asked pointedly whether they wished to drive the Ministers out of public life, and he said, "I do not. It is not for me to judge what action it may be necessary for them to take." He added that if they possessed the confidence of their colleagues he did not see that the expression of the views of the House of Commons made any difference to them. Then he made a fighting speech of the kind that at this time was characteristic of him.

> We say that they have done things which in their position— remember that is the key of the whole matter—they ought not to have done, and that they have shown a want of moral courage in their attempt to conceal from the House what they have concealed.

He showed once more the association between the two companies and the reasons why it was certain the Attorney-General bought on special terms. He said it was difficult to draw the line between speculation and investment, but not difficult here, and he explained that, apart from any other consideration, investment stocks do not rise or fall two or three hundred per cent in two or three days. But it was when he spoke of the concealment from the House that he was most forthright.

> The Attorney-General quite frankly said that the question had been carefully considered: therefore not telling the House was deliberate. Remember that. It was not accidental. . . . That is not all. Here is a curious thing. Neither the Attorney-General, nor the Chancellor of the Exchequer, nor the Prime Minister gave us any explanation as to why they did not at once ask to be called before the Committee. . . . They gave no explanation. Can anyone understand at all why they did not do that? No one who listened to the speeches of those two right hon. gentlemen yesterday, and I looked at them while they were

234

speaking, could fail to have, as I had, great sympathy for them, or to feel what they must have suffered all these months by these charges lying over them. . . . Surely, then, the first thing they would have wanted to do was to say to themselves: "This has all got to come out, and the sooner it comes out the better: let us at once go to the Committee and make a clean breast of it."

Bonar Law then suggested that they had not done this because at the back of their minds was the feeling that perhaps in the end "we may never have to tell."

At all events I think that is the probable explanation. If you say it is not, if you say these Ministers meant at all costs, whatever happened in the Committee . . . to go to the Committee and tell it—remember this, that that defence of those two right hon gentlemen is the condemnation of Lord Murray. It puts him on the black list by himself. . . . Is it not really probable that the reason that the House of Commons and the country were not told was that the Ministers hoped that it might never be necessary to tell them.

He asked the House what they thought of the partial disclosure to two members of the Committee, saying that they knew what the two members themselves thought, by their efforts to prevent it being known. Then he continued:

And we know what the Prime Minister thought of it. I listened . . . to a question the other day with absolute amazement. The question was put to the Prime Minister: "Was it with his knowledge and consent that this communication was made?" "The answer," he said, "was in the negative." An hon. friend of mine then rose and asked him: "Do you approve of it?" His answer was: "That is a question I am not called upon to answer." But in giving the answer he did answer it, and the answer was listened to without protest by certainly one and probably both of his colleagues, an answer in reality which condemned something they had done in a vital matter, a condemnation by the head of

235

their own Government, and they accepted it in silence.

When Falconer interrupted, Bonar Law turned on him.

> The hon. Member spoke this afternoon for, I think, nearly two
> hours, and he did not give us the smallest explanation as to why that
> communication was made. But he did tell us that there was a kind of
> analogy with a Court of Law. . . . I am under the impression that if
> there was an analogy to a Court of Law, he was in the position of a
> juryman, and I am under the impression that if anyone interested in
> the case were to have any communication of any kind with a member
> of the jury, he would render himself liable to criminal procedure.

When Bonar Law sat down it was obvious that no agreement could be
reached and that the House would divide. Sir Edward Grey, the Secretary of
State for Foreign Affairs, nevertheless, succeeded in holding Members'
attention.

He said that, if the Opposition Amendment was accepted, he thought it
would entail the resignation of the Ministers and it might even close their
political careers. If the House had had nothing under review but their transaction, it might have gone to the extreme limit of language which it thought
errors of this kind deserved.

> But we are also conscious of this, that gross charges of corruption,
> unfounded, made with a recklessness which if it occurred often would
> go far to make public life intolerable, have been levelled against them.
> Under these they have suffered for months past, and, if justice is to be
> done by the House, the first thing to be emphasised is to do away, as far
> as lies in the power of the House, with the imputation of those charges
> and the effects of them.

He thought that, in the Amendment before the House, "regret" was put
on record, and he said:

> What you want is not to lay down any absolute rule, but to ensure

236

that you have men in public life who can be trusted, when private interest does conflict with public duty, to put private interest on one side.
Those men are men who are sensitive about their reputations, and
unless the House repudiates, and repudiates vehemently, reckless
attacks when they prove unfounded, those are the sort of men to whom
you will make public life impossible.

When he sat down the mechanical majority moved into action and the day
was won, the Ministers' careers saved, by a vote of 346 to 268. The
Government majority was 78 as compared with 98 the week before on the
Home Rule Bill. On the Tory side there were two abstentions—Sir Edward
Carson and F. E. Smith. On the Government side the eight O'Brienites of the
Irish Party abstained and so did five Labour Members, Messrs Thorne,
O'Grady, Snowden, Jowett and Walsh. Three Liberals voted with the
Opposition, Messrs D. M. Mason, J. Martin and Munro Ferguson, the last-
named cancelling his pair and travelling a long way to do it.

(17)

Aftermath

1

For the chief participants the Marconi case came to an end with the great
debate on 18 and 19 June 1913. The echoes of the great scandal did not cease
altogether to be heard, however, until in August 1914 they were completely
overcome by the guns of Europe. During the intervening year certain events
took place as a direct result of the case, occurring with an eccentricity worthy
of the main case itself.

In the first place two more Committees of Inquiry have to be recorded. The
first was an inquiry by the Committee for General Purposes of the Stock
Exchange into the flotation of the shares of the Marconi Telegraph Company
of America. This Committee summoned before them in November 1913 the
firm of jobbers Messrs Heybourn & Croft, and several firms of stockbrokers,
including Messrs Grenfell & Co, who as Billett, Campbell & Grenfell were
brokers to the Company. They accepted the explanations of the firms of stockbrokers and on two counts the explanations of Messrs Hey-bourn & Croft.
But, on a third count: "Whether there was any breach of trust between Messrs
Heybourn & Croft and the Brokers who left orders with them," having
heard the evidence of Mr Heybourn, they inflicted a heavy punishment.

Messrs Heybourn, Croft and William Bagster Jun., partners in the firm, were suspended from entering the Stock Exchange for a period of five years. And, in announcing this verdict, the Committee published the following resolution:

> The Committee condemns in the strongest terms the manner and method of the introduction of the shares of the Marconi Telegraph Company of America in the Stock Exchange, and they give notice that all introductions of this character will render members concerned in them liable to be dealt with under the Disciplinary Rules.[1]

The second inquiry, which took place in March of the following year, was conducted by a Select Committee of the House of Lords into certain charges and allegations made in the public press against one of their number—Lord Murray of Elibank. The elusive Lord Murray returned to this country in the spring of 1914 to find their Lordships in this inquiring mood. The main features of the conduct of the case by the House of Commons were then repeated all over again. There were, however, many In the debate on the Motion to appoint a Committee of Inquiry spades were called spades with a richness and accuracy of description that must have startled not merely Lord Murray but also Sir Rufus Isaacs. The House of Lords was a predominantly Conservative body and the majority, which in the House of Commons had been used to safeguard the Ministers, was used here to overrule Liberal objections to the Motion. Lord Crewe, for the Liberals, expressed the view that the Committee was superfluous and said he would assume no responsibility for it, nor take any active part in its formation. In spite of this loss of co-operation, an eminently judicial Committee was formed, consisting of the Earls of Halsbury, Loreburn and Desart, Lord Charnwood and Lord Sanderson. Of these, the first two were former Lord Chancellors, the former Conservative the latter Liberal, while Lord Desart, a former Director of Public Prosecutions, and Lord Sanderson, Permanent Under-Secretary for Foreign Affairs from 1894 to 1905, sat on the cross-benches, and Lord Charnwood had been a Liberal Member of Parliament.

---

[1] *The Times,* 12 November 1913.

In fulfilment of Lord Lorebum's request that the charges should be formulated, Counsel appeared to support charges brought by the proprietors of the *Morning Post,* and by L. J. Maxse, proprietor of the *National Review.* Lord Murray was also represented by Counsel.

Lord Murray has been heard off-stage from the beginning to the end of this drama, and his part in the performance has always been of an ambiguous, if not a discreditable, character. He was a well-known figure in the London of his day and here is a description of him in the words of one of his contemporaries. J. A. Spender says:

> Long intimacy blinded me to the faults which his enemies alleged; I found him always cheerful and considerate, and willing to put himself to any trouble to do me a kindness. His ample figure and full-moon face, with its fringe of curls, were always a pleasant vision, and he had a persuasive manner that was hard to resist. He was in some ways *the* character of these times, and his chronic good humour soothed many savage breasts. Beside Elibank I felt myself a mere beginner in the art of smoothing. He knew exactly what to say to Redmond, and when to say it; he kept Lloyd George from boiling over, and raised Asquith's temperature when it seemed to be falling. He soothed the rich Liberals who were uneasy about Limehouse, and got large cheques out of them to be used for their own despoiling. When two people quarrelled, he was at infinite pains to bring them together again, and could make each of them seriously believe that the other was pining for a reconciliation. It was pleasant to be in his company, if only to realise for the first time in one's life what charming things other people, who were very disagreeable to one's face, were saying about one behind one's back.
>
> Yet behind this pleasant mask was a very determined, astute and wary man. From the moment that he appeared on the scene as Chief Whip, he was laying his plans and filling his coffers for two elections ahead.[2]

---

[2] *Life, Journalism and Politics,* 1, 235.

As a witness in his own defence Lord Murray showed an admirable candour. He relied on the principle recommended by Balfour: whenever blunders are fallen into, the best that those concerned can do is, without any attempted explanation, simply to say they made a profound mistake and are very sorry for it.

When Mr Upjohn, K.C, appearing for the *Morning Post*, and questioning him on his original purchase, asked: "You . . . never intended to make it an investment?" Lord Murray replied: "Partially an investment."

Q. To what extent?

A. I cannot say. That would depend on many things; but what we actually did—the first portion of it—was a speculation. It resulted in our retaining a certain number of shares which I hold today.

Later, when questioned on his part in the October 11 debate, he refused to defend himself and said:

There appears to be a conflict of opinion between myself and those two gentlemen who were recently my colleagues. But what was in my mind was the impression of the man in the street, that somehow or other Ministers were mixed up in Marconis, and they never drew much distinction between these various Companies . . . I can only say that the general impression on my mind was that there were Marconi rumours about Ministers. . . . If there is a distinction between what was understood by other Ministers and myself I must take the consequences.

And finally, questioned upon his failure to appear before the Select Committee, he said:

I quite frankly say that I did not volunteer my evidence because I was in hopes that it might not be necessary for the transactions with the Party Funds to be made public. That has been my feeling which I have not concealed all along.

As a result of considerable exuberance in Maxse's compliance with the request to formulate charges, several accusations were made against Lord Murray which were untrue and these were rejected by their Lordships; but on the main charges of having bought shares for himself and for the Liberal Party they found he had been guilty of a "grave error." They referred to his "most unwise reticence," and after adding that he had been perfectly candid throughout the Inquiry and freely blamed himself, they concluded:

> His secrets were not wholly his own, but we think he ought to have arranged for the information to be laid before the House of Commons Committee.

Their Lordships acquitted Lord Murray of conduct reflecting on his personal honour, but in conclusion they stated:

> We think it is within our province to express our strong opinion that there should be henceforth an inflexible rule to preclude those who hold any public office from entering upon speculative transactions in stocks or shares in any circumstances whatsoever, and that this rule should be by them inculcated on their subordinates both by precept and example. The evils that may arise from a violation of this principle are incalculable.

The absconding Mr Fenner had left debts of more than £40,000 to the Liberal Party Funds. Lord Murray of Elibank shouldered all this debt and personally repaid it.

In addition to these two inquiries a great lawsuit spread itself over the columns of news sheets for many months to prevent the public forgetting the Marconi case. It may be remembered that during his summing up in the Isaacs *v.* Chesterton case Mr Justice Phillimore had suggested that there might be a claim by shareholders in the English Company against Marconi and Godfrey Isaacs to get any profits made on their transactions. None of the shareholders who might have been deprived by the good fortune of Isaacs's friends had had recourse to the law, but Mr Oliver Locker-Lampson, M.P., and a Mr P. S. Wright, inspired by the curious altruism of the common informer, had each subsequently bought one share in the

Marconi Company—they later increased their holdings to ten—in order to represent the body of shareholders in an action in which Godfrey Isaacs, Marconi, Harry Isaacs, Messrs Heybourn & Croft and Messrs Billett, Campbell and Grenfell were the defendants. When this case came into court an array of advocates faced each other that made legal history.[3] Hardly had Mr Gore-Brown, K.C, begun his opening speech, however, when Sir John Simon rose to interrupt him and to announce that a settlement had been reached out of court.

The terms of this settlement were not disclosed at the time, but later, in the course of a lawsuit on a different matter, the public learned that, although the explanations given by the defendants had been accepted, the unlucky Mr Heybourn had, on the understanding that it should not be made public, contributed £14,000 to the costs incurred by the plaintiffs.

2

It is against this background of continued sensation that the immediate careers of the main participants in the Marconi case must be regarded. Sir Rufus Isaacs only a few months later came back into the news.

On the last day of the session that had seen the Marconi debate Bonar Law rose in the House of Commons to ask the following question:

> I wish to ask the Prime Minister whether it is true, as reported in today's Press, that the Lord Chief Justice (Lord Alverstone) has resigned, or has tendered his resignation; and if so, when such resignation was tendered and when accepted; also whether the right hon. gentleman has advised the appointment of any successor, and, if not, when does he intend to do so?

To this Asquith replied:

---

[3] The seventeen Counsel included Simon, Frank Russell, Gordon Hewart, Maugham, Hogg, Upjohn and Harold Smith.

So far as I am aware the Lord Chief Justice has not resigned. The last communication I had from him, I am glad to say, led me to entertain the hope that he would in course of time be able to resume his active duties.

At which a Nationalist member interjected the comment: "Another mare's nest."

Beneath the form of words the question Bonar Law asked was whether the rumours that Sir Rufus Isaacs had been appointed or was about to be appointed Lord Chief Justice were true; and Asquith replied that they were not. The cheers with which his answer was greeted were an indication of the feelings of large sections of Parliament and the public with regard to these rumours.

However, it was not a mare's nest. In little more than two months Lord Alverstone's resignation had been accepted and Sir Rufus appointed Lord Chief Justice.

Asquith was clearly in a difficulty about this appointment. Since by precedent the Attorney-General was almost heir-apparent to the office of Lord Chief Justice, any other appointment would have been a clear admission that he felt there were reasons why common procedure could not be followed—the Marconi case would have been fought, as far as this participant was concerned, in vain. Had Sir Rufus refused the appointment this would have involved the same implied admission. There is evidence that both men considered the point, and both decided that the only possible course was to withstand the protest which this promotion to one of the highest offices in the land was bound to provoke. Commentators at the time and historians since have expressed astonishment at the insensitivity that enabled them to go through with it.

Isaacs was much respected at the Bar, and there were many of his colleagues who approved of the appointment, but feeling in the press and among the public was scandalised and bitter. This section of opinion found a terrifying spokesman in Rudyard Kipling. Millions of words have been written about the Marconi scandal and all that is left lies yellowing in the British Museum. But *Gehazi* is a poem of hate written by a genius and has an evil life of its own. Kipling had followed the case with intensity right from the start and now he used the power he had been given to express his scorn of the new Lord Chief Justice and his feelings of outrage at the appointment.[4]

Lord Reading's subsequent career, which culminated as Viceroy of India, is too well known to need discussion here. It is only necessary to say that when in 1918 he represented England as Ambassador to the United States, while still holding office as Lord Chief Justice, it was Balfour who as Foreign Secretary sent him the following telegram.

> We cannot think, in the circumstances, the judiciary would insist on your early return to your high office, as, however great their deprivation may be, it is after all domestic, while duties you are now executing are essential to effective prosecution of the War and cannot be performed by another.[5]

Lloyd George did not easily recover from the Marconi scandal. One of his biographers suggests that he never really regained his position or his spirits until the Great War. At a dinner at the National Liberal Club ten days after the Marconi debate he made plain his feelings in a hysterical if characteristic speech.

> There is one martyrdom I have always felt the least endurable of all, and that is where the victim had his hands tied and arrows were sped into his body from all quarters. He could neither protect himself from the arrows, tear them out nor sling them back. Well, I can understand something of that martyrdom now. . . .
>
> There is a great story in the greatest of books of a man who spent his life fighting the Philistines, and one day he was assailed by a wild beast, whom he slew. Returning to the scene of the conflict in a few

---

[4] I have been refused permission to quote *Gehazi* but it can be found in the inclusive edition of Kipling's verse, and also in all the following works: Birkenhead, *F. E.*; Churchill, *Lord Derby*; Ward, *Chesterton*.

[5] *Dictionary of National Biography.*

days, he found the carcase full of honey. My right hon. friend and I have been assailed by a hideous monster that sought our lives. Not by our own right arm, but with the help of friends we have slaughtered it, and, unless I am mistaken, out of its prostrate form will come something that will sweeten the lives of millions who hitherto have tasted nothing but the bitterness and the dust of the world.[6]

This fanciful interpretation of history provoked Amery to the speech entitled St Sebastian of Limehouse, afterwards printed in the *National Review* and already quoted on page 106, in which he dealt precisely with these pretensions and with the facts of the whole case. Where Balfour in the House of Commons had taken the most lenient view of the Ministers' transactions, Amery took the harshest. In this speech he also referred to something never officially explained. The Select Committee, originally called to investigate the contract with the Marconi Company, failed to publish a report on it. Amery said:

Well, you know that those gentlemen have now, in spite of the protest of the Unionist members, summarily shut down the proceedings of the Committee. They have decided to present no report on the negotiation and completion of the contract, although that was the task specifically assigned to them by Parliament. They no doubt realised that the incompetence shown by the Post Office in those negotiations could not be concealed by any report of theirs, however ingeniously they might have endeavoured to gloss it over. They knew, in fact, that the resources of the whitewash pail were exhausted, and that after the liberal helping given to Mr Lloyd George and Sir Rufus Isaacs there would not be enough left to furbish up poor Mr Samuel.

E. T. Raymond in a biography suggests that Lloyd George may never have forgiven Asquith for befriending him in this affair.

---

[6] *The Times*, 2 July 1913.

To put a proud man under a vital obligation is a great imprudence. Mr Asquith, in standing staunchly by Mr Lloyd George and Sir Rufus Isaacs throughout the Marconi affair, had been unfortunate enough to wound a very sensitive pride. . . . Mr George, embarrassed and hampered, must have resented equally the sense of obligation and the equally inevitable sense of lessened freedom and importance.[7]

Cecil Chesterton died from influenza in a hospital in France in 1918, after enlisting as a private, being wounded in battle and serving his country with gallantry. His brother and his wife kept the *New Witness* alive for several years until it died for lack of funds. In 1924 it was re-started as *G.K.s Weekly*, but now, in an interview that was obviously a great embarrassment to him and of which different versions are given in *The Chestertons* and in Maisie Ward's biography, he told his sister-in-law that he no longer desired her services as assistant-editor.

Mrs Chesterton, after an experimental adventure in which she dressed in the poorest clothes and lived without money as a "down-and-out" in London, wrote a book on her experiences entitled *Darkest London*, and then founded the Cecil Houses for women—public lodging-houses where any woman could get a bed and hot water, tea and biscuits for the sum of a shilling, or if necessary from a charitable fund founded for the purpose. She spent much of her life working for the foundation and administration of this admirable charity.

3

And so we end as we began, with the Marconi Company and the contract for a chain of wireless stations. The interminable history of negotiations, committees, agreements and reversals of agreement that were to take place before Britain at last achieved an Imperial network must be related to the progress of wireless telegraphy in other countries, in particular those so soon to become enemy territory.

---

[7] *Mr Lloyd George*, 161.

In 1910, when the Imperial Chain was first discussed in England, the German Government created a company which was financed by the principal banks and subsidised by the Government. No discussion took place in Parliament, but stations were built in each of the German colonies. War was declared at midnight on 4 August 1914. At five o'clock that afternoon, seven hours before the expiry of the British ultimatum, a message passed from one station to the other to be sent out to sea. This message was: "War declared upon England; make as quickly as you can for neutral port." Germany saved the greater part of her mercantile marine, and it was later estimated that the salvation of one big ship would have paid the cost of the whole system of wireless stations.

In England Mr Herbert Samuel, who alone seems to have appreciated the urgency of the matter, with great political courage negotiated a new contract with the Marconi Company immediately after the events related in the last chapter, in spite of much dissuasion from members of his own party. C. F. G. Masterman, then Financial Secretary to the Treasury, wrote to him:

> Spicer came to me yesterday and told me that he thought under *no* condition ought we to have any further negotiations with the Marconi Company, especially with Godfrey Isaacs. I think too that there would be strong feeling in the House if it were known we were still negotiating with them.[8]

In July 1913 the House of Commons ratified this contract, after determined opposition to it. The sites now selected for stations differed from those originally proposed, because during the preceding year many stations had been built by other countries. In August 1914 only two stations, one at Leafield in England and one in Egypt, had been begun, and these were unfinished. The masts at Leafield were converted for use in a network of interception receiving stations which was quickly set up, and a temporary strategic transmitter was installed on the Egyptian station.

---

[8] Bowle, *Viscount Samuel*, 100.

At the end of 1914, no adequate reason being given, the Post Office cancelled the contract with the Marconi Company. The Company immediately instituted legal proceedings to recover their costs and for breach of contract. The proceedings dragged out over years, but in 1919 they were awarded the sum of £600,000 in compensation. Since by this time the urgency for an Imperial Chain was no less, and progress in wireless telegraphy made it certain that both the Admiralty and the Post Office would be heavily engaged in the installation of wireless systems, it seems incredible that, rather than pay this huge sum in damages, the Government should not have entered into negotiations with the Marconi Company to find means of employing their services on one or other of their undertakings.

In 1919 the Company approached the Post Office with a new offer to establish direct communication between all parts of the Empire by means of a main trunk-route, with networks of lower-power feeding-stations serving the outlying territories. The Government replied by appointing a Select Committee to consider the matter under the chairmanship of Sir Henry Norman. Since Sir Henry, during the year of opposition to the original contract, had developed settled opinions—opinions of which he made no secret but which never received the backing of any technical committee considering the matter—there could hardly have been a worse choice. In May 1920 this Committee rejected the Marconi offer and reported that in their opinion no monopoly should be given to private enterprise, and the Post Office should undertake the scheme. The Post Office had already taken over the two stations at Leafield and Cairo and were installing Poulsen arc-transmitters, and it was suggested that these two stations should function as the first link in the chain.

During this period Godfrey Isaacs, addressing the Marconi shareholders, said:

> Let us examine their programme. They say: "For transmission we will erect Poulsen arcs, the original patent of which expired last year." The French Government say: "We have tried this; it is a failure. We are pulling out the Poulsen arcs." But that does not matter; we, the Post Office, will avoid paying Marconi royalties at any cost. For reception we will use the expired Marconi patents. For avoiding interference we will

249

use the Admiralty secret patent—an abandoned Marconi invention of 1903.[9]

In fact Parliament rejected the report of the Norman Committee, but work was, nevertheless, continued at Leafield and Cairo. No great advance was made because when the Poulsen transmitter began to operate it effectively "jammed" the services of several European countries.

In 1921 and 1922 some of the Dominions entered into arrangements with subsidiaries of the Marconi Company for their own installations, while in England committees still sat to consider the matter, and the problem of the central link of the chain was still unsolved. On 9 January 1923 the *Daily Telegraph* remarked:

> We who live in the British Empire are forced to be spectators of the triumph elsewhere of a physical science which we did much to bring to perfection, while remaining ourselves silent, or almost silent.

Then in March of that year Bonar Law announced the Government's decision to issue licences to private enterprise for the erection of wireless stations in this country for communication with the Dominions, Colonies and foreign countries, subject to the conditions necessary to secure British control. In the interests of security one State-owned station was also to be erected.

"Private enterprise," *The Times* said on 6 March, "means the Marconi and associated Companies."

The Marconi Company once more entered into negotiations with the Post Office to agree terms for the licences, and once more no agreement was reached.

In 1924 a change of Government brought yet another Committee, under the chairmanship of Mr Robert Donald, to consider the Imperial Chain. This Committee recommended that all stations in the British Empire should be owned by the Post Office, with a partial exception in the

---

[9] *The Times,* 8 August 1919.

case of Canada where a service by private enterprise already existed, and secondly that all services other than Empire services should be left to private enterprise.

During all this time the Marconi Company, which throughout remained the only company that could certainly have undertaken the work, was neither consulted nor asked to give evidence. The deadlock produced by this determination to reject the only means by which progress could be made was finally and decisively broken by the genius of Marconi. With the discovery of the possibilities of short-wave directional transmission and reception, all other methods of wireless communication became so outdated that the Government were forced to co-operate in a trial of the system, and to come to an agreement with the Marconi Company to erect a station for communication with Canada and capable of extension to communicate with South Africa, India and Australia. As a result of the outstanding success of this experiment, by the autumn of 1927 the British Empire at last achieved a complete system of wireless communication. The stations were owned by the Governments concerned, but built by the Marconi Companies.

It would be interesting to explain why the difficulties in establishing the wireless chain proved for so long insoluble. There were only two disputable points, and almost every country in the world disposed of these in one way or another. First, the choice had to be made between private enterprise or State-owned stations. Secondly, a company had to be approved to undertake or co-operate in the work. During the whole of the time the Marconi Company had no serious rival and was still the only company with the necessary resources. It is impossible to avoid the conclusion that the obstacle to agreement must be looked for in the management of the Marconi Company—in the character of the managing director himself.

Clearly some people had formed a bad impression of Godfrey Isaacs during the course of the Marconi case, but as the years went on and the urgency increased it cannot have been only the memory of this case which defeated every attempt to bring about an essential State service. If Isaacs's reputation had been damaged he was not alone in that, and nothing had been conclusively proved against him except, perhaps, doubtful taste in his choice of business associates and the fact that he had made an offer to the

Attorney-General of England which the latter—after thought and at one remove—had accepted. Consequently, his subsequent history must be looked at.

Isaacs always stood high in the regard of his colleagues. During the course of the Locker-Lampson case, addressing a meeting of shareholders and explaining the charges that were being brought, Marconi said:

> I am told that Mr Locker-Lampson and Mr Wright have been and are industriously busying themselves in an endeavour to obtain the support of other shareholders. To what extent if at all their efforts have been successful is a point upon which I desire complete enlightenment, and my method of obtaining it is by retiring from the Board and offering myself for re-election. Your managing director will do the same. It is not my turn to retire and the managing director is never under an obligation to retire.[10]

Both officers were re-elected with only one dissentient.

Isaacs was, however, a dangerous man and he had one unusual quality which by itself might have made many people reluctant to deal with him. He was a natural litigant. Most people will go to any lengths of negotiation or compromise to avoid a lawsuit, but there are men, suffering perhaps from an exaggerated sense of persecution, and sufficiently aggressive, who regard the law-court as the obvious place for the setttlement of a dispute. So constant is their confidence in the justice of their own cause that they never doubt its success. Isaacs was one of these.

Directly he became managing director of the Marconi Company he instituted proceedings for infringement of patents all over the world. In addition, he has already made his appearance in the Chesterton case, the Locker-Lampson case and the case against the Government for breach of contract. In the years from 1912 to 1919 no year passed without his name appearing once more in the headlines connected with sensational litigation.

---

[10] *The Times,* 22 July 1914.

There was the Seager case, in which Seager sued for breach of contract and lost because the judge ruled that, although there had been a breach, the contract had been entered into in circumstances strongly suggestive of blackmail.[11] There was the Hamilton case, in which Hamilton successfully pleaded wrongful dismissal. There was the Jackson case, in which Jackson received three years for blackmail, his crime having consisted in offering Isaacs shares in the *Financial News* with the suggestion that their purchase would ensure that the Marconi Company's shares were quoted and that adverse comment on the Company's affairs was prevented.

Finally and most serious, there was the case against Sir Charles Hobhouse, who had had dealings with Isaacs as Postmaster-General. Isaacs accused Hobhouse of having attempted to persuade the Telefunken Company of Germany to enter into competition with the Marconi Company of England. Hobhouse said in the House of Commons that this was completely untrue. Isaacs then challenged him to repeat the statement in an unprivileged place, Hobhouse complied and Isaacs took him to law. In court Isaacs produced a letter from the Telefunken people warning him that Hobhouse, accompanied by Sir Henry Norman, had visited them. Hobhouse did not deny the visit, but, after producing evidence that it would have been impossible for him to make overtures to the Telefunken Company, because there was a published agreement between them and the Marconi Company not to trespass upon each other, he said the visit had been to acquire knowledge of the most up-to-date wireless techniques. He suggested that the letter was a deliberate attempt to make mischief.

The case turned on a private interview between the two men. Isaacs gave evidence that at this interview Hobhouse had said:

---

[11] During the course of this action Godfrey Isaacs admitted that in March 1911, on board ship on his way home from America, he had given Seager odds of ten to one that Marconi shares would touch £10 before the end of April. He also admitted that on April 22 of that year he had sent for Seager and, telling him that he was anxious Marconi shares should not fall below the price at which they stood, had sent him on to Heybourn in order that he should deal in the shares and support the market.

You recognise I suppose that you have your foot on my neck. Are you going to crush me, which will mean my leaving the Government, or are you disposed to help me?[12]

Hobhouse denied it.

In the Seager case, the Jackson case and the Hobhouse case the jury had to decide between the word of two men as to what had happened at a private interview. Mr Justice Darling expressed the dilemma as follows:

The issue is simple. One of these two people is committing the blackest perjury. The question is which of the two it is.[13]

Godfrey Isaacs won the Seager case on the strength of his evidence and his personality as a witness.[14] He won the Jackson case because he took the precaution of having a detective-inspector concealed in a cupboard in his office for three days. He lost the Hobhouse case because Hobhouse had made a memorandum of the interview at the time. The judge directed the jury that if they gave the verdict to Isaacs it involved believing not merely that Sir Charles Hobhouse lied, but that he had subsequently and fraudently concocted this memorandum.

In each of these cases there was an issue of sufficient complexity to exercise the minds of counsel, judge and jury for many days. Nevertheless, it seems likely that each could have been settled with a little good will and the smallest humour, but for Isaacs's addiction to the law. In any case, as year after year he appeared in court to give evidence of a private interview, it would not be surprising if an impression began to prevail that one unrecorded word with him inevitably led to an opposing array of counsel and an

---

[12] *The Times*, 17 July 1918.

[13] *The Times*, 20 July 1918.

[14] There is no doubt that Godfrey Isaacs was an attractive witness; he always sincerely believed in his case. In an Appeal to the Seager case, Lord Justice Phillimore, the only dissentient to a verdict in Isaacs's favour, went out of his way to comment favourably on his appearance in the Chesterton trial. "He gave his evidence very well . . . in a manner which commended itself to me." *(The Times,*17 December 1915.)

appearance in the witness-box. There is no evidence to suggest that this impression had any bearing on the chronic indecision of British Governments, but it may well have had.

4

In 1924 Godfrey Isaacs resigned his post with the Marconi Company and in 1925 he died, leaving £195,490 (net personalty £139,428). In the later years of his life he entered the Roman Catholic Church. At the time of his death he received full honours. *The Times* in an obituary referred to the Marconi case and also to his continual appearances in court, and remarked that he had not always been exempt from criticism, but it said:

> It is hardly too much to say that the Company owes as great a debt to Mr Isaacs on the business side as it does to Mr Marconi on the scientific side. He will be long remembered as a man of remarkable gifts and boundless enthusiasm for the new science with which he had linked his commercial fortunes.[15]

However, Godfrey Isaac's name had not yet passed from the news. Two years after his death *The Times* once more found it necessary to devote a leader to the affairs of the Marconi Company.

> Yesterday, by a substantial majority, the shareholders of Marconi's Wireless Telegraph Company passed the scheme put before them by the board for the reconstruction of the concern and of the directorate.
>
> On the facts disclosed at the meeting no other decision could be justified. The general public may therefore approve it; but their uppermost feeling will probably be one of regret that the name of one of the great inventors of the age should be associated—not for the first time, and through no fault of his marvellous discovery—with recrimination

---

[15] *The Times*, 18 April 1925.

and scandal. . . . It was a tale of reckless mismanagement. Over a period of years, substantial profits were reported, inordinately large fees paid to certain directors, and shareholders were lulled into a false sense of security by receiving appreciable dividends. Yet all the time, as it now turns out, the company was in fact suffering heavy losses by unwise investments (several of which had nothing whatever to do with the company's business), by advances to subsidiary companies which turned out to be bad debts, and by foolish speculation in foreign currencies.

These things happened for the most part during the period that the late Mr Godfrey Isaacs was managing director of the company. Altogether the losses have involved the writing down of the assets to the extent of approximately £6,000,000. That has stripped the company entirely of its reserves and renders necessary the reduction of the capital by one-half. Seldom in the history of a joint-stock enterprise have losses of this magnitude been sustained by a single company in a few short years.

So long ago as 1920 the directors were warned by the auditors in their certificate attached to the balance sheet that the values stated in the latter document required revision. Every year since then the auditors have repeated their warning in terms which should not have been misunderstood by the directors, even although amongst the public there were apparently but few discerning minds who understood the meaning of the qualified certificate. In short the record of the company for the past seven years affords no cause for satisfaction for anyone associated with it. The explanation of yesterday's decision is really to be found in the fact that shareholders felt, after listening to the managing director's statement, that the present management was not responsible for the policy that led to the staggering losses, but, on the contrary, had done their best to put the company's affairs on a sound basis.[16]

---

[16] *The Times,* 16 March 1927.

To end this strange story it is only necessary to add that the losses sustained by the Marconi Company included £117,000 written off in the Carreg-y-Llam Quarries (slate quarries in Wales); £25,000 written off in Gauntlets Ltd (a tin-making company); £32,000 written off in Hamonite Ltd (a company for making artificial coal) and £225,000 written off between the British Hungarian Bank and the Compass Allgemeine Guarantee Bank.

Author's Reflections

The Marconi case is often discussed and usually inspires the remark: "It couldn't happen today."

One is tempted to add importance to this book by suggesting that, if it could not happen now, our more unyielding standards of public behaviour are a direct result of that case. This is a difficult position to sustain, however, because one cannot help feeling that, even without the events that took place then, the rules that govern public life would be much as they are. If there is anything in the Marconi case that throws light on our greater inflexibility, it can, I believe, only be found beneath the wild exaggerations of Hilaire Belloc.

It was the rise to power of the Labour Party and all the social changes this brought in its train that made rigid a code the principles of which had been accepted long before the Marconi case. The moment one Party in Parliament seriously believes the other to be composed of individuals given to indulgence in trivially peccant acts—manipulation of railway vouchers, over-valuation of bottles of sherry—while the other Party regards its opponents as a related gang of bankers, landlords and nepotists (practitioners on a consummate scale), the honour of both Parties will become exceedingly sensitive and the rules of behaviour self-imposed and very nice. Thus we have Dr Dalton resigning in circumstances which in retrospect, and certainly in comparison with the Marconi case, seem simply silly. If we are now in a period of civilising the barbarian, if in future the members of the two Front Benches come, as before, from much the same world, speak the same language, meet in the same houses, we may see a slight drop, not in the principles that govern public life, but in the severity with which they are enforced.

The Marconi case was an isolated incident without, it seems to me, much historical significance. But I have found it a fascinating study, an endless field for speculation.

Everyone assumed at the time that if, in the debate of October 11, the Ministers had made a frank statement, all would have been at an end; that they spun the case out for months and jeopardised their careers by a foolish error of judgment on that occasion. And yet I cannot believe it.

This assumption could be correct only if the admissions they would then have made were of a kind completely acceptable to the House of Commons; and this could hardly have been the case. They had speculated in shares of a company associated with a company in contractual relations with the Government, and on information received from the managing director of the contracting company; and, although these were the points the House of Commons eventually debated, they did so after months of preparation and when the news was staled by familiarity.

Any statement on October 11 would have been made in the atmosphere created by false rumours and slander, the fact of a statement would have implied an admission, and the Opposition would have been left to interpret there and then the difference between the transactions of which the Ministers had been accused and those in which they had taken part. Witnesses were to say again and again that at that time the ordinary man did not distinguish much between the various Marconi Companies. Almost certainly Sir Rufus Isaacs, quite possibly Lloyd George, would have had to resign.

It seems probable they acted initially from instinct and without much premeditation. When they considered whether they should go down to the House of Commons and say: "No, we none of us bought shares in the English Company, but we did buy shares in the American Company" after all those months of rumour and slander, while the Opposition sat silently listening, and the avid and heartless journalists waited in the gallery above, they probably felt they could not do it. The terrible nature of political life makes it so difficult to confess to an error because it must always be done in public and because of the advantage one's enemies will take.

After this I think there must have been an implicit decision to bluff it out. I find it impossible to believe they intended whatever happened—even if the journalists failed to make a case—to go before the Select Committee and make a full statement, although I think there may never have been an overt agreement not to. But this is an expression of personal opinion, for they were unequivocal in their statements on this matter.

Although they showed complete unity in all their actions, and also in their reactions to the long chain of events, which, by a single thoughtless moment, they had precipitated, the minds and the characters of the two men were very different. Both had an overweening personal ambition, but in Lloyd George this was sustained by a just confidence in his own powers, as well as by a disregard for accepted ideas of integrity in political relationships, which ensured that, although it was a factor to be reckoned with, it ran easily in harness with the character and talents of this unique personality. Sir Rufus Isaacs was governed by more conventional standards of morality and behaviour. He was respected, trusted and liked, and it seems probable that he cared more than Lloyd George for the opinion of his fellows. Throughout his life, however, there recurs the suggestion that, at the turning-points of his career, at those moments when some great future opening out before him had yet to be secured, or when, as in the Marconi case, he felt himself seriously threatened, his desire for self-advancement became a passion which drove this reserved and disciplined man.[1]

So in the Marconi case Lloyd George was merely impatient and angry, felt resentful and put-upon. By nature confident and unscrupulous, unconcerned with the niceties of honour, he never seems to have understood or even tried to understand that he was other than the victim of hostility and political feeling. It seems likely that if, instead of himself, some friend or colleague had been involved, he would still have seen the whole thing as a great pother about nothing. Sir Rufus was quite a different case. He had an acute analytical brain and an area of understanding from which he could easily have appreciated every nuance of the argument against him. Yet when he made his

---

[1] For illustration of this characteristic, see *Two Memoirs* by J. M. Keynes, p. 23, and *The Chief, the Biography of Gordon Hewart* by Robert Jackson, p. 126.

statement on 11 October he had had six months to assess the relationship of the two companies and his exact position. The extent to which he then deceived the House of Commons and the public must be taken as the measure of the extent to which he deceived himself. Proud and sensitive, he was constitutionally unable to believe that he had put himself so badly in the wrong; and his mind rejected reasoning that, if applied to another, he would have found self-evident.

He cannot be considered merely as a moral coward. Again and again he showed formidable courage in publicly challenging a critic to state that he meant, by a question or a remark, something he clearly had meant.

Nor, within its self-imposed limits, did his mind fail to evaluate every detail in his long-sustained ordeal, or to turn what it might to advantage. When he decided to make the truth public in the *Matin* case, he was probably frightened into it because Maxse appeared to have definite information. But he was also quick to seize a favourable opportunity. A barrister goes into court to represent a client and he is honourably bound to make the best of his case, whether by emphasis on the facts that tell in his favour or by omission of others. When Sir Edward Carson announced the purchase of the American shares as a small matter of no importance, but one the Attorney-General desired known—"he wishes to state everything . . . and keep nothing back"— he lent the force of his magnificent personality, his great position and the climate of His Majesty's Law Courts to the farce. More important, he saved his clients the humiliation of a personal statement. Serious humiliation can be followed only by resignation.

When it is added that the case was chosen because the libel was both specific and untrue, instead of one in which the libel, although equally untrue, was aimed broadly at the whole integrity and honour of public men—which would have made nothing less than complete innocence of any compromising act seem adequate—and finally that it was undefended, it is difficult to see how the ground could have been chosen more adroitly.

The case was settled in the end by a majority vote, a vote that could not have been given had the Ministers not secured the backing of the Prime Minister. Asquith saved Lloyd George and Sir Rufus Isaacs, and he did it voluntarily. This is a point that must be discussed because it has been obscured.

From start to finish he was in an unusual position. We know that he thought it "lamentable" and "so difficult to defend" because he said so to the King,[2] but indeed one would have assumed this without his testimony. The political atmosphere was such—the case ran concurrently with the Third Home Rule Bill—that any Prime Minister of the day would have had to back his Ministers or test very severely the power of his Government. But Asquith's difficulties were much increased because he was a man of fine character.

We know that he was unusually loyal and would not therefore easily have forced his Ministers' resignations if he believed them guilty of indiscretion and not of dishonour, particularly at a time when they had been so vilely accused of things they could never have done. Far more inhibiting than that, he was faced with this devilish circumstance. One of the two Ministers concerned was his nearest and most dangerous rival. Lloyd George had long before emerged as a great public figure and already enough was known of him for Asquith to be unable to suppose that, should it ever occur to him that his duty was to take over the leadership of the Liberal Party, he would be deterred by personal considerations. The Prime Minister had either to associate himself completely with the "Marconi Ministers," or rid himself of a threat to his own position by a means despicably easy and irrelevant to the issues of the day. It is no wonder that his biographers say that "to the end of his days he regarded this as the most difficult and painful personal incident he had had to deal with in the course of his life."[3]

On the other hand many people believe that he was not informed of the facts until the public were, at the *Matin* case, or alternatively very shortly before this; by which time he would have been faced with a major political issue and, as Prime Minister, would have had no choice but to fight it out.

Asquith himself seems to be responsible for this. The passage in his memoirs quoted here on page 55 is very smooth and carefully worded, but it gives the impression that he knew nothing of the facts at the time of the debate of October 11. His biographers go further in the following passage:

---

[2] See page 102.

[3] *Spender and Asquith*, 365.

Asquith had convinced himself that there was not the slightest foundation for either of the foregoing allegations, and he was quite confident that they would be blown out of court by the Select Committee. But unfortunately the Ministers had bought shares in the American Marconi Company . . . and they omitted to mention this fact when on 11th October they spoke in the debate on the appointment of the Select Committee. It became known, however, in the following year when Sir Rufus Isaacs disclosed it in giving evidence in the action which he and Mr Herbert Samuel brought against the French newspaper *Le Matin*, for repeating the original allegations. The *Matin* admitted its mistake and made a full and frank apology, but the new fact thus disclosed, though not bearing on the original slanders, was undoubtedly a very unpleasant surprise which threatened serious consequences in Parliament.[4]

Finally Asquith told the King that the Ministers "confessed" to him in January 1913.

In fairness to Lloyd George and Sir Rufus Isaacs it is necessary to establish the facts.

Asquith was told by Mr Samuel and by the Master of Elibank in late July or early August 1912. He was not told the circumstances in which the purchase was made, but this cannot be thought important. At the time great publicity was being given to the contract, to the rumours about Ministers (the Prime Minister was consulted about the *Eye–Witness* libel in a letter from Rufus Isaacs) and to the relationship between the managing director of the Marconi Company and the Attorney-General. Moreover, in Mr Samuel's account he makes it clear that, immediately he was told of the share transaction, Asquith appreciated the implications.[5]

He was ill at the time of the debate of October 11 and—this may be a point of some significance—he was not consulted about, or told in advance of, the statements that were then made, and which, intentionally or not, so

---

[4] 1, 362.

[5] See page 55.

much misled the House; but, unlike his enemies and his friends, he had the key to them.

Finally, in January 1913—the only authority I have for this is Sir Harold Nicolson's account of Asquith's interview with the King—the Ministers sought an interview with him at which they told him all the details and offered their resignations.

Mr Winston Churchill always supported the Ministers and indeed from his public utterances one might reasonably suppose his attitude to the purchase of American Marconi shares to be hardly different from Lloyd George's. All the more interesting, therefore, is a conversation recorded by Duff Cooper in which Mr Churchill is reported as saying that if the affair had been properly handled by the Tories they might have brought down the Government, but "some of them were too stupid and, frankly, some of them were too nice."[6]

One of the most teasingly interesting figures in the Marconi case is Godfrey Isaacs. How reconcile, as Cecil Chesterton asked, the "iron front," the great financier and man of business with the idiot pursuit of gold? (There is no doubt that Isaacs in the early days of his employment showed enormous ability and put the Marconi Company on a sound basis or that he made possible the vast expansion of wireless telegraphy.) What, on his record, caused Marconi to recognise his qualities in the first place?

The answer seems to be that he was a classic example of an octagonal peg suddenly slotted into an octagonal hole. Marconi was a man who believed he would one day speak directly and without the use of wires to someone on the other side of the Atlantic. Probably it was just the balance, the sense of reality Godfrey so conspicuously lacked that he found most obstructive in the rest of the world. The science of wireless telegraphy was "the one new thing in twenty" likely to succeed. In these conditions Godfrey Isaacs's qualities shone unrestrained by the balance of probability. Greater men than he have waited half a lifetime for a special set of circumstances to surround and animate their marvellous potentialities.

---

[6] *Old Men Forget,* 46.

Appendix A

The Sign of the World's End:
An Open Letter to Lord Reading

My Lord—I address to you a public letter as it is upon a public question: it is unlikely that I should ever trouble you with any private letter on any private question: and least of all on the private question that now fills my mind. It would be impossible altogether to ignore the irony that has in the last few days brought to an end the great Marconi duel in which you and I in some sense played the part of seconds; that personal part of the matter ended when Cecil Chesterton found death in the trenches to which he had freely gone; and Godfrey Isaacs found dismissal in those very Courts to which he once successfully appealed. But believe me I do not write on any personal matter; nor do I write, strangely enough, with any personal acrimony. On the contrary there is something in these tragedies that almost unnaturally clarifies and enlarges the mind; and I think I write partly because I may never feel so magnanimous again. It would be irrational to ask you for sympathy; but I am sincerely moved to offer it. You are far more unhappy; for your brother is still alive.

If I turn my mind to you and your type of politics it is not wholly and solely through that trick of abstraction by which in moments of sorrow a man finds himself staring at a blot on the tablecloth or an insect on the ground. I do, of course, realise, with that sort of dull clarity, that you are in practice a blot on the English landscape, and that the political men who made you are the creeping things of the earth. But I am, in all sincerity, less in a mood to mock at the sham virtues they parade than to try to imagine the more real virtues which they successfully conceal. In your own case, there is the less difficulty, at least in one matter. I am very willing to believe that it was the mutual dependence of the members of your family that has necessitated the sacrifice of the dignity and independence of my country; and that if it be decreed that the English nation is to lose its public honour, it will be partly because certain men of the tribe of Isaacs kept their own strange private loyalty. I am willing to count this to you for a virtue as your own code may interpret virtue; but the fact would alone be enough to make me protest against any man professing your code and administering our law. And it is upon this point of your public position, and not upon any private feelings, that I address you today.

Not only is there no question of disliking any race, but there is not here even any question of disliking any individual. It does not raise the question of hating you; rather it would raise, in some strange fashion, the question of loving you. Has it ever occurred to you how much a good citizen would have to love you in order to tolerate you? Have you ever considered how warm, indeed how wild, must be our affection for the particular stray stockbroker who has somehow turned into a Lord Chief Justice, to be strong enough to make us accept him as Lord Chief Justice? It is not a question of how much we dislike you, but of how much we like you; of whether we like you more than England, more than Europe, more than Poland the pillar of Europe, more than honour, more than freedom, more than facts. It is not, in short, a question of how much we dislike you, but of how far we can be expected to adore you, to die for you, to decay and degenerate for you; for your sake to be despised, for your sake to be despicable. Have you ever considered, in a moment of meditation, how curiously valuable you would really have to be, that Englishmen should in comparison be careless of all the things you have corrupted, and indifferent to all the things that you may yet destroy? Are we to lose the War which we have already won? That and nothing else is involved in losing the full satisfaction of the national claim of Poland. Is there any man

268

who doubts that the Jewish International is unsympathetic with that full national demand? And is there any man who doubts that you will be sympathetic with the Jewish International? No man who knows anything of the interior facts of modern Europe has the faintest doubt on either point. No man doubts when he knows, whether or no he cares. Do you seriously imagine that those who know, that those who care, are so idolatrously infatuated with Rufus Daniel Isaacs as to tolerate such risk, let alone such ruin? Are we to set up as the standing representative of England a man who is a standing joke against England? That and nothing else is involved in setting up the chief Marconi Minister as our chief Foreign Minister. It is precisely in those foreign countries with which such a Minister would have to deal, that his name would be, and has been, a sort of pantomime proverb like Panama or the South Sea Bubble. Foreigners were not threatened with fine and imprisonment for calling a spade a spade and a speculation a speculation; foreigners were not punished with a perfectly lawless law of libel for saying about public men what those very men had afterwards to admit in public. Foreigners were lookers on who were really allowed to see most of the game, when our public saw nothing of the game; and they made not a little game of it. Are they henceforth to make game of everything that is said and done in the name of England in the affairs of Europe? Have you the serious impertinence to call us Anti-Semites because we are not so extravagantly fond of one particular Jew as to endure this for him alone? No, my lord; the beauties of your character shall not so blind us to all elements of reason and self-preservation; we can still control our affections; if we are fond of you, we are not quite so fond of you as that. If we are anything but Anti-Semite, we are not Pro-Semite in that peculiar and personal fashion; if we are lovers, we will not kill ourselves for love. After weighing and valuing all your virtues, the qualities of our own country take their due and proportional part in our esteem. Because of you she shall not die.

We cannot tell in what fashion you yourself feel your strange position, and how much you know it is a false position. I have sometimes thought I saw in the faces of such men as you that you felt the whole experience as unreal, a mere masquerade; as I myself might feel it if, by some fantastic luck in the old fantastic civilisation of China, I were raised from the Yellow Button to the Coral Button, or from the Coral Button to the Peacock's Feather. Precisely because these things would be grotesque, I might hardly feel them as incongruous. Precisely because they meant nothing to me I might be satisfied with them, I might enjoy them without any shame at my own impudence as an alien adventurer. Precisely because I could not feel them as dignified, I should not know what I had degraded. My fancy may be quite wrong; it is but one of many attempts I have made to imagine and allow for an alien psychology in this matter; and if you, and Jews far worthier than you, are wise they will not dismiss as Anti-Semitism what may well prove the last serious attempt to sympathise with Semitism. I allow for your position more than most men allow for it; more, most assuredly, than most men *will* allow for it in the darker days that yet may come. It is utterly false to suggest that either I or a better man than I, whose work I now inherit, desired this disaster, for you and yours. I wish you no such ghastly retribution. Daniel son of Isaac, Go in peace; but go.

Yours,

G. K. Chesterton.

Appendix B

Report of the Select Committee
of Inquiry

Part 1

At the commencement of the sittings your Committee publicly announced that they were prepared to consider all evidence relevant to the subject-matter of the Enquiry, and invited all persons in possession of such evidence to communicate with the Clerk to the Committee.

Among the circumstances attending the formation of the Contract which your Committee had occasion to investigate were certain allegations or suggestions originally circulated in the form of rumours, which became current before the date of the acceptance of the Tender upon which the Agreement was based.

The allegations or suggestions, which reflected on the conduct of several Ministers of the Crown, notably the Right Honourable Sir Rufus Isaacs (the Attorney-General), the Right Honourable David Lloyd George (the Chancellor of the Exchequer), and the Right Honourable Herbert Samuel (the Postmaster-General), ranged themselves under two main heads. It was stated or implied: *First*, that a member or members of the Government, acting in the interests of Marconi's Wireless Telegraph Company Limited, hereinafter referred to as the English Company, and in disregard of the public interests, had exercised undue influence to procure for the Company a Government contract, or had, in some way, exercised improper or undue influence, direct or indirect, in the course of the negotiations for such a contract; and, *Secondly*, that a member or members of the Government, with a knowledge acquired in his or their official capacity of the nature of the negotiations and of the probability that an Agreement would be completed of great value to the English Company, during the progress of the negotiations had purchased shares in that Company with a view to selling them at a profit on the announcement of a favourable result of the negotiations.

On October 11, 1912, on the occasion of the motion for the appointment of your Committee, Sir Rufus Isaacs, speaking on behalf of himself and his colleagues, took the opportunity of publicly informing the House of Commons that all such statements or suggestions were baseless fabrications. He expressed himself in the following words:

> The one (i.e. charge) is that some person has used his influence to obtain a contract for the Marconi Company with the Government, or has in some way acted to the advantage of the Marconi Company in the negotiations which took place with reference to this contract. I want to say in reference to myself that I have never, from beginning to end, in any shape or form, either by deed, act or word, or anything else, taken part in the negotiations in reference to this company. . . . Let me go to the next charge, which is, I think, a worse charge. It is that some member of the Government not named, but hinted at—some member or members of the Cabinet—knowing that these negotiations were taking place, knowing that there was a contract in contemplation, and thinking the shares would go up when the announcement of the contract came to be made—the price of the shares being then 14s. or 15s., and eventually rose to £9 after the announcement of the contract was made—thereupon and in consequence of the information which some member of the Government had got bought shares in this company at a low price, in order to sell them at the higher price when the contract was announced.

I desire to say frankly, on behalf of myself, that that is absolutely untrue. Never from the beginning, when the shares were 14s. or £9, have I had one single transaction with the shares of that company. I am not only speaking for myself, but I am also speaking on behalf, I know, of both my right hon. friends the Postmaster-General and the Chancellor of the Exchequer, who, in some way or other, in some of the articles, have been brought into this matter.

It has been proved to the Committee that there is no foundation for any of the charges made against these Ministers.

In addition to issuing the public invitation referred to, the Committee during the months of January and February 1913 summoned to appear before them the Contributors, Editors and Proprietors of the journals who were responsible for the publication of the charges referred to, and Sir Theodore Angier, who was reported in the Press to have repeated similar charges against members of the Government. All of these have appeared before the Committee with the exception of Mr Cecil Chesterton, who asked to be excused on account of the state of his health and also on the ground that he was being prosecuted on a charge of criminal libel and could not give evidence on the matters in question without prejudicing his defence to that action, and Sir Theodore Angier, who has asked to be excused on account of the state of his health and has gone abroad.

The charges referred to appear to have originated in rumours on the Stock Exchange, which commenced in January 1911 or January 1912.

They were first published in the *Outlook* in a series of articles contributed by Mr W. Ramage Lawson, which commenced with an article on July 20, 1912. They were repeated in various forms in subsequent numbers of that journal, and in the *Eye–Witness*, the *New Witness*, the *National Review*, and the *New Age*, and they were also referred to in the *Spectator*.

In these journals the suggestion was repeatedly made and referred to that the contract in question was obtained by the English Company through the influence of the Attorney-General, who is the brother of Mr Godfrey Isaacs, the managing director of the Company. It has been proved to the Committee that there is no foundation for such a suggestion, and that the Attorney-General had no negotiations, direct or indirect, either with the

Postmaster-General or with any official or member of the Government.

The journals also made repeated references to alleged transactions by Ministers in the shares of the English Company during the course of the negotiations which took place with the Postmaster-General prior to the acceptance and publication of the Company's tender on March 8, 1912.

No evidence of any kind has been submitted to the Committee to justify any of these charges, and they have been denied on oath by the Postmaster-General, the Attorney-General and the Chancellor of the Exchequer.

Mr Lawson admitted that he was never able to verify any of the rumours or to discover any definite ground for them. All the other witnesses responsible for their publication who have appeared before us have also failed to specify any ground on which they could be justified or to produce any evidence in support of them.

It has also been suggested that the Postmaster-General unduly pressed for the approval of the Agreement before the rising of the House of Commons on August 7, 1912.

The Committee cannot adopt this view. The construction of the Imperial Chain of Wireless Telegraphy was declared by the Imperial Defence Committee to be a matter of extreme urgency; and this was also the view of the Admiralty and the War Office. Statements to that effect were made to the Committee by representatives of both Departments in public and their evidence was further explained and emphasised at meetings with them held in private.

Having regard to the urgency of the matter and to the fact that he regarded the Agreement as a satisfactory one, the Committee consider that the Postmaster-General was bound to do everything in his power to secure the approval of the Agreement at the earliest possible date.

Your Committee beg to submit a Special Report in relation to the matters bearing upon the allegations affecting members of the Government. Your Committee finds as follows:

No evidence has been forthcoming or disclosed to your Committee, nor have they been able to discover any evidence to support any allegation, or in any way lend colour to any suggestion that any member of the Government has or had exercised undue or any influence to procure for the English Company a Government Contract, or has or had directly or indirectly sought to exercise any such influence, or has or had otherwise acted in the private interests of the Company, or in disregard of the public interests.

Nor was there any evidence forthcoming or disclosed to your Committee to support any allegation, or lend colour to any suggestion, that any member of the Government has or had taken advantage, or sought to take advantage, of any knowledge acquired by him in his official capacity in relation to the purchase or sale of shares in the English Company, or otherwise.

Your Committee further find and report that there was no evidence adduced before them to support any allegation or suggestion that any member of the Government purchased or sold, directly or indirectly, either by himself or his agents, or was in any wise concerned in the purchase or sale of, any share or interest in the English Company, either with a view to securing a profit to himself or otherwise at all in fact.

Your Committee further find and report that the charges made against Sir Rufus Isaacs, Mr Lloyd George and Mr Herbert Samuel are absolutely untrue and that the persons who are responsible for their publication had no reason to believe them to be true.

The Committee cannot too strongly condemn the publication in such a way of unfounded charges against the honour and integrity of public men. The combined and persistent action of the journals named has given widespread currency to a slander of a particularly vile character on the Ministers against whom it was immediately directed and on the whole public life of the nation.

Part 2

The Committee have also investigated the circumstances relating to a purchase by the Attorney-General from his brother, Mr Harry Isaacs, on April 17, 1912 of 10,000 shares in the Marconi Wireless Telegraph Company of America (hereinafter referred to as "The American Company"), and the purchase from the Attorney-General on the same day of 1000 of these shares by the Chancellor of the Exchequer, and of 1000 of them by Lord Murray of Elibank, and the subsequent purchase of 3000 shares by the Chancellor of the Exchequer and Lord Murray on May 22, 1912, and also to separate purchases made by Lord Murray of 2500 shares on April 18, 1912, and 500 shares on May 14, 1912.

The Committee find that in these transactions there is no ground for any charge of corruption or unfaithfulness to public duty, or for any reflection on the honour of any of the Ministers concerned.

In purchasing shares in the American Company Sir Rufus Isaacs acted in perfect good faith and with a sincere conviction that his personal interests conflicted in no wise with his public duty, believing as he did from enquiries which he made and information which he received that the American Company was not in any way concerned with the solvency or success of the English Company or with any of its contracts or undertakings. Mr Lloyd George and Lord Murray in acquiring shares in the American Company acted on the faith of the assurance given to them by Sir Rufus Isaacs that the American Company was in no way concerned with the English Company.

The first purchase of shares in the American Company took place on April 17, 1912, more than five weeks after the tender of the English Company had been accepted by the Postmaster-General and its acceptance had been published, and the second purchase took place nearly ten weeks after the publication of the acceptance. Neither of these purchases could therefore have any connection with the negotiations prior to the acceptance of the tender or with the origin of the rumours before referred to, which commenced in December 1911 or January 1912, and related to dealings in English Marconi shares during the negotiations.

The circumstances under which the shares in the American Marconi Company were purchased by the Attorney-General, and the subsequent dealings with them, were stated by him in an action raised in the English Courts at his instance against *Le Matin,* a French newspaper, and the whole circumstances relating to all the dealings by him and the Chancellor of the Exchequer were fully stated by them to the Committee, and it was explained by them that they had hoped to have had an opportunity of placing these circumstances before the Committee shortly after its appointment.

In addition to the Attorney-General and the Chancellor of the Exchequer, the Committee examined Mr Harry Isaacs and Mr Godfrey Isaacs, and also a number of witnesses who were concerned in the issue of the shares of the American Company. In the opinion of the Committee, these witnesses gave their evidence fully and frankly.

Owing to the absence of Lord Murray from England the facts regarding the separate purchases made by him were proved to the Committee by his brother, Captain Arthur Murray, and Mr F. S. Salaman, the trustee of the estate of Charles Edwin Fenner, stockbroker, and other witnesses. These shares were purchased by Lord Murray on behalf of a political fund at his disposal. Copies of the cablegrams which have passed between Lord Murray and the Chairman of the Committee are printed in the Appendix to this Report.

The Committee have examined the two agreements between the English Company and the American Company dated April 18, 1902, and March 29, 1912, with the view of ascertaining whether the American Company would have any interest in the proposed agreement between the English Company and the Government if it were entered into, and they are satisfied that the American Company would not have any interest in the agreement. They are not parties to it, and could have no interest in the construction of the stations to be erected under it or in any profit which might be derived by the English Company from the construction or from the operation of these stations when constructed.

The agreements provide for the exchange of messages between New York and London by means of a station to be erected in New York by the American Company, and a station to be erected in London for the English Company, but these stations, if erected, would not form any part of the Imperial Chain or have any connection with it.

In regard to these transactions the Committee report as follows:

(1) They find that before any purchase was entered into by the Attorney-General he made special enquiry, and was satisfied that the American Company had no interest in the agreement between the Postmaster-General and the English Company, and that there was no ground on which a purchase of its shares by a British Minister would be open to objection. He informed the Chancellor of the Exchequer and Lord Murray of the result of his enquiries when offering shares to them.

(2) That the Ministers concerned, when entering into the purchases, were all bona fide convinced that the American Company had no interest in the agreement, and that there was no ground on which the purchase of shares in the American Company would be open to objection.

(3) That the American Company is a company formed and registered in New York; that its organisation and operations are confined to the United States of America; that it has no interest, direct or indirect, in the proposed agreement with the British Government, and no interest, direct or indirect, in any profits which might be derived therefrom.

(4) That neither the English Company, nor its managing director, Mr Godfrey Isaacs, was a party to any of the transactions in question, or in any way directly or indirectly interested in them.

(5) That in connection with the transaction between the Attorney-General and Mr Harry Isaacs, neither the Attorney-General nor the Chancellor of the Exchequer, nor Lord Murray, received any favour, advantage or consideration of any kind, either from the English Company or from Mr Godfrey Isaacs. The shares were acquired by the Attorney-General from his brother, Mr Harry Isaacs, who had no connection with or interest in the English Company. They were bought by the Attorney-General on April 17, 1912, at £2 per share, which the Attorney-General had ascertained from Mr Harry Isaacs to be the market price at the time. Other sales at or about that price (some being slightly below and some slightly above) took place on the same day, and although the price of the shares rose rapidly on the 18th and 19th, this was owing to an exceptional rush on the part of the public to buy.

(6) That neither the Attorney-General nor the Chancellor of the Exchequer, nor Lord Murray, nor Mr Harry Isaacs, was a party to or in any way concerned in any arrangement or understanding with any other person or syndicate with regard to the purchase or sale of shares.

Part 3

On the whole matter, relating to the conduct of Ministers which have come before the Committee, the Committee find that all the Ministers concerned have acted throughout in the sincere belief that there was nothing in their action which would in any way conflict with their duty as Ministers of the Crown.

Appendix C

Lord Robert Cecil's Report

1. It was apparent from the debate which resulted in the appointment of the Committee that our enquiry fell into two parts. We had to consider whether the Marconi system was the right one to be adopted for the Imperial Wireless Chain and, if so, whether the terms proposed were fair and reasonable from a public point of view. And we had, further, to ascertain whether there were any financial transactions of an improper character by Ministers or others with the Marconi Company or anyone connected therewith, and in particular whether certain charges and suggestions which had been made in the Press and elsewhere had any foundation. It is with the last named portion of our enquiry that this Special Report is concerned.

2. The negotiations between the Marconi Company and the Government for the construction of a chain of longdistance wireless stations round the Empire were opened by a proposal made by Mr Godfrey Isaacs, the managing director of the English Marconi Company, in March 1910, and were continued during 1911 and the beginning of 1912. On March 7, 1912, the Post Office signified its acceptance of the general terms of the Marconi Company's tender. After a series of further discussions between the different Government Departments and between the Post Office and the Marconi

Company an agreement was signed on July 19, 1912, subject to ratification by the House of Commons. This agreement, in the opinion of the Company, as expressed in its annual report, dated June 8, 1912, was one the importance of which to the Company "could not be exaggerated." Apart from any profit on the construction of the stations, the profits from the royalty on the first six stations have been estimated at various figures from £4000 to £31,000 a year, a figure which would be increased if further stations were erected by the Company.

3. But the indirect advantages of the contract were, in our opinion, far more important than the direct ones. The contract was in itself a striking recognition of the strategical and commercial importance of wireless telegraphy in general and of the Marconi system in particular. The erection of a chain of stations extending half-way round the globe would not only provide an additional traffic to existing long-distance stations on the Marconi system within the range of any of the Imperial stations, but would, in our opinion, constitute an inducement for the erection of future stations public or private, on the Marconi system rather than on any other. It would, in fact, as stated in the Company's circular of March 7, 1912, "contribute to a material increase in the Company's general and telegraphic business in all parts of the world."

Further, the actual terms of the contract, involving as they then did a five years' monopoly of the erection of all stations in the British Empire, as well as a heavy penalty by way of continued royalties, unless all patented Marconi apparatus were eliminated, were calculated to give the Marconi Company a position of great advantage over all possible future competitors, and to act as a powerful lever to induce inventors to sell their patents to the Marconi Company and thus strengthen its position still further. All these important indirect advantages were, we consider, advantages not only to the parent Marconi Company, but to all the subsidiary companies of the Marconi system, and these companies were all, consequently, in a greater or lesser degree interested in the ratification of the contract.

4. The financial importance of the agreement is clearly indicated by the effect of the course of the negotiations upon the price of the Company's shares. During 1910 and the opening of 1911 the £1 shares of the Company had stood at 5/8 to 7/8, and in order to secure the necessary capital to carry on its business considerable blocks of shares had been issued at 25 per cent

discount. From the beginning of the active negotiations with the Government, which may be dated from the decision of the Cables (Landing Rights) Committee on March 23, 1911, that an Imperial Wireless Chain was desirable, and that the Marconi Company should be approached as to the terms on which they would co-operate with the Government, the shares began to rise and continued to do so with no very serious setback until they reached the price of 9\8 on April 19, 1912. The movement in the shares of the parent Company was in its later stages closely reflected in the shares of other Marconi Companies, such as the Canadian and Spanish, which were successively brought on to the London market.

5. It is not suggested that this rise was wholly due to the Government negotiations and agreement. There were other important contributory causes, such as the successful patent action against the British Radio-Telegraph and Telephone Company in February 1911, the acquisition of the Lodge-Muirhead patents, the payment of a 10 per cent interim dividend in the course of 1911, and the successful American negotiations in March 1912. But a comparison of the crucial dates in the negotiations with the market movements of the shares indicates that the Stock Exchange was not only kept well informed of the progress of the negotiations, but that their success was regarded as likely to be of great financial importance to the Company. Thus the great rises that began in May 1911, in December 1911, and at the end of January 1912, were each of them preceded by a definite step forward in the negotiations with the Government.

On May 18, 1911, the Cables (Landing Rights) Committee adopted a draft report previously prepared by the Post Office definitely recommending a wireless chain, stating that the Marconi Company alone had experience of longdistance commercial working, and entertaining the Company's proposed terms subject to modification. The shares rose almost continuously from 11/4 at the beginning of May to 2 1/2 at the end of June. On December 18, 1911, the Post Office and Mr Godfrey Isaacs practically came to an agreement as to the chief terms on which the Marconi Company would undertake the erection of the wireless stations. The shares which stood at 2 3/4 in the middle of December, went to nearly 4 by January 9, 1912.

On January 24 the Post Office informed the other Government Departments that the Poulsen system could not be considered, and that it would not be advisable to defer the conclusion of an agreement with the Marconi Company. The negotiations were in fact brought to such a point that Mr Godfrey Isaacs informed the Press on that date that he hoped the agreement with the Government was about to be signed. This date may be regarded as approximately the starting point of the great boom which culminated on April 19. The actual acceptance of the tender on March 7 was not followed immediately by any very remarkable rise. But it seems to us that the acceptance had no doubt been largely anticipated, and that the further tendency to rise would naturally, for the moment, be checked by realisations. We cannot accept the view that the movement of shares during the days immediately following March 7 indicates the whole effect of the contract, and that the further rise during the next few weeks was unaffected by it.

6. In this connection it is necessary to draw attention to the fact that upon the acceptance of the tender the Company published in a circular of March 7 a version of it which omitted all mention of the right of the Government to terminate the royalty period at any time, upon using a system entirely independent of the Marconi system, and which was calculated to convey the impression that the Marconi Company had secured a complete monopoly of all wireless stations in the British Empire for eighteen years. This misleading version of the tender was the only version accessible to the public for over four months. The Post Office apparently made no attempt to insist upon a correction, and the Postmaster-General did not take the opportunity to clear up the matter properly, either in answer to repeated questions or in his otherwise detailed account of the contract in the debate on the Post Office Estimates on May 20.

Mr Godfrey Isaacs told us that he omitted from the circular any reference to the provision that if the Government made use of a system entirely independent of the Marconi system the payment of royalty should cease, because he regarded it as practically meaningless, upon the ground that no wireless system could be independent of the Marconi system without abandoning the transmission of signals by ethereal waves. We are unable to accept this curious explanation. It is clear from the notes of the interviews of January 19, February 9, and March 5, 1912, between Mr Isaacs and the Post Office, that both parties intended the condition to relieve the Government from the payment of royalties if they ceased to use Marconi apparatus, and Mr Isaacs, in fact, regarded the condition as of so much importance that at first he asked that it should be kept secret.

7. Before the acceptance of the tender for the Imperial Chain negotiations had been in progress for an arrangement between the Marconi Company and the United Wireless Company of America. This Company, according to Mr Godfrey Isaacs, "really commanded practically all business of value in the United States." But the validity of its patents was in dispute, its directors were in prison for financial irregularities, and its affairs were being carried on by trustees in bankruptcy and by a shareholders' reorganisation committee. The terms suggested on behalf of the United Wireless Company were not satisfactory to the Marconi Company, which decided to proceed with the American Marconi Company's action for infringement of patents. This was fixed for March 25, and Mr Godfrey Isaacs and Mr Marconi sailed for New York on March 9, two days after the acceptance for the tender of the Imperial Chain.

8. On their arrival in New York on March 16 a banquet was organised in honour of Mr Marconi by the *New York Times,* and as a feature of the banquet certain eminent persons in England, including the Attorney-General, were induced to send congratulatory wireless telegrams. The message of the Attorney-General to the *New York Times* was in these words: "Please congratulate Marconi and my brother on the successful development of a marvellous enterprise. I wish them all success in New York, and hope that by the time they come back the coal strike will be finished." It has been suggested that this telegram had some connection with the financial proceedings of Mr Godfrey Isaacs in America, but no evidence to sustain this suggestion was brought before us, and the Attorney-General denied that any special significance was to be attached to it. This denial we accept.

9. Meanwhile the United Wireless Company's representatives had decided to come to terms, and approached Mr Godfrey Isaacs as soon as he reached New York, and agreements were signed on March 21 by which the representatives of the United Wireless Company admitted infringement, submitted to a perpetual injunction, and agreed to sell all its patents and assets to the British Marconi Company for 700,000 dollars in fully-paid shares of the American Marconi Company, whose total capital it was now decided to raise from 1,511,200 dollars to 10,000,000 dollars. The object of this increase of capital was mainly to provide a series of longdistance stations at New York,

Cuba, Panama, San Francisco, Hawaii, and the Phillipines and elsewhere on American territory, which would put the United States into wireless communication with all parts of the world. As a part of this scheme the English Marconi Company undertook, in its agreement of March 29, 1912, with the American Marconi Company, that (subject to the licence of the British Postmaster-General) it would erect in or near London a high-power station for the purpose of wireless communication from America to places in and beyond London, and from England to places in and beyond America.

In order to secure facilities for the collection and distribution of the traffic passing through these stations, an agreement was made on April 1, 1912, between the British and American Marconi Companies on the one hand and the Western Union Cable Company and North-Western Telegraph Company of Canada on the other, by which these latter companies agreed to collect and distribute Marconi messages at the reduced rates enjoyed by the cable companies. In securing these agreements the Marconi Company was, we cannot help thinking, materially assisted not only by the prestige of the agreement with the Post Office, but by a consideration of the fact that if the practical occupation of the field of wireless telegraphy in the Eastern Hemisphere by the Marconi system could be supplemented by a similar occupation of the Western Hemisphere, the advantages already gained in respect of the former would be still further enhanced and an exceptionally strong position created.

10. To raise the capital required in America was, however, a difficult matter, as the American public had already lost heavily over both the American Marconi and the United Wireless Companies. The former company had never paid a dividend, and its shares, after having been reduced from 100 dollars to 25 dollars, were at that time standing at a nominal figure of 10 dollars, but were practically unsaleable. The British public, on the other hand, were eagerly buying Marconi shares of all descriptions. Canadian Marconis had doubled their price between March 8 and the end of the month. Spanish Marconis had risen from 30s. in February to 42s. at the end of March. British Marconis had begun a fresh upward rise on rumours of successful negotiations in America, and their movement was apparently stimulated by cables from Mr Heybourn, a member of the firm of Heybourn and Croft, the leading jobbers in the Marconi market, who had accompanied Mr Isaacs and Mr Marconi to New York in the expectation that some large

284

financial reorganisation would be required. There was little doubt that the greater part of the new American issue could be floated on the London market.

11. The total amount of the new capital to be subscribed was 7,000,000 dollars, the British Marconi Company under the agreement with the American Company of March 29, 1912, receiving from the American Company 1,488,800 dollars in fully-paid shares for the assets of the United Wireless Company and for its services in the reorganisation. According to the laws of New Jersey the existing shareholders of the American Company were entitled to apply for the whole of the new issue at par, and it was decided to offer them the whole of the new shares at the rate of five dollars' worth of new shares for one of the old. Of these shareholders the British Marconi Company was the largest, holding shares to a nominal value of 875,000 dollars (35,000 25-dollar shares). The rest of the old shares were held by several thousand small holders scattered all over the United States.

By this agreement the British Company bound itself to take-up at least 1,250,000 dollars (250,000 five-dollar shares) of the new issue at par, and secured an option for twelve months over the whole balance of the issue not applied for by existing shareholders within fifteen days of the offer to them of the right to subscribe. The British Company thus secured complete control for a year of all operations in the shares of the American Company, save such as might be actually taken up during the first fifteen days by the small American shareholders or those to whom they might transfer their shares.

Under these conditions Mr G. Isaacs arranged with Mr Marconi to place 500,000 of the new shares in readiness for their introduction on the London market immediately after the meeting of the American Company to autho-rise the new issue which was fixed for April 18. Of these he placed 250,000 with Mr Heybourn, originally at 1 1/18, the par equivalent in pounds of five dollars, a figure subsequently altered to 1 1/4. Another 150,000 were placed with certain financiers in New York at par. The remaining 100,000 were placed by Mr Isaacs immediately after his return to England on April 8, 56,000 with Mr Harry Isaacs, 10,000 with Mr Marconi, and the rest among the directors and staff of the Marconi Company.

12. According to Mr Isaacs, the English Company, or rather Mr Marconi and himself on behalf of the English Company, were compelled in order to

induce the American directors to sanction this very large increase of capital, to guarantee the issue of the whole 1,400,000 new five-dollar shares, and this was, in effect, so stated by Mr Marconi at the annual meeting on July 9, 1912. Mr Godfrey Isaacs, however, on being pressed admitted that the formal agreement between the English Company and the American Company was only that they should take 250,000 shares and that the guarantee was in the nature of a "moral obligation." The fact that the British Marconi Company had a twelve months' option on all the shares not taken up by the original shareholders was only disclosed when the actual agreements and minutes of the English Company were subjected by Mr Isaacs, very reluctantly, to the consideration of the Committee.

As regards the 500,000 shares which he undertook to place, Mr Isaacs in his evidence informed the Committee that these shares had been sold to him outright and that he was entitled to deal with them as he pleased and to make any profit he could out of them, but that, as a matter of fact, he had passed on £46,000 of profits so made out of the sale to Mr Heybourn to the credit of the Company. He stated that a record of this sale of 500,000 shares to him would be found in the minutes of the English Company. On inspection, however, it turned out that no such minute existed, it being merely stated that the managing director reported the placing of 500,000 shares and 200,000 more on option on certain terms.

We feel compelled to state that Mr Isaacs's account both of his own position with regard to these share dealings and with regard to the whole of the transactions connected with the introduction of these American shares upon the London market was not satisfactory. Owing to a decision of the majority of the Committee we were precluded from recalling Mr Isaacs in order to explain the discrepancy between his statements and the records produced.

13. On April 8 Mr Isaacs reached London. He told us that directly he returned he was informed that the rivals of the Marconi Company who were interested in the Poulsen system intended "to make a very strong attack indeed upon the Marconi contract" in order to prevent its ratification. He was even told that a powerful syndicate had been formed with this object, including Members of Parliament and other influential persons. On April 9 he invited the Attorney-General and another brother, Mr Harry Isaacs, to lunch with him. He told his brothers of his proceedings in America, and

particularly of the contracts with the Western Union Company and Great North-Western Company, which were not to be made public for the present, and he told them further that he had still about 100,000 shares to dispose of, for which he was personally responsible, and that they could "take any number of them they liked." He further said that it was considered that they would be thought well of and would certainly go to a premium. The Attorney-General asked about the relation between the English Company and the American Company and was told that the American Company was not interested in the profits of the English Company or in the agreement with the British Government. He, however, declined to take any of the American shares on two grounds, firstly, that to do so might be a very risky transaction, as the issue of capital was a very large one, and secondly, that he thought it better in the circumstances, as a matter of delicacy, not to have any dealings with the English Company or with Mr Godfrey Isaacs. He then went away leaving his two brothers still talking over the matter.

14. As the result of a long discussion between them, Mr Harry Isaacs agreed to take 50,000, later increased to 56,000, shares at par, that is to say, at 1 1/16. Mr Godfrey Isaacs told us he had never made any similar offer to his brothers in connection with any of the other Marconi Companies, and that he offered the shares on this occasion because he thought they were likely to be of considerable value.

15. Meanwhile the British Marconi shares were still rising, and on April 11 reached 8 1/2 1/2 or double the price at which they had stood on March 7. Though no official information as to the terms of the agreement concluded in America was given by the Marconi Company until after the American Company's meeting on the 18th, enough was allowed to be known to cause considerable demand for the American shares. The eagerness of the public was still further intensified by the *Titanic* disaster, details of which began to come in on the 15th and 16th, and gave striking evidence of the value of wireless telegraphy.

16. The Attorney-General was at this time living on terms of the closest personal intimacy with the Chancellor of the Exchequer, and the present Lord Murray, then Master of Elibank, the Chief Whip of the Liberal Party. He told them both of his conversation with his brothers. Between April 9 and 17 Mr Harry Isaacs saw him more than once, and urged him to take

287

some of his American shares, and on April 17, in the evening, he persuaded him to take 10,000 shares at 2. The figure 2 was based on the statement of Mr Harry Isaacs that the price then was "round about 2". The question of selling was then discussed. It was contemplated by the Attorney-General and Mr Harry Isaacs from the first that there would be sales of the shares belonging to each of them, and it was agreed between them that any sales made by either of them should be treated as sales made on account of both.

17. The shares had not actually come into existence. The American Company was to hold its meeting on April 18, at which the new issue was to be sanctioned, and it had been arranged that Messrs Heybourn and Croft were to "introduce" the shares on the London Stock Exchange on the morning of the 19th. In such a case it is unnecessary in law to issue a prospectus giving the statutory particulars as to underwriting contracts and so on, and the public had thus no means of knowing how many shares were available or who controlled them.

As a matter of fact, until the 19th, the available total was strictly limited and controlled. Apart from the 500,000 placed by Mr Godfrey Isaacs, the only shares not under the control of the British Marconi Company were those for which the old American shareholders might apply. So far as we can ascertain, some, but apparently not a great many, of these had sold their rights to dealers in New York. The rest were scattered all over America, and could not in the most favourable circumstances be informed of their rights or dispose of them until the morning of the 19th in America, that is the afternoon of the 19th in England. Of the 500,000 placed by Mr Godfrey Isaacs, 250,000 were, as already mentioned, placed with Mr Heybourn, and the remaining 250,000 were placed among three small groups—namely, certain American financiers who took 150,000, Mr Harry Isaacs and the directors and staff of the Marconi Company.

Even in the absence of any direct restriction upon the right of any of these to dispose of their shares to the public before the 19th, they may all be presumed to have known enough to see that their obvious interest was to await the successful opening of the market before realising. A certain number of speculators do appear to have ordered from America through the arbitrage dealers shares which the New York dealers were able to secure from American shareholders. The dealings do not seem to have been very large, but they were sufficient to cause the price of the shares to rise rapidly in the New York market.

On the 15th they reached 8 3/4–9 dollars (36s. 6d.–37s. 6d.) with a total volume of 4000 shares sold, and on that day an investor with inside information was able to secure an option on 5000 out of 10,000 shares asked for at 9 1/2 dollars *(39s. gd.)*.

On the 16th they varied between 9 1/8 dollars and 9 1/2 dollars; on the 17th between 9 3/4 dollars and 11 3/4 dollars (4.0s. 9d–49s.) and on the 18th between 13 1/4 dollars and 16 dollars (55s. 2d.–66s. 8d.).

A leading arbitrage dealer stated before the Committee that if he had been given an order for 10,000 shares on the evening of the 17th he would have had to pay 14 dollars (58s. 4d.). Even, therefore, if the transaction had been carried out in New York through arbitrage dealers, a purchase of 10,000 shares could not have been made at 2 on the evening of the 17th.

18. But the general public in this country do not seem to have been given the opportunity of buying in New York. The leading brokers and dealers in Marconi shares appear to have agreed not to deal in the American issue until the 19th. The brokers were all referred to Messrs Heybourn and Croft, who consequently received for days prior to the 19th large orders for the purchase of the new shares at the opening price. The result was that if an ordinary member of the public had gone to his stockbroker with an order to buy 10,000 American Marconi shares on April 17, the order would not have been carried out until April 19, when the shares were formally introduced to the English market by Messrs Heybourn and Croft and the purchaser would have had to pay 3 1/4 or over. Moreover, such member of the public would not, on April 17, have had any authoritative information about the agreement made with the Western Union and Great North-Western Telegraph Companies to which Mr Godfrey Isaacs attached so much importance.

19. The Attorney-General, therefore, on April 17, had information from Mr Godfrey Isaacs not authoritatively announced to the public. He himself stated that he "would not have bought those shares in the market for the reason that he would have been knowing something which the other person did not know." He urged, indeed, that in buying from his brother "he was knowing nothing but what he knew," but we cannot see that this, in fact, diminished the advantage which he enjoyed over the general public. He

289

further got his shares at a lower price than could have been obtained by a member of the general public even if such a person had known how to get any shares at all on that date. These advantages accrued to him through the instrumentality of his two brothers, Mr Harry Isaacs and Mr Godfrey Isaacs, the managing director of the Marconi Company.

20. On the evening of April 17 the Attorney-General saw the Chancellor of the Exchequer and the Master of Elibank and offered to them 2000 of the 10,000 shares at the same price at which he had agreed to take them. He informed them that the American Company had no interest in the British Government contract or the British Company. He gave them substantially the same information as had been given to him by Mr Godfrey Isaacs. Among other things he told them of the contract with the Western Union Cable Company, that the purchase of the shares at that price was a very good invest-ment, that it was thought that they would undoubtedly rise in value, and that his information came from Mr Godfrey Isaacs. He said "that if they went up at all considerably he should sell part of his shares so as to reduce the price he had paid, but that he intended to hold at any rate half and probably more as a definite investment." He was asked about payment for the shares and inti-mated that payment need not be made immediately.

Mr Lloyd George and the Master of Elibank agreed to take the shares and it was apparently arranged between the three that the Attorney-General should sell for all of them, at any rate so far as one-half of the whole number of shares was concerned. With respect to the other half the position is not clear. In his earlier answers the Attorney-General appeared to indicate that all the selling was left to him. Later, he explained that that only applied to 1000 of the 2000 shares sold to his colleagues, and that with respect to the other 1000 "they were entitled to deal with them as they liked."

21. On the 18th the American Company formally agreed to issue the shares, and the price rose still further in America and in street dealings in England. During the course of this day the demand for shares became so great that Mr Hey-bourn bought from the English Company through Mr Godfrey Isaacs two more lots of 50,000 shares at 2 1/8 and 2 7/16 respectively.

Late on that evening Messrs Heybourn and Croft issued notices to the various stockbrokers who had sent in orders for shares, stating that the applications had been so numerous that it was impossible to let them have for their clients more than 15 per cent of their orders at opening price. They at the same time sent to a certain number of persons letters offering them for their personal account shares in the Marconi Company of America at the rate of 1 1/2. This was described by one of the witnesses as a sale on "ground-floor terms," and it was explained that the recipients had been earlier promised such shares in order to secure a free market.

We were told that it was not unusual in the City to distribute shares on "ground-floor terms" among those whom it was desired to conciliate. In this case the recipients of the shares at the rate of 1 1/2 were able to sell them again the next day at a profit of £2 per share and were consequently, in effect, given that amount of money on each share. This practice must be borne in mind when considering the nature of the transactions between Mr Godfrey Isaacs, Mr Harry Isaacs, and the Attorney-General.

22. On the morning of the 19th the shares were formally "introduced" to the Stock Exchange by Messrs Heybourn and Croft at a price of £3 5s. and an official announcement was made as to the agreement concluded in America and as to the objects of the new issue. Owing to the large number of orders received by stockbrokers which had not been satisfied by Messrs Heybourn and Croft before the market opened, the price quickly rose until it touched £4, and then fell away again on receipt of selling orders from America.

On the same day Mr Lloyd George informed his broker that he was interested in American Marconis. His broker, Mr Rice, said he was sorry as he did not consider it a desirable investment, basing his opinion on the past history of the Company, the methods of flotation, and the panicky state of the market, and he urged the Chancellor to sell. The Attorney-General also informed his broker of his purchase and was advised strongly to sell, as the price at which the shares stood was too high. The Attorney-General sold on that day, first 5000 and later 2000 more. On the 20th Mr Lloyd George sold on behalf of himself and the Master of Elibank 1000 at the price of 3 5/32, and on May 3 the Attorney-General sold another 1000.

Meanwhile Mr Harry Isaacs had sold 11,700 of his shares, and since he and the Attorney-General had agreed that any sales made by either of them should be treated as sales made on account of both, the net result was that the

Attorney-General was treated as having sold 3570 shares out of his 10,000 at an average price of £3 6s. 6d. Of these shares 357 were credited by the Attorney-General to Mr Lloyd George's account and 357 to that of the Master of Elibank. These figures, however, are only right if it be assumed that as between the Attorney-General and his brother, the Attorney-General was still in possession of the shares sold by Mr Lloyd George on April 20, and that the sale of these was, in fact, an independent transaction.

23. If the sale on April 20 is treated as a sale of shares bought from the Attorney-General, the transactions, so far, had resulted in a clear profit to the Chancellor of the Exchequer and the Master of Elibank of £743 each and left them each with 143 shares, costing them nothing. So far as the Attorney-General was concerned he had 5144 shares left, and on the shares that he had sold he had made a profit of £3808.

On May 22 Mr Lloyd George bought for account of himself and the Master of Elibank 3000 more American shares at a price of 2 5/82 and these they still hold. After setting off against the cost of these the proceeds of the 1000 shares sold on April 20, there remained a balance of £3486 due to Mr Lloyd George's brokers in respect of these shares. One-third of this amount, viz. £1162, was paid by Mr Lloyd George to his brokers in October and the rest of the amount due he borrowed from his brokers at rates of interest varying from 5 1/4 per cent to 7 per cent. The shares have never been delivered to Mr Lloyd George but are still held by the brokers as security for the loan.

The Attorney-General did not pay Mr Harry Isaacs until January 6, 1913, when he paid him the £8129 due to him in respect of the balance of the shares bought by the Attorney-General. Nothing has been paid to the Attorney-General by the other Ministers, nor has he, in fact, transferred to them any shares.

Very late in our enquiry we discovered that in addition to the transactions already mentioned, the Master of Elibank on April 18, 1912, bought 2500 American Marconi shares at 31/14, and another 500 at 2 7/16 on May 14. These were paid for by three cheques, the first for £3000 on June 9, the second for £1900 on June 19, and the third for £4519 8s. on June 20, making altogether £9419 8s. These purchases were made through Mr Fenner, the broker through whom the Master of Elibank had invested

292

Liberal Party funds, and were made on behalf of those funds.

24. In forming a judgment as to the propriety or otherwise of the transactions described above, certain considerations should be borne in mind. In the first place the agreement with the British Government was, in our opinion, an essential factor in the whole structure of Marconi finance. Its value to the English Company and to the subsidiary Marconi Companies we have already pointed out. We do not doubt that it played an important part in the American negotiations. As the Attorney-General said, in answering a question about the effect of his telegram of March 16, "If they (i.e. Mr Godfrey Isaacs and Mr Marconi) wanted that Company (i.e. the English Company) to appear strong could they get anything stronger than to say that the Postmaster-General, the responsible head of the telegraphs in this country, had accepted the tender which they had offered?"

In any future business negotiations, whether with the United States or any other foreign Government or the cable companies &c, that would be equally true. And if for any reason the agreement ultimately were to break down a serious injury would be inflicted on the whole Marconi system.

Secondly, on April 9, 1912, the agreement was by no means secure. The Attorney-General indeed told us that in April he "never thought there was any question about it or its ratification," and as a description of his state of mind at that time we accept what he said. But as a matter of fact the view expressed by the Postmaster-General that until July "it was not a contract—it was merely the acceptance of a preliminary tender"—seems to us more accurate. There was in truth a most elaborate series of communications and conferences between the Admiralty, the War Office, the Colonial Office, the Treasury and the Post Office before the contract was signed on July 19, and as late as July 18 there was apparently some risk of the negotiations between the parties breaking down. Even when signed it had still to be ratified by the House of Commons, and in point of fact it has not yet been ratified.

Thirdly, Mr Godfrey Isaacs told us that on April 9 it was "very very common talk in the City" that "those who were attempting to float the Poulsen Company were arranging a strong attack upon the contract." It is true we were not able to get any information of this assertion, and it may not be accurate. But it is at least an indication of the frame of mind of Mr Godfrey Isaacs on April 9.

26. Nor must it be forgotten that each of the three Ministers might have had to deal with the contract in his official capacity after April 17. The legal difficulties in connection with various clauses, more particularly the five years' monopoly provisions of Clause 3, might at any moment have been brought before the Attorney-General, and his decision might have seriously affected the value of the contract to the Marconi Company.

27. If the objections raised by the Treasury officials to certain provisions in the contract had been somewhat more strongly pressed they would have come before the Chancellor of the Exchequer himself, and he would have had to decide whether they constituted sufficient ground for withholding Treasury sanction from the contract.

28. If the Government had persisted with the intention of carrying through the contract in the House of Commons in the summer of 1912 it would have been Lord Murray's duty, as Chief Whip, to persuade Liberal critics of the contract to restrain their criticism and to vote its ratification.

29. It was in these circumstances that the managing director of the English Marconi Company offered to his brother, the Attorney-General, an unde-fined portion of 100,000 shares in the American Company, on "ground-floor" terms. Had Sir Rufus taken, say 50,000 of them, he could, as things turned out, have made over £100,000 profit in ten days' time. So great a rise was certainly not in the contemplation of the parties on April 9, but "it was considered . . . that they would certainly go to a premium," and something like 10s. per share was mentioned.

It must be remembered that at this time the boom of the English shares was in full swing. On March 22 they had been about 5; on this date, April 9, they were between 7 and 8, and they were still rising rapidly. The Canadian and Spanish Marconi shares were also booming. The atmosphere of reckless speculation and excitement was well reproduced by a series of quotations from the *Financial Times* given to us by Mr Godfrey Isaacs, which incidentally show that the rise in the Marconi group was in part at least due to the news coming from America.

It must further be borne in mind that, as already explained, Mr Godfrey Isaacs had made such arrangements with Mr Heybourn as practically to give to those two gentlemen the control of the market in the American shares when they were introduced. Assuming that there was a demand for the American shares, as it was tolerably certain there would be, these arrangements enabled Messrs Isaacs and Heybourn to regulate the price within fairly wide limits. The offer, therefore, of April 9 to the Attorney-General was almost equivalent to an offer of a considerable though uncertain amount of money.

30. Finally, it must not be forgotten that the rights to the shares offered to him actually belonged to the English Marconi Company. It is true that Mr Godfrey Isaacs told us that they had been sold to him. This account of the arrangement is not borne out by the minutes of the Company, very reluctantly produced by Mr Godfrey Isaacs, nor did Mr Marconi's recollection on the subject appear to be very clear. In any case Mr Godfrey Isaacs's rights, whatever they were, to the shares offered to the Attorney-General were subject to his undertaking to place them, and they never actually came into his possession. When issued they belonged to the English Marconi Company, and were at the disposal of Mr Godfrey Isaacs as the agent of that Company.

Sir Rufus seemed to attribute the offer made to him by Mr Godfrey Isaacs entirely to fraternal affection. It may have been so. But having regard to all the circumstances of the case, and particularly to Mr Godfrey Isaacs's evidence as to the rumours which he heard immediately upon his arrival in England of a strong Parliamentary attack to be made upon the Government contract, we cannot feel certain that his offer to the Attorney-General was not in part due to other and less creditable motives. We have no doubt that this view of the transaction did not present itself to the Attorney-General.

31. As a matter of fact, Sir Rufus refused, as we know, the offer made by Mr Godfrey Isaacs, partly upon the ground that he did not wish to have any dealings with the English Company or its managing director. Mr Harry Isaacs later pressed him to take some of the shares which he had bought through Mr Godfrey Isaacs, and after several interviews the Attorney-General agreed to take 10,000 at 2 under conditions which, as we have explained, put him at an advantage over the ordinary public.

Sir Rufus thought that the fact that he dealt with Mr Harry Isaacs instead of Mr Godfrey Isaacs made all the difference. We cannot agree with him. The transaction appears to us to have been gravely improper, because a Minister of the Crown made an advantageous purchase of shares upon advice and information not then fully available to the public given to him by the managing director of a company which was in course of obtaining from the Government a contract of the greatest importance; and we do not think that the intervention of a person in the closest confidence of both of them makes any difference to its impropriety. While we do not think that the Attorney-General in fact allowed or intended to allow the discharge of his public duty to be affected by his purchase of American Marconi shares, we are of the opinion that by accepting and acting upon the advice and information of Mr Godfrey Isaacs he did place himself, however unwittingly, in a position in which his private financial interest or sense of obligation might easily have been in conflict with his public duty.

The acceptance by a public servant of a favour of any kind from a Government contractor involves so grave and obvious a danger of corruption that if the Attorney-General's action is to be condoned by Parliament we feel that a wide door will be open to corruption in future.

32. The same reasoning applies to the Chancellor of the Exchequer and the Master of Elibank. It is quite true they were not brought into personal contact with Mr Godfrey Isaacs. But the Attorney-General was quite clear that he told them substantially what Mr Godfrey Isaacs had told him and from whom he had obtained his information. They must be taken therefore to have acted on the same advice and information as moved the Attorney-General, and if his action was gravely improper, as we think it was, it was certainly no less improper on the part of the Finance Minister and the Chief Party Manager.

The possibility of future corruption in the case of such important Ministers is more serious even than in the case of the Attorney-General. As regards the last-disclosed transactions of the Master of Elibank, it is not certain to what extent he acted on the advice and information of Mr Godfrey Isaacs. But it is at least possible that he did so, and to that extent the transactions appear to us open to the same criticism as applies to the other transactions of the Ministers.

It is true that the transactions turned out badly, but that was obviously not foreseen when they were entered into. It is also true that the Master of Elibank intended to benefit his party and not himself. But that, in our view, makes the transactions the more dangerous. Experience shows that to allow government contractors to make contributions, however indirect, to Ministerial party funds leads to a very insidious form of corruption.

33. It was very much pressed upon us that the Ministerial transactions in American Marconi shares were unobjectionable because the American Company had derived and could derive no benefit from the contract between the English Company and the Government. The American Company, it was said, had nothing whatever to do with the English Company, was not interested in its profits, and was not in any way concerned with the undertakings of the English Company. Even if this were true, it would not in the least affect the considerations we have just set forth. The impropriety of which Ministers, in our opinion, were primarily guilty, was that of making an advantageous purchase of shares upon information received from a government contractor, and that impropriety would remain the same whatever the character of the shares purchased.

34. But quite apart from this, the contention, in our opinion, is not in itself a sound one. The American Company was founded by the English Company, which, until April 1912, held the majority of its shares and nominated three of its directors. The acquisition of the assets of the United Wireless Company by the American Company the arrangement with the cable companies, and the subsequent financial expansion of the American Company were all initiated and in the main carried through on behalf of the American Company by the English Company, whose prestige and financial position were essential to the success of all these operations. Moreover, the patents belonging to the American Company were the same as those of the English Company.

Anything which increased the reputation of the system covered by the English patents must have reacted favourably upon the reputation of the same system under the American patents, and conversely anything occurring here, such as the failure of the Government contract, which was adverse to the value of the system in this country, must have had a prejudicial effect on the value of the system in the United States. We were told by Mr Godfrey Isaacs that practically every important business throughout the world for which he had been in negotiation for the last two years was standing over in consequence of the inquiry into the British Government contract. It is true that he later said that this did not apply to America, but it is difficult to believe that even in America a definite failure of the British Government contract would not have adversely affected the fortunes of the Marconi system there.

We have already pointed out the great indirect advantages conferred by the contract upon the whole Marconi system, and we think that to the American Company would accrue a full share of these advantages, and, indeed, that it was largely on the strength of these advantages that the new capital for the American Company was raised. As regards actual operation it seems to us that, at any rate as far as any long-distance communication is concerned, the Marconi system is in effect a single system.

35. For these reasons we are of opinion that the conclusion of the Government contract was a matter of importance to the American Company, and in particular that the value of its shares would or might have been affected by the value of that contract. It was, therefore, in our judgment very undesirable for Ministers of the Crown to take shares in the American Company while the fate of the Government contract with the English Company was still in suspense, even if they had bought the shares in the open market without any advice or information from Mr Godfrey Isaacs.

36. A good deal of discussion took place before us as to whether the transactions of the Ministers were in the nature of an investment or a speculation. Without attempting any definition of what exactly constitutes speculation, we think it clear that there was a speculative element in the whole of the transactions, since some of the shares were bought in order to be sold again, at a profit for the purpose of "lessening the price" of the remainder.

We are also of opinion that the sale by the Chancellor of the Exchequer of shares on April 20, which had not yet been delivered to him, the allocation of 1000 of the shares bought on May 22 to meet this sale, the borrowing of money at a high rate of interest from his broker to pay for the balance of the shares then bought, and the fact that no payment has ever been made to the Attorney-General for the shares sold by him to his two colleagues make it absurd to describe the transactions of Mr Lloyd George and Lord Murray as in the main investments.

In this connection it must not be forgotten that the transactions were in shares which had become the subject of a scandalous Stock Exchange gamble, and that Mr Lloyd George's broker advised him immediately he heard of it that it was not a desirable investment for the reasons already stated.

37. We made such efforts as we could to satisfy ourselves that no other public official was in any way connected with Marconi or other wireless

finance. But we were much hampered in this Inquiry by a decision of the majority of the Committee which precluded us from making any real investigation into the transactions in these shares by Messrs Heybourn and Croft, who were by far the largest dealers in them. All we therefore can say is that we are satisfied that none of those public officials who appeared before us had any connection with Marconi or other wireless finance except Mr Taylor, whose transactions have already been published. This observation applies equally to the Members of Parliament who gave evidence before us.

38. Ministers urged very strongly before us that we were bound to enquire into the truth or falsehood of the charges made against them in the Press, particularly in the *Outlook* and the *National Review*. These charges were not very definite, but we think that in substance they included allegations that Ministers had been widely accused of being[1] influenced in their conduct of the negotiations with the Marconi Company by the fact that they were interested in its shares, and had utilised information coming to them from official sources for the purpose of investment or speculation in the Marconi Companies.

We believe the charges thus stated to be without foundation. No evidence was brought before us in support of them, and they were denied by the Attorney-General, the Chancellor of the Exchequer, the Postmaster-General and the First Lord of the Admiralty. With respect to the last two Ministers it is right to say that any rumours connecting them with any transactions in the shares of any Marconi Company here or abroad we believe to be baseless.

Other charges were made by the *Eye–Witness* and later the *New Witness* and some other less important papers. We have no reason for thinking these charges were true, but owing to the fact that the Editor of the *New Witness* was being prosecuted by Mr Godfrey Isaacs for criminal libel, we did not think it right to insist on his giving evidence before us. We desire to place on record that we reprobate very strongly the recklessness with which many of these charges were made. At the same time it is right to add that, in view of the very definite and persistent rumours connecting Ministers with Marconi shares

---

[1] According to *The Times* the words "accused of being" were accidentally omitted from the official text as published.

which prevailed in the City for some considerable time before any references to them were made public, the statements in the Press cannot all be set down as due to mere malicious invention.

39. The Attorney-General asked our assistance to trace these rumours, and we did our best to do so. But we found great difficulties. Even the date on which the rumours became prevalent is doubtful. Some witnesses told us that they had existed as early as January or February. Others did not hear of them till May or June. On the whole, we are of opinion that the rumours did not come into existence, to any great extent at any rate, until after the dealings of the Attorney-General and the Chancellor of the Exchequer in American Marconi shares, and we believe that a distorted account of these transactions really set the rumours going.

Mr Godfrey Isaacs gave evidence suggesting that the rumours were the invention of the adherents of the Poulsen system and that they were set about with the view of discrediting the Marconi system, and with this charge he connected, more or less directly, two Members of Parliament—Mr Norton Griffiths and Major Archer-Shee. Later on he told us that he did not intend to make any charge against either of those gentlemen, but those who heard him give evidence on the first day could have had no doubt that some insinu- ation of the kind was intended against them. We accordingly enquired closely into the matter and were satisfied that there was no truth whatever in the suggestion.

Neither Mr Norton Griffiths or Major Archer-Shee had any pecuniary interest in the Poulsen system and neither they nor any of those connected with the Poulsen system appear to us to have had anything to do with organis- ing or spreading the rumours, and it is to be regretted that Mr Godfrey Isaacs should have given currency to any such suggestion.

40. The rumours themselves continued to prevail in some form or another right through the year 1912 and the beginning of the present year, and we are unable to say that they have ceased at the present time. For this persistence we think Ministerial reticence must bear the chief blame. The Chancellor of the Exchequer and the Attorney-General as early as July in last year appear to have told some of their colleagues, including the Prime Minister and the Postmaster-General, that they had had dealings in American Marconi shares. In spite of this fact the Postmaster-General thought it right to make

300

determined efforts to get the contract ratified before the adjournment of Parliament in August of that year without any disclosure of the transactions of his colleagues. He even carried his attempt so far as to suggest to Major Archer-Shee late in the evening of August 6 that he would press for ratification the next day, notwithstanding the Prime Minister's undertaking, given earlier on August 6, that the ratification should not be pressed until October.

41. On October 11 the whole question of the contract and of the rumours was discussed in the House of Commons on the Postmaster-General's Motion for the appointment of a Select Committee to investigate the circumstances connected with the negotiation and completion of the contract and to report on the desirability of the contract. In the course of the discussion Mr Samuel, Sir R. Isaacs and Mr Lloyd George, while withholding all reference to what had actually taken place with regard to the dealings in American shares, made declarations or interjections which, even if on a careful scrutiny they can be seen to refer only to the specific charge of having bought British Marconi shares, were calculated to convey an impression, and did in fact generally convey the impression, that none of them had ever had any interest, direct or indirect, in Marconi shares of any kind.

It is impossible to admit the plea that any mention of the actual dealings in American shares would have been irrelevant because Ministers were only concerned in denying the specific charges brought against them. No specific charge of any kind had in fact been formulated in the House of Commons. But there was a general uneasiness as to the possibility of anything in the conduct of Ministers being accountable for the existence of rumours. That uneasiness demanded an immediate, full and straightforward statement. In evading such a statement, Ministers failed to treat the House of Commons with the frankness or the respect to which it is entitled.

42. When the Committee was appointed it provisionally arranged its procedure in such a fashion as to allow of all criticisms of the contract and all possible charges against Ministers to be definitely formulated before asking Ministers to reply. This procedure would obviously not have been adopted if the Committee had been in possession of the facts, and we regret that Ministers committed another grave error of judgment in not communicating the facts to the Chairman at once and asking to be called to give

evidence without delay, particularly as Lord Murray was to leave England early in January of this year, which he in fact did.

A mere intimation of readiness to be called, which the Attorney-General did make, was not sufficient; and a communication to two members of the Committee, treated by them as confidential, merely emphasised the failure to make a full disclosure to the Committee as a whole.

43. It further appears that even the Prime Minister was not told the full facts until January of this year. On March 19, 1913, came the action for libel against the *Matin*, one of the main objects of which was, we were told, to enable Ministers to explain exactly how matters stood. Even then, however, a very incomplete account of what had occurred was given. Nothing was said of the later transactions by Mr Lloyd George in purchasing 3000 shares on May 22 or of his sale of 1000 shares on April 20.

We were told that this was due to the advice of counsel. But phrases were used by the Attorney-General in giving evidence at that trial which certainly appeared to suggest that the position of the Chancellor of the Exchequer was precisely similar to his own. Moreover, the Attorney-General did not in that case say from whom he bought the shares or what he gave for them. Even when he came to give evidence before us he unfortunately used language on the first day of his evidence which appeared to indicate that it was left to him to sell Mr Lloyd George's shares as well as his own and that he was really doing the whole transaction, and it was only at the end of the second day that he casually dropped out that Mr Lloyd George had sold 1000 shares in his own name, and it was not until the next day that he told us of the second purchase by Mr Lloyd George on May 22.

The transactions of Lord Murray on behalf of the Liberal Party funds do not appear to have been disclosed to any of his own colleagues, not even to his successor in the position of Chief Party Whip. Indeed, he intended apparently to conceal them altogether from the Committee. With that object he did not hand over to his successor the certificates of the shares he had bought with the money belonging to the Party, meaning to keep them until the Marconi business had been "cleaned up." But for the accident that the broker through whom these transactions were conducted defaulted, neither the Committee nor the public would have ever heard anything about them.

302

44. We feel that this apparent shrinking from a full disclosure of the whole of the transactions by Ministers in American Marconi shares is largely responsible for an uneasy impression that perhaps even now the whole truth is not known, and this impression has been strengthened by the acceptance on the part of Ministers of an arrangement proposed to them by the majority of the Committee by which only the Chairman and an expert were allowed to see the passbooks which Ministers had originally tendered for the inspection of the Committee, and by the very regrettable failure of Lord Murray to present himself for examination as witness before the Committee, in spite of more than one invitation to do so.

45. We therefore beg to report that we have come to the following conclusions:

(1) So far as we have been able to ascertain, no Minister, official or Member of Parliament had been influenced in the discharge of his public duties by reason of any interest he may have had in any of the Marconi or other undertakings connected with wireless telegraphy, or has utilised information coming to him from official sources for the purpose of investment or speculation in any such undertaking.

(2) We are of opinion that the Attorney-General acted with grave impropriety in making an advantageous purchase of shares in the Marconi Company of America upon advice and information not then fully available to the public given to him by the managing director of the English Marconi Company, which was in course of obtaining a contract of very great importance—a contract which even when concluded with the Government had to be ratified by the House of Commons. By doing so he placed himself, however unwittingly, in a position in which his private interest, or sense of obligation, might easily have been in conflict with his public duty.

(3) We think that the Chancellor and the then Chief Ministerial Whip, in taking over a portion of the Attorney-General's shares on the same advice and information, are open to the same censure; and we hold this to be also true of the purchase of the shares for the Liberal Party funds by the Chief Whip, so far as such purchase was due to the same advice and information.

(4) We find that the purchase of shares by Ministers on April 17 was made at a time when the shares could not have been bought in the ordinary course on the Stock Exchange and at a price lower than that at which an

ordinary member of the public could have then bought them. The Attorney-General obtained these advantages because he took the shares from Mr Harry Isaacs, who had to his knowledge taken them on even more advantageous terms from Mr Godfrey Isaacs. We think these circumstances increase the impropriety of the transaction.

(5) We are of opinion that the Marconi Company of America was materially interested, although indirectly, in the conclusion of the agreement between the English Marconi Company and the British Government, and it was therefore in any case, apart from any question of purchase on special information, or on special terms, highly inadvisable for Ministers to take shares in the American Marconi Company while the agreement was still pending.

(6) We hold that the transactions of the Chancellor of the Exchequer were in the main in the nature of speculation rather than investment, and that this applies in a less degree to the transactions of the Attorney-General.

(7) We think that the circular distributed by the Marconi Company on March 7, 1912, gave a misleading account of the tender which had been accepted by the Government, in omitting one of its most important terms, and we regret that the Postmaster-General did not take adequate steps to correct this omission.

(8) We think that the action of the Postmaster-General in trying to obtain the ratification of the agreement by the House of Commons without enquiry, after he knew of the share transactions of the Attorney-General and the Chancellor of the Exchequer, was regrettable.

(9) We find that the rumours current in the City of London as to the connection between Ministers and Marconi shares, however recklessly and inaccurately expressed, arose chiefly from distorted accounts of Ministerial dealings in the shares of the American Marconi Company, and that they were not the mere invention of journalists.

We find no justification for the suggestion that any Member of Parliament or any persons connected with the Poulsen system were responsible for the origination or dissemination of the rumours.

(10) We are of opinion that the persistence of rumours and suspicions has been largely due to the reticence of Ministers, particularly in the debate in October 1912. We regard that reticence as a grave error of judgment and

as wanting in frankness and in respect for the House of Commons.

(11) Except as above stated there is no ground for thinking that any Minister or official (apart from Mr Taylor, whose case has already been dealt with) or Member of Parliament who appeared before us had any financial dealing direct or indirect in any Marconi or other undertaking connected with wireless telegraphy.

List of Works Quoted and Referred To

ASQUITH, EARL OF OXFORD AND: *Memories and Reflections*, Cassell, 1928.

BEECHAM, SIR THOMAS, BART: *A Mingled Chime*, Hutchinson, 1944.

BELLOC, HILAIRE : *The Cruise of the Nona*, with a new introduction by Lord Stanley of Alderley, Constable, 1955.

BELLOC, HILAIRE AND CHESTERTON, CECIL: *The Party System*, Stephen Swift, 1911.

BIRKENHEAD, SECOND EARL OF: *F.E.*, Eyre and Spottiswoode, 1960.

BOWLE, JOHN: *Viscount Samuel*, Gollancz, 1957

CECIL OF CHELWOOD, VISCOUNT: *All the Way*, Hodder and Stoughton, 1949.

CHESTERTON, MRS CECIL: *The Chestertons*, Chapman and Hall, 1941.

CHESTERTON, G. K.: *Autobiography*, Hutchinson, 1936.

COOPER, DUFF: *Old Men Forget*, Hart-Davis, 1953.

DUGDALE, BLANCHE E.: *Arthur James Balfour: First Earl of Balfour, K.G., O.M., F.R.S.*, Hutchinson, 1936.

DUNLAP, ORRIN E., JR.: *Marconi: The Man and his Times*, Macmillan, New York, 1937

HASSALL, CHRISTOPHER: *Edward Marsh*, Longmans, 1959.

JACKSON, ROBERT: *The Chief, the Biography of Gordon Hewart, Lord Chief Justice of England, 1922–40*, Harrap, 1959.

KEYNES, J. M.: *Two Memoirs*, Hart-Davis, 1948.

MASTERMAN, LUCY: *C. F. G. Masterman,* Nicholson and Watson, 1939.

MAURICE, MAJOR-GENERAL SIR FREDERICK, *The Life of Viscount Haldane of Cloan,* Faber, 1937.

MORTON, J. B.: *Hilaire Belloc, a Memoir,* Hollis and Carter, 1955.

NICOLSON, HAROLD: *King George V,* Constable, 1952.

OWEN, FRANK: *Tempestuous Journey: Lloyd George, His Life and Times,* Hutchinson, 1954.

RAYMOND, E. T.: *Mr Lloyd George,* Collins, 1922.

READING, MARQUESS OF: *Rufus Isaacs, First Marquess of Reading, P.C., G.C.B., G.C.S.I., G.C.I.E., G.C.V.O.,* Hutchinson, 1942.

SAMUEL, RT. HON. VISCOUNT: *Memoirs,* Cresset Press, 1945.

SPEAIGHT, ROBERT: *The Life of Hilaire Belloc,* Hollis and Carter, 1957.

SPENDER, J. A.: *Life, Journalism and Politics,* Cassell, 1927.

SPENDER, J. A. AND ASQUITH, CYRIL: *The Life of Lord Oxford and Asquith,* Hutchinson, 1932.

[SPICER]: *Albert Spicer, 1847–1934, A Man of his Time,* by One of his Family, Simpkin Marshall, 1938.

TIMES, THE: *The History of The Times,* Vol. IV, 1912–1948, Part II, Appendices, The Office of The Times, 1952.

UPTON, MONROE: *Electronics for Everyone,* Faber, 1956.

WARD, MAI SI E: *Gilbert Keith Chesterton,* Sheed and Ward, 1944.

WOOLF, LEONARD: *Sowing,* Hogarth Press, 1960.

Dictionary of National Biography, 1931–40.

Parliamentary Debates: Commons: 4th series, 3–15 December 1900, vol. 88; 5th series, 7–25 October 1912, vol. 42; 10–28 March 1913, vol. 50; 31 March–18 April 1913, vol. 51; 16 June–4 July 1913, vol. 54.

Lords: House of Lords Sessional Papers. No. 66 1914.

Reports from the Select Committee on Marconi's Wireless Telegraph Co. Ltd. Agreement.

Lady Donaldson of Kingsbridge (1907–1994), a British writer and biographer, was the daughter of Freddie Lonsdale, a playwright. In 1935 she married John George Stuart Donaldson, Baron Donaldson of Kingsbridge (known as Jack), a left-wing intellectual, social worker, and dilettante Gloucestershire farmer. As the daughter of the playwright Frederick Lonsdale, she grew up in the frivolous world of 1920s café society, yet she became a committed socialist. As the wife of Lord Donaldson, who was on the board of both London Opera houses and was subsequently Minister for the Arts, Frances Donaldson was at the cultural centre of British life.

Her body of work included topics such as farming, and biographies of writers Evelyn Waugh and P. G. Wodehouse, as well as of her father, Freddie. Her biography of King Edward VIII won the Wolfson Literary Award and was the basis for a six-part television series, "Edward and Mrs. Simpson," starring James Fox and Cynthia Harris.